Smith Island, Chesapeake Bay

SMITH ISLAND,

Chesapeake Bay

BY FRANCES W. DIZE

Tidewater Publishers : Centreville, Maryland

The author gratefully acknowledges the assistance of Jennings Evans in the preparation of the map of Ewell, Smith Island.

Research on the history of Smith Island was partially funded by a grant from the Maryland State Arts Council through the Somerset County Arts Council, Princess Anne, Maryland.

The Library of Congress has cataloged the casebound edition of this book as follows:

Dize, Frances W., 1932–
    Smith Island, Chesapeake Bay / by Frances W. Dize. — 1st ed.
        p.   cm.
    Includes bibliographical references.
    ISBN 0-87033-399-2 (casebound); ISBN 0-87033-492-1 (paper)
    1. Smith Island (Md. and Va.) —History.   I. Title.
    F187.C5D59
    975.5′15—dc20   89–40301
                                              CIP

Manufactured in the United States of America

First edition, 1990; second printing (first paperback), 1996

For the people of Smith Island,
who welcomed me into their hearts and homes,
as if I belonged.

Contents

Smith Island, Chesapeake Bay

I

An Introduction to an Island

Twelve miles out in the Chesapeake Bay from land's end
at Crisfield, . . . Smith Island lies awash in the tides, history, isolation, fundamentalist faith, and comforting
forces of a cohesive community.

—William H. Rodgers

SMITH Island is a place of raw, untamed beauty, a locale
whose setting is limited only by the boundaries of nature.
It is a private, beautiful world that is like no other in Maryland.

Isolated geographically from the rest of the state, Smith
Island is actually a cluster of small islands with only a few acres
of dry land. A maze of waterways cuts through the marshy
terrain to connect three separate communities whose yards
and lanes are often awash in tidal waters. There are no tall
buildings here, no steep hills, and no patches of forest to break
the winds that blow in from the Chesapeake Bay. It is truly a
"Wet and Windy Kingdom."[1]

Besides being isolated, wet, and windy, Smith Island is a
place that does not have mainland conveniences. There is no
movie theater here, no supermarket, no gymnasium or swimming pool, and no drugstore or hospital emergency room. And
there are times when fierce weather or frozen waterways make
it difficult, or even impossible, to reach the mainland. But the
people who live in this watery world are accustomed to life
without these modern conveniences.

These are people who have adapted to their environment;
they have learned to bend with the wind and flow with the tide.
They are hardy and self-reliant people who make their living

3

from the water that surrounds them, and although generations of island living have set them apart from the rest of
Maryland, they have a life-style that enriches the culture of
the entire state.

This is a life-style that has evolved through more than three
hundred years of history. Nearly all of the islanders are the direct
descendants of the first settlers who dared to claim this little bit
of land. They bear the same names and retain the manners and
customs of their English and Cornish forefathers. On Smith
Island there is a conscious link with the past, a sense of belonging,
a remembrance of tradition, a contentment with old ways, and a
loyalty to a way of life that may soon pass into history.

Less than a century ago, Smith Island was only one of
several inhabited offshore islands. Watts Island, a short distance south of Smith, was once rich farmland that sustained
a dozen homes, a church, and a store.[2] The last of its occupants
left Watts in 1931. Smith Island's nearest neighbor, Holland's
Island, once supported an entire community; it had its own
schoolhouse and post office. Holland's was once called the
"Show Place of the Chesapeake," but by 1914, high tides and
wave action had washed away large chunks of the island, and
the people began to move away.[3] Today, even the graveyard is
underwater, and only one house remains on what is left of the
island. Jones' Island is completely gone, and the only structure
left on Fox's Island is a hunting lodge. These islands and others
like them have all been abandoned, left to the mercy of the Bay.

Virginia's Tangier and Maryland's Smith Island are the last
of the Chesapeake's inhabited offshore islands. Only on these
two islands can be found the unique culture that sets its people
apart from the rest of society. This is a culture that is steeped
in tradition and enduring folkways, a way of life molded by the
islanders' encounters with the forces of nature and with their
fellowman.

Nearly all of the islanders are independent watermen who,
because of past experiences with outsiders, do not fully trust
the strangers they call foreigners. Over the years, they have
learned to take care of themselves and one another. In their
secluded environment, they live together in peace and harmony, and although they purchase most of their supplies from
the mainland, they rely almost entirely upon themselves. It has
not always been so, for at one time, Smith Island was at the
crossroads of the Chesapeake.

4

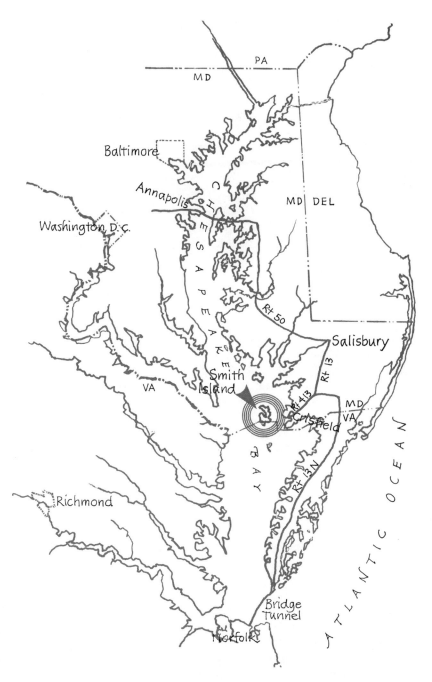

Vicinity map of Smith Island, Maryland, showing highway routes to
Crisfield, Maryland, departure point for the Smith Island ferry.

5

Smith Island, Chesapeake Bay

Over three centuries ago, the Chesapeake afforded the early colonists their highway and their marketplace. They "traded on it, travelled on it, fought and frolicked on it . . . Neither on the James River, nor the Hudson, Long Island Sound, nor at Port Royal, did the waters offer such thoroughfare, nor even they anywhere so much made use of."[4]

Plantations were scattered along the shores of the Bay and on the banks of the rivers that emptied into it. Accomac, Virginia, lay to the south and east of the island; to the west, the Potomac led the way to the first Maryland settlement, the Citie of St. Maries. To the northeast were the Big and Little Annamessex rivers and the Pocomoke; while farther north, the Choptank and the Patuxent led to the plantations and settlements on the middle Bay.

In the wilderness of Maryland and Virginia, good roads were virtually nonexistent; the Bay was the highway that linked the people. Its branches were the rivers that carried tall ships laden with colonists, their servants and slaves, and goods to be traded for tobacco. The settlers used the highway, too. Nearly everyone had navigable water close by, and in their small boats, they traded goods and services, or just visited.

Smith Island, located halfway between the shores of the Bay, was a way station on the great highway of the Chesapeake. The few settlers who lived there were not just farmers; they were skilled craftsmen—coopers and carpenters, boatbuilders, shoemakers, wheelwrights, and blacksmiths.[5] They traded their services for sugar and salt and other necessities that they could not produce for themselves.

But as civilization progressed in the New World, more towns were built closer to each other, and ships from the Old World brought skilled tradesmen to set up shop in those towns. As the settlements grew, Indian trails became roads, and travel by land became easier. The colonists began to use these roads and the facilities in nearby towns, and Smith Island was visited less often.

Until the advent of modern transportation and communication, the island retained the atmosphere of early centuries. On the mainland, methods of agriculture were modernized; factories began turning out finished products; institutions of higher learning were established. Cities grew, and the people grew with them.

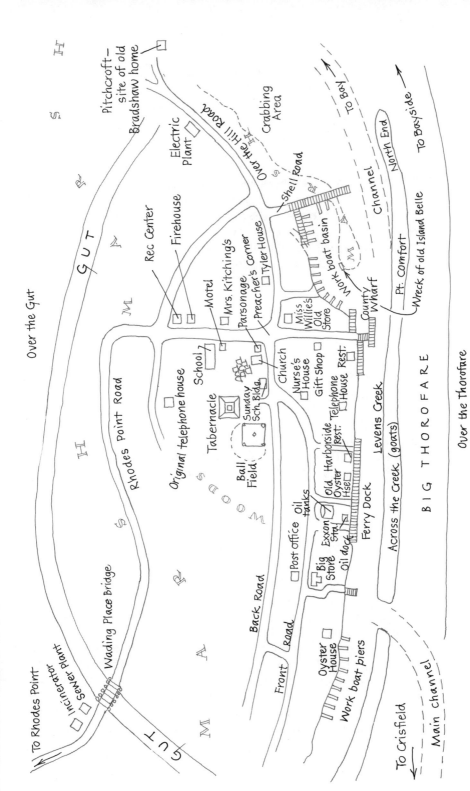

Over the Gut

To Rhodes Point
Incinerator
Sewer Plant
Wading Place Bridge

GUT

MARSH

Rhodes Point Road

Back Road

Front Road

Original telephone house

WOODS

Tabernacle

Ball Field

Sunday Sch. Bldg.

School

Rec Center

Firehouse

Motel

Mrs. Kitching's

Parsonage

Preacher's Corner

Tyler House

Electric Plant

Pitchcroft – site of old Bradshaw home

Over the Hill Road

Crabbing Area

To Bay

Shell Road

Work boat basin

County Wharf

Channel

North End

Pt. Comfort

Wreck of old Island Belle

To Bayside

MARSH

GUT

Post office

Oil tanks

Big Store

Exxon Stn.

Oil dock

old Harborside Oyster Hse.

Telephone Rest.

Nurse's House

Gift Shop

Telephone House Rest.

Church

Miss Willie's Old Store

Ferry Dock

Levens Creek

Across the Creek (goats)

Oyster House

Work boat piers

To Crisfield

Main channel

BIG THOROFARE

Over the Thorofare

Street map of Ewell, Smith Island, Maryland. (Prepared with the assistance of Jennings Evans.)

Smith Island, Chesapeake Bay

On Smith Island, time stood still. The people there continued to grow their own food, turning the earth with hand plows. With seafood supplementing their diet, they required little from the outside world. Using the works of Shakespeare and *Pilgrim's Progress*, they taught their children to read.[6] Their families grew, but the island remained sparsely populated until the nineteenth century.

These early islanders did not feel isolated; this was their home. They were men and women of strong character and pioneer spirit, the same spirit possessed by the men and women who inhabit the island today. As one old islander says, "We eat well, we sleep well, and everywhere we turn, there's something beautiful."[7]

Although the island retains its Old World culture, it is rapidly catching up with the twentieth century, and there have been many changes. The islanders no longer grow their own food; most of it is brought over from the mainland. The men of the island are not farmers anymore; they are commercial fishermen. And today, Smith Island is once more a way station on the highway of the Chesapeake.

Twice daily, packet boats take seafood across Tangier Sound to Crisfield and return laden with freight and passengers. Lavishly equipped tour boats bring tourists, people who have heard about Smith Island and want to see it for themselves. They roam the narrow lanes, visit the seafaring villages, sample a bit of island cooking, and then return to the mainland.

From Tangier Sound, the island is first seen as a long, thin shadow on the horizon; its ragged shoreline barely rises above sea level. But as the ferry nears the marsh-lined channel that leads to the harbor, the shadow begins to take shape. Bayberry, loblolly pines, and cedar trees begin to climb toward the sky, and the tall church steeple becomes a landmark. Off in the distance, clusters of houses rise above the waterline, and just outside the channel, scraping boats, their captains clad in oilskins, bob up and down with the waves.

The marsh-lined channel is the Big Thorofare that leads to the dock at Ewell. A row of low, rustic buildings lines the wharf, and along the finger piers that rim the cove, sturdy workboats tug against their moorings. At the water's edge, weather-beaten crab shanties march out on pilings, linked to each other across the marsh by a network of sagging planks. Just beyond the dock, stacks of crab pots and piles of paddles and corks lean against work sheds.

Stepping off the ferry is like taking a step backward to a time long past. While sea gulls screech through the air, robust children call out to each other in lilting voices. In the workboat basin, a waterman tinkers with his engine; another trundles a wheelbarrow filled with baskets down the lane. They speak to each other in what seems to be a different language—a mixture of colloquialisms spoken with a soft British, almost Shake-spearian, accent. No one seems to hurry, yet each villager seems to have a determined quality to his stride.

The village of Ewell is quiet and lovely. Rows of prim white houses with brightly painted shutters and squatty chimneys line narrow roads. Flowering shrubs border neatly kept green lawns, and plots of vegetables nestle against the outbuildings. Low-hanging branches of shade trees brush against picket fences, and cats are everywhere—beautiful cats, sunning themselves on doorsteps, nestled in the flower beds, and curled up in the windows looking out over the street.

Beyond the rows of homes built on ridges that are just a little higher than the surrounding marshland, there is a raw, windswept beauty. The ruggedness of the landscape is some-how softened by the light reflected from sky and water. The fields of reedy marsh grass ripple in the wind like fields of grain, taking their shadowy colors from the sky.

One visitor was so taken with the stark beauty of the island that he described it as having "astonishing light patterns, exuberant colors, and vistas to the horizon that are reminiscent of Holland and the Dutch masters."[8]

Ewell is the largest of the three villages that make up Smith Island. Each village is on its own separate island; each has its own store, post office, and church, and each has its own places of interest.

Ewell is the trade center for the island; most of the pack-inghouses are located here. So are the Telephone House and the Wilson-Butler Tabernacle and Campground. The Tyler house is also here, on the road that leads to the site of the first settlement. The Tyler house is a residence that has been converted to a visitor's contact point for the Glenn L. Martin National Wildlife Refuge.

Tylerton is the smallest community, and the most isolated. Accessible only by boat, it is separated from the rest of the

9

island by a broad expanse of water, and seems remote and vulnerable to the high tides that frequently inundate its yards and roads. The Chesapeake Bay Foundation maintains an estuarine study center at Tylerton. The center conducts seminars on Bay processes, marine biology, pollution, and law. There is also a small museum with a remarkably beautiful door that was handcarved by a local artist.

The village of Rhodes Point also seems remote. It is reached by a long, narrow road that ambles through the marsh and across a wooden bridge that spans Wading Place, the gut that separates this island from the community at Ewell. Erosion has narrowed this spit of land; water laps at the side of the road that leads to the very tip of the point.

At this tip is the Railway, a boatyard operated by ship's carpenters and boatbuilders who are descendants of the same family that started the yard generations ago. Here, perched on metal milk crates and wooden blocks, sit workboats in various stages of cleaning and repair. A squatty, low-sided scraping boat, peeling bottom exposed, waits to have barnacles scraped from her hull.

A long, sleek round-stern sits high in the air, while workmen clad in overalls bustle about with hammers and nails, caulking compound and cotton, and paint cans. Other boats, from the square-sterned, wooden-hulled workboat to the modern, graceful fiberglass wonder, wait with damp bottoms for the tender loving care that their owners will give them.

At the foot of the railway, a wide ramp slopes down into the basin, a slip of water enclosed and protected by pilings driven deep into the bottom, and fenced off against wave action. In the slip, a stout workboat waits, its engine quietly idling. A tall travel lift maneuvers into position, and two strong, wide slings are placed just under the boat's hull.

The lift operator gives the signal; the boat's engine surges to life, and its captain eases his craft gently forward over the broad straps. Then he cuts his engine, and jumps ashore while hydraulic winches slowly haul their dripping burden out of the water.

The workboat's owner, a Smith Island waterman, walks alongside with anxious eyes. While workmen handle the winches and the lift, it is the waterman's hand that reaches out to gently guide the progress of his own boat as it is moved along and placed on a cradle of blocks. It is his eyes that first scan the hull for signs of rot and worm, his fingers that feel for loose boards or worn wood. When painters and carpenters get to work, he is also there, scraping and cleaning, a part of the team that is giving his boat her regular maintenance—recaulking, mending, and applying protective paint. And he is there watching with bated breath as the slings are replaced under the hull. The motors of the hydraulic winches hum, and once again, his own workboat is lifted tenderly back into the water where she belongs.

This workboat represents a lifetime investment for the islander, but it is not the monetary value that is important. His boat is an extension of himself, a member of his family. He knows his vessel, her every board and nail, her quirks and her capabilities. For him, she lives and breathes; she has feelings. She responds to his command; she gives him power and speed when he needs them, and she lies gently in the water to let him work.

A waterman's boat is his lifeline to the world, his transportation, his workshop, and his only means of making a living. His boat gives him a sense of balance with wind and wave, when together, they confront the hazards of their occupation. For, even today, when modern citizens band and VHF radios link boats and homes, his occupational hazards are danger and discomfort. But with a stoicism drawn from a long line of water-rooted forebears, he constantly faces possible death or disaster with a sense of humor and the ability to laugh in the telling of a close call.

The modern-day Smith Island waterman has been described in many ways. He is stubborn, tenacious, and self-reliant. He is proud of his independence, wanting neither advice nor interference. He faces life squarely, head on into the wind. He is firm in his belief that he knows where he is going and how to get there. He is hardy and calloused, and fierce when angered, yet his heart is easily touched. He clings to old beliefs and superstitions; he is suspicious of strangers and skeptical of progress. Engaged in one of the most precarious and competitive of businesses, he is still his own boss. He works hard, lives hard, and plays just as hard as he works.

His occupation, that of waterman, is defined as one who works with a boat on the water. That is simple enough as a definition, yet the Smith Island waterman is a complex individual. He has special qualities that set him apart from other men. In the modern, twentieth-century world, he displays ancient characteristics that help him survive the rigors of his working conditions.

The islander's knowledge of the weather and other elements of nature is a science to which he was born. It is the knowledge gleaned from the observations of generations of islanders. He knows when the oysters will be lean, and when they'll be fat. He reads the signs for a peeler run, and senses from the feel of the air when the crab will bury. He knows when to take his boat out, and when to keep it in safe harbor.

Daily, he sets out on the water to face the raw elements of nature with a courage that, to him, is merely a part of going to work. Cold rain and sleet, biting wind, and icy temperatures are his winter companions; steamy heat, sunburn, and sudden squalls face him in the summer. But it is all a part of the job that he was born to do.

Although the tools of his trade have been modernized, much of the island waterman's business is conducted as it was a hundred or more years ago. Bicycles and wheelbarrows are still used to transport gear to the landing; crabs are still dipped up and packed by hand. Hundreds of soft crabs and buckrams are cleaned and wrapped, one by one, to be frozen for later shipment. Flat-bottomed skiffs are still used to gather "sea'ors"—crab grass that has been washed ashore—to be dried and used for padding crab boxes.

The waterman's business is a family business, especially during crab season. Preparation for this season begins long before the first run of crabs. Part of the long winter is used in the making of crab pots, a job sometimes done by island women while their husbands are out oystering. Making pots is a long, tedious process, but each pot is made with skill and care, for a well-made pot is one that catches crabs. All through the winter, the stack of pots in the yard grows, row by row, taller and taller, waiting for spring, when each pot will be rigged with lines, paddles, and corks.

As the weather begins to warm up and the pots are all finished, spring's real work begins. Attention is turned to shanty and boats. Built on pilings in the marsh just offshore, the shanties house the crab floats used for shedding soft crabs.

Each shanty is self-contained, having a worktable, a freezer or two, an ice machine, and from six to ten floats. The floats, plywood boxes with short sides, are waist high, arranged side by side with a plank walkway between the rows. To keep the crabs alive and healthy, a constant spray of water is pumped into the floats from overboard. Used water drains back overboard through small screened drains.

But before the shanty can be used, all must be made ready. Pumps have to be put in working order, wires checked for corrosion, electricity turned on, equipment cleaned up and oiled—the list seems endless. Each float must be scoured with a wire brush, allowed to dry, and a fresh coat of white paint applied.

Wharves, walkways, and shanties are checked over for any damage done by winter storms; rotten or loose boards are repaired or replaced. Whole families can be seen at work down by the water's edge, where small boats are overturned and propped up on posts stuck in the soft earth. All are helping to scrape, repair, paint, and launch. Finally, bags of sea'ors are gathered and piled under the shanty's workbench, and the new season begins.

When crabbing is on, the day begins early for the waterman and his wife. Long before dawn, both are up and about. While he's getting ready for his busy day, she's preparing breakfast and packing his "bail"—his lunch bucket. Before setting out for the day's crabbing, he'll make a stop at the shanty to fish up and pack the crabs that have shed during the night.

Back at the house, chores are finished as quickly as possible, before it is time to fish up again, this time by the islander's wife. The crabs in the floats need watching; they have to be fished out of the water soon after emerging from their hard shells. Tending the shanty takes first priority, and the island wives often carry their babies with them to watch over the floats. Between trips to the crab shanty, they tend their houses, gardens, and yards.

The work is simple, but physically demanding and time consuming. After they are fished up, the crabs must be sorted according to size, and packed in shipping boxes cushioned by sea'ors, covered with sheets of white paper and more sea'ors, and sprinkled with chipped ice to keep them alive, but quiet, and to prevent their soft backs from getting hard. They lie in rows in their boxes, resting with their blue claws neatly folded, quietly blowing bubbles, until shipping time, when the island freight boat makes the rounds of the shanties.

The watermen's wives are as knowledgeable about crab sign as their men. As the day's catch is brought to the shanty,

13

they help with the sorting. Rank crabs are put in one float, green ones in another, and busters in still another. The rank crab has a blood-red rim on its back fin, meaning that it is nearly ready to shed. The green ones have a white sign that will soon turn pink, then a rank red. In each stage of molting, the crabs are kept separate to prevent the green ones from nibbling the others.

Busters (crabs that are in the actual process of shedding) are treated very tenderly and are carefully watched. When they ease out of their old shells, they are allowed to rest a few minutes, then they are lifted out of the water, their soft new backs silky to the touch. It is now that each crab must be packed away on a bed of sea'ors to be shipped off to market.

When the packing's done, shanty chores are still not finished. Some crabs are injured by the molting process, and some, if left in the water too long, get a stiff papery shell called buckram. The injured crabs must be fished up, killed and cleaned immediately, then wrapped and quick-frozen. They are stored in the freezer until fall, when they are sent off for the winter market.

Buckrams, too, have a special use. They are killed and cleaned; their backs, as stiff and coarse as the fabric they are named for, are removed. Then each is wrapped separately and stored in the home freezer. Buckrams, when french-fried to a crisp, golden brown, make a much welcomed addition to the islander's winter table.

By early evening, most of the shanty work is done. The pace has slowed, but the crab does not stop shedding just because the day is drawing to a close. After supper, one more trip to the shanty has to be made before the tired waterman and his wife can call it a day.

To an outsider, the women of Smith Island may seem undertrod and overworked. Not so. They do work hard, but it is their choice to do so. They are well aware of their importance to the family operation, and they are proud of the fact that they are a vital part of the seafood industry. They are also aware that their husbands value them, not only as wives and mothers, but as partners in a family enterprise.

The island helpmate has the same feeling of fulfillment that a career woman on the mainland has. And she manages to run her home efficiently, in spite of the demands on her time and energy. Added to the satisfaction of a job well done, she has

14

the extra contentment of knowing that she and her husband are working together to build their family's future.

When winter comes, the oyster season is easier for island women, at least physically. They have more time to themselves. The shanty work is over; the children are back in school; the lawn takes less care. They are now free to make trips to the mainland, to participate in social events, or just to visit each other and relax a little.

But winter is also a time of worry and stress. Fierce winter storms bring harsh wind that keeps the boats in harbor for days; sometimes the Bay freezes over for weeks at a time. Every waterman's wife is well aware of winter dangers: fog, wind, and ice. But it is part of her role to wait, to watch the weather signs, to listen to the citizens band radio, and to set aside her fears and provide the loving atmosphere that her family needs.

Some island watermen still go away from home in the winter, especially during a poor oyster season, when they take their boats up the Bay in search of more productive beds. Some have jobs on tugboats; others have places on dredge boats, the Chesapeake's skipjack fleet. Some come home only on weekends, but most are in home port by late afternoon each day.

Gone are the days when whole fleets stayed away for months at a time, sometimes getting caught in a faraway harbor. An old log kept by a Captain Evans from Smith Island contains this bit of nostalgia:

> Lying here in Brittain's Bay. All across the mouth the ice has jammed. We can't get out. You can see the lonesome acomin' right aboard.

Captain Evans was one of the island men who had become accustomed to leaving home in late fall. Long before gasoline engines replaced sail power, nearby oyster beds were being depleted by wanton harvesting. At the beginning of oyster season, the bugeyes and the sloops, the brogans and the pungies, were rigged up for dredging and stores put on board. The island fleet would sail away, not to return until Christmas week.

While their men were gone, island wives took full responsibility for home and family. They carefully husbanded winter stores, for no one knew if the oyster season would be profitable. An elderly island woman who used to be a midwife remembers hearing her mother talk about the old days. She said, "They stayed home, they did. That was their job, to take care of things at home while their men was out makin' a livin'. They just took care of everything till the men come home again."[9]

During the last few days before Christmas, excitement would build, while anxious eyes scanned the horizon for homecoming sails. When the fleet finally landed, Christmas came, too. If the harvest had been good, shouts of joy rang out as captain and crew unloaded boxes and bags of supplies, fruits and candies, and gifts from Santa Claus—bolts of fabric, bonnets and shoes, gewgaws, and ready-made toys from the shops in Baltimore.

If the fleet had not been successful, it was still a joyous time, for husbands and fathers were safely home once more. It meant only that families must tighten their belts a little more, and make do with whatever was available—homemade gifts and toys given with love and thanksgiving. Often, a homecoming mariner would be greeted with a unique Christmas gift, a new son or daughter, born during his absence.

Back then, Christmas lasted a whole week, a week filled with merrymaking and hymn singing. But the day after the New Year came in, the sails faded away on the horizon as the fleet went in search of more oysters, leaving the women alone again on a wintry island to care for family, home, and each other.

Each generation of island family has its own stories of courage, of heroes and heroines, of storms weathered, crises passed, and difficulties overcome. And each family has its stories of valiant women. There were the midwives, the granny women who passed their skills from mother to daughter, women who left their own families to deliver babies and care for new mother and child until that mother was well enough to care for her own.

There were the women with so much knowledge about illness and injury that they were respectfully called doctor. They grew their own herbs for medicines, gathered roots, bark, and berries, and called upon the lore of mother and grandmother to heal the sick. And there were the matriarchs who made decisions and dispensed advice to those who were weaker.

Each island family can boast of a grandmother, or at least a great-grandmother who chopped wood, killed and dressed wildfowl, attended to family emergencies, or bailed out the skiff and poled that skiff up icy guts to help tend a sick and needy neighbor. One of those women, the wife of an oyster boat captain, was so revered by island people that she is remembered to this day, and spoken of with awe.[10]

According to Smith Island legend, Aunt Caroline was a saint. She was always ready to lend a helping hand, to give of her own stores to a needy family, and to give wise counsel when necessary. Aunt Caroline's story goes like this:

As Christmastime drew near one exceptionally cold winter, families grew anxious about the oyster fleet. A severe winter storm with gale force winds had kept the boats from returning home. Finally, on Christmas Eve, the fleet was sighted a little more than a mile off Rhodes Point. The storm had blown itself out the night before, but the temperature had plummeted. The Bay was full of ice, the harbor chockablock. Out off Bayside, a section of the island northwest of the Big Thorofare, the fleet was stuck fast, frozen in by treacherously sharp piles of ice. The fleet could not move, and the tide was grinding the sharp edges of the ice against the wooden hulls.

As the news spread from house to house, women began to gather on the shore at Rhodes Point, agonizing over the sure fate of their men. When Aunt Caroline arrived to join the cluster of women, she knelt on the cold ground, her shawl clutched around her, and raised her voice to heaven. One by one, the women knelt beside Aunt Caroline to join with her in prayer, and as they prayed, the ice began to rumble. From the shore to the fleet, a pathway opened up through the ice, and the oyster boats sailed safely into harbor. All of the boats were saved; not a man was lost.

Aunt Caroline is buried on Smith Island. Her grave is tenderly cared for by her grandchildren and great-grandchildren, who remember her good deeds through story and legend as the works of Saint Caroline.

The island women have retained a sense of this type of devotion; sometimes, their love surpasses devotion. It is not uncommon to see an island wife, after her own hard day's work, drawing her husband's bath and laying out his clothes, just as his mother did. This is not servitude; it is her choice.

As one island wife says, "He goes out and risks his life for me and our family; I want to do all I can for him. Every time he goes out, I don't know if it's the last chance I'll ever get to do

17

something for him."[11] It is her traditional role to provide for her husband's comfort, and upon occasion, to tolerate his rowdiness. But without being told, she knows that she is indispensable, and she accepts circumstances that would create rebellion in today's women.

But these are not today's women; they are still yesterday's women—island watermen's wives. Their homes have all the modern appliances, all the latest gadgets that are advertised on television; they are tastefully furnished and decorated. Their clothes are the latest fashion; they know how to use makeup and style their hair. They enjoy going off to the mainland for a few days, to stay overnight in a motel and shop in the big shopping centers. They are comfortable in supermarkets.

Most of them are familiar with long distance travel; some have been as far away as New York, Florida, or the Bahamas. But most are happy to return to their island, far away from noise or glamour, where they can live simply, in the same quiet atmosphere, in the same peaceful neighborhood, where they can still feel their grandmothers' presence.

Island watermen are content with their existence; so are their wives. It is the life they know. Through contact with the mainland, they see the difference between their lives and the lives of others. But to them, there is no comparison.

When asked why he stayed in such an out-of-the-way place, an elderly waterman gave this answer: "God gave us this island. He brought us here. He took care of our granddaddies and showed 'em how to use the water and the creatures in it, and this is where we belong." Another says, "The islands catch aholt of you like nothin' that can be explained."

And one island waterman's wife has been heard to say, "This is where I belong to be."

II

From the Beginning

Later in the colonial history, the packet boat was always preferred to the stage coach and the freight wagon in all the bay counties of Maryland, and it was this free, open, safe and pleasant navigation of the Chesapeake Bay and its many inlets, which not only gave to our people a freedom and facility of intercourse with one another . . . but shaped their manners and regulated their customs to an extent which is difficult to exaggerate.

—J. Thomas Scharf

DOWN through the years, nature and the Smith Island people have come to a near perfect balance. By learning to work with their environment, generations of islanders have forged an indestructible bond between man, the land, and the sea, and in the process, have built a culture that is unique.

Island society is a closed society, a community of uncommon people drawn together by their work, their religion, their family ties, and their heritage. On Smith Island, there is a feeling of communion with the universe, of security in the midst of turmoil, of being a part of the whole, yet set apart.

The development of an island culture does not begin with the first settlers who chose to live in this environment. It begins with the formation of an archipelago and the prehistoric people who inhabited Maryland's coastal plain.

Long before the first Europeans traveled the highway of the Chesapeake and found "many isles both great and small,"[1] this chain of islands was part of a wilderness. They were an extension of the mainland, part of a ridge bordered on one side by the Nanticoke River, on the other by the Susquehanna. Smith

Island was a part of this ridge, which was a continuous landmass that sloped downward through the Susquehanna River Valley.[2]

During the last Ice Age, huge sheets of ice spread over the northern continent and rested there until a warming trend began. The ice slowly melted, and the water level of the earth's seas began to rise. Gradually, water spilled over into the Susquehanna Valley, and eventually formed the Chesapeake Bay. As the salty water rose, tidal marshes spread and the coastline was altered; the higher elevations were left exposed in the surrounding water.

The newly formed Chesapeake possessed many of the qualities of the ocean, and the natural processes of flooding, wave action, and erosion created a ragged coastline with smaller bays, coves, and inlets. Bit by bit, destructive storms and turbulent water etched out the archipelago that includes Smith Island.

Before these islands were formed, the early peninsula was lush and green, with oak and hickory forests, grassy slopes, and freshwater streams. There were nuts, berries, and low-lying brush to feed and shelter animals. Herds of deer and elk grazed the grasslands, while bear and cougar, rabbit, fox, raccoon, beaver, and mink made the ridge their home. Prehistoric people, archaic traditional cultures of seasonal hunters and gatherers, inhabited the area.[3]

As seawater encroached upon the land, vegetation changed; fresh water became brackish. Gradually, grazing land turned into low, marshy ground. The trees that had supplied food gave way to pine forests; the larger land animals moved inland and were replaced by an abundance of sea life and waterfowl. The Indians who had freely roamed the peninsula sought higher ground; hunting and gathering camps moved inland.

In pre-Columbian times, the Alonquin Indians settled on what is now called the Delmarva Peninsula. As separate tribes, or bands, broken off from the main body, the Pocomokes, Nanticokes, and Assateagues settled along the banks of the Pocomoke and Nanticoke rivers. Unlike the Potomacs of the far shore, they were gentle-natured, agricultural tribes.

These tidewater Indians depended upon their knowledge of the land and water for their subsistence. Cultivated crops were their primary source of food; fields and gardens stretched

20

beyond their crude huts. They were accomplished farmers who knew the secrets of cultivation and fertilization. As they tilled their fields, they worked refuse, dead fish, and scraps of food into the soil. The fairly mild climate produced two crops of vegetables during the growing season.

They were hunters and gatherers as well as farmers. From their main villages, foraging parties, usually made up of women and children, went out to gather food. They gathered wild onions and salad herbs, watercress and sorrel, shallots, dock, and dandelion greens. They dug for roots of burdock, and harvested cattails and the tender sprouts of wild vegetables. Fields of wild strawberries, hips of wild roses, and the berries that grew on thorny bushes added sweetness to their diet. The tall trees yielded nuts that they ground into flour or stored until the winter winds came.

During the winter season, hunting parties set up temporary camps. Using snares and bows and arrows, they trapped and killed deer, bear, and smaller animals to add to their food supply.

Fishing was also an important part of their existence. Although the people lived in permanent villages along the Bay and the tidewater rivers where fish and wildfowl were abundant, the stockpiling of food for the long winter was vital. During the warm months, parties of fishermen rowed out to the offshore islands to set up camp. These Indians were among the first to experience the pull of island living.

With weirs, nets, lines, and spears, they harvested seafood, then roasted, smoked, or dried it to take back to their village. Until the oncoming winter forced them to return with their cache of seafood, they stayed on the islands, feasting on crabs, fish, and oysters.

The busy Indians who used Smith Island for hunting and fishing found peaceful shelter. As they explored the island, they found patches of woodland with trees big enough to be felled for canoes. They found a variety of marsh grasses to be woven into nets and baskets. They also found the mosquitoes and gnats that swarmed in from the marsh, and they coated their bodies with rancid grease to ward off the biting insects.

The Pocomokes and the Assateagues were peaceful tribes that humbly gave way when threatened. As white settlements encroached on their territory, the Indians dispersed. They moved on to the north and east, and by the late seventeenth century, there were few Indians living in the area that became Somerset County of the Eastern Shore. But they left evidence of their camps on Smith Island: refuse sites and kitchen middens, large piles of shells, broken tools, and shards of pottery, all valuable prehistoric resources.

Prehistoric resources are defined as archeological remains composed of artifacts or natural objects that relate to human activities before recorded history.[4] While historic remains in Maryland date from the time of European exploration and settlement, prehistoric remains result from the earlier native life in the territory. Data from archeological studies show the subsistence and settlement patterns of the early Indians and their cultural habits.

According to a reconnaissance made by the Thunderbird Research Corporation of Virginia, three prehistoric sites on Smith Island have been reported to the Maryland State Archeologist.[5] All lie between Twitch Cove and Little Thorofare. One site contains Woodland period artifacts, including shell-tempered pottery and side-notched projectile points, or arrowheads. A six-inch-thick shell midden is located on the beach, with the artifacts scattered close by.

The state archeologist's office also has reference to an oyster midden at Hog Neck, on the southwestern section of the island. The variety of artifacts found at the sites provides proof that Smith Island was used long ago by ancient people, and even more recently by transient Indians.

Present-day islanders make a hobby of walking the shoreline to search out Indian artifacts. Many have extensive collections of pipes, arrowheads, spear points, tools, and broken pottery. The collections include triangular, fluted, notched, and stemmed points, some bone, some stone, and some flint.

The islanders are always eager to show their collections, but they keep to themselves their favorite hunting grounds. Every defined archeological period is represented in the collections, including artifacts found in historic burial sites from the colonial period.

Indians were still using the islands as seasonal campsites when the first European explorers came to the Bay. As early as 1498, John Cabot sailed into the Chesapeake, and in 1570, Spanish expeditions explored the area. Later, Sir Ralph Lane, governor of the first colony on Roanoke Island, made a voyage to tidewater Virginia and became the first Englishman to enter the Bay. Then, in 1603, Bartholomew Gilbert, a nephew of Sir Walter Raleigh, was killed by the Indians on Virginia's Eastern Shore.[6]

The next exploration was that of Captain John Smith, who had journeyed to the New World with the first of the Jamestown settlers in 1607. In June of the next year, he and a crew of fourteen set out to explore the Bay. When he discovered the marshy islands of the Eastern Shore, the captain named this group of islands for the physician who accompanied him, and charted them as the Russell Isles.

Just off the islands, they encountered a summer squall: ". . . . the winds and the waters so much encreased with thunder, lightening, and raine that our mast and saile blew overboard, and such mighty waves overracked us in that small barge that with great labour we kept her from sinking by freeing out the water."[7] Such was the description of the first recorded Smith Island "camp meetin' squall."

During his exploration, Captain Smith mapped almost two hundred Indian villages on the shores of the Chesapeake and its adjacent rivers. Later, he published a description of his journey along with charts and maps and his observations of the distribution of native groups according to their location, strength, and numbers.

During the next few years, the Virginians concentrated on expanding their settlement at Jamestown. Under royal rule, Jamestown prospered, and more colonists came to the New World. Among them was William Claiborne, who was authorized by the governor to make explorations of the Bay.

Claiborne sailed on past the Russell Isles toward the upper Bay, where he bought an island from the Indians. He named his island the Isle of Kent, obtained a trading commission from the king, and established a trading post.

The tranquillity of the Russell Isles was barely disturbed by Claiborne's activities, but before long his Isle of Kent was to become a source of conflict between the Virginians and the next group of Englishmen to travel the highway of the Chesapeake.

In 1632, Charles I granted to Cecilius Calvert, second Baron of Baltimore, the territory now known as Maryland. Lord Baltimore's charter gave him "all that part of the peninsula lying between the ocean on the east and the bay of Chesapeake on the west, divided from the residue of the same by a right line drawn from the promontory or headland called Watkin's Point, situated near the bay aforesaid, near the river Wighco on the west, unto the great ocean on the east, and between that boundary on the south, unto that part of the estuary of Delaware on the north, which lieth under the 40th degree of latitude north of the equinoctial, where New England is terminated, passing from said estuary, called Delaware, in a right line, unto the true meridian of the first fountain of Potowmack."[8] From there, the line was to follow the southern bank of the Potomac to a place called Cinquack near the river's mouth, and thence by a straight line back to Watkins Point.

Almost immediately, Virginia took exception to this charter that claimed rights to land already settled by William Claiborne in 1631, and objected to the possibility of interference with his profitable Indian trade. Virginia laid claim to the Isle of Kent, and sent a protest to the king.[9]

In the meantime, Lord Baltimore sent his brother with the first settlers to the new province. The *Ark* and the *Dove* sailed up the Bay and turned into the mouth of the Potomac. These colonists chose the site of an old Indian village for the first permanent settlement in Maryland, and named it the Citie of St. Maries.

Soon after the establishment of St. Marys (as it is now spelled), Lord Baltimore published a pamphlet containing a translation of his charter and maps of his province, and issued a proclamation against trading in Maryland waters without a license from the lord proprietor. When Claiborne's vessel, the *Longtayle*, was seized for unauthorized trading, that act led to the first of many armed conflicts between Virginians and Marylanders over their common boundary.[10]

In an attempt to recover his vessel, Claiborne fitted out his ship, the *Cockatrice*, with an armed crew. Lord Baltimore's two armed pinnaces, the *St. Margaret* and the *St. Helen*, overtook the *Cockatrice* in Pocomoke Sound just east of the Russell Isles. In the ensuing battle, the commander of the *Cockatrice* and two of his men were killed; one Marylander lost his life.

Virginia's claim to the Isle of Kent was temporarily ended by the decision of the King's Commissioners of Plantations when they proclaimed that the absolute right and title belonged to Lord Baltimore. Sir John Harvey, who was then governor of Virginia, ceded Virginia's claim and went even further. He declared the Onancock River to be the northern boundary of

24

his colony, and prohibited his people from trading with the Indians north of this river.[11] The Onancock is far south of the cluster of islands that would be named Smith Island, yet within a few years, Virginia would take possession of a large part of the Russell Isles.

During this same period, settlements on the Eastern Shore had extended northward to the Accomack area. Recognizing a need to organize settlement near his boundary on the peninsula, Lord Baltimore urged his governor and general assembly to take special care that no encroachment be made on his territory. To ensure that Virginians would remember the boundary, he ordered Governor Calvert to "encourage some English as soon as you can to take up such land as shall be due them."[12]

Soon afterward, Virginia's drastic law against Quakers and other religious nonconformists led to the exodus of those people from Virginia.[13] They, too, were offered grants of land on the Shore adjoining Accomack.

Lord Baltimore had hoped to prevent any controversy that might arise between the two colonies. But once again, Virginia took exception to Baltimore's charter. The surveyor general of his majesty in Virginia claimed that the land he was granting did not belong to Maryland; it rightfully belonged to Virginia.[14]

While Maryland and Virginia were squabbling over their common boundary, traffic on the Chesapeake increased, and the Russell Isles caught the attention of passersby. In 1652, Nicholas Waddelowe patented four hundred acres of island land, named it Gabriell's Island, and sold a piece of it to John Watts.[15] Thomas Wellbourne obtained Fox's Island northeast of Watts, and Charles Scarborough and John West acquired land called "a western island of Chesapeake Bay," the island that would become Tangier.[16] The first piece of land on the island that was to become Smith Island was patented to Robert Cager of St. Marys in 1665—two hundred acres just south of the straits now called Kedges.[17]

The Bay islands offered an excellent opportunity for Cager to raise stock. They were covered with plenty of marsh grass in the lowlands, plus succulent sweet grass on the higher ground. Brush thickets and patches of woods provided shelter for the cattle, and since the land was completely surrounded by water, no fencing was necessary. Large round holes were dug to furnish watering places.

Unfortunately, Cager did not live long enough to see the results of his island cattle-raising experiment. His son inherited the estate, and in 1675 bequeathed all of the Cager property to "the inhabitants of St. Georges and Poplar Hundred in the aforesaid (St. Mary's) County and to their successors and Survivors forever."[18]

There is no way to determine the exact date that the first permanent settler arrived on Smith Island. However, it is known that Cager, a citizen of Maryland, was the first to own part of it. The second piece was granted to a Virginian, the third and fourth to Marylanders, and a little later, a patent for 3,804 acres of islands, including nearly all the Russell Isles, was issued to a group made up of two citizens of Maryland and one prominent Virginian. In all this confusion, it is apparent that the grantors "did not know which was Maryland and which Virginia territory, or they had forgotten where the line of 1668 was run."[19]

This line of 1668 was the line agreed upon by Governor Calvert and Edmund Scarborough.[20] It crossed the peninsula and the Bay, cutting through the Russell Isles on its way toward the western shore, giving part of the chain to Maryland and part to Virginia.

When Henry Smith was rewarded for bringing twenty servants into the colony, Virginia gave him one thousand acres; the land grant was recorded as "scituate lying and being in Accomack County." When Colonel William Stevens received his thousand acres from Lord Baltimore, one of his boundaries was the divisional line drawn betwixt Maryland and Virginia.[21]

A short time later, Colonel Stevens consigned all his acreage, all that parcel of land called Pittcraft, to Smith. This land was surveyed, boundaries fixed, and the certificate of survey returned to the land office at St. Marys. Henry Smith became the owner of nearly all the island below what is now called the Big Thorofare, and the island became known as Smith's Island.

Very little is known about the first occupants of Pittcraft, but in the original indenture, Pittcraft is called a plantation. It is also known that Stevens named his plantation for his wife, the former Elizabeth Pitt. The indenture mentions houses, yards, orchards, and gardens, as well as meadows and marshes, pastures and "wayes," and fishing places. From this document, it can be assumed that a dwelling had been built at Pittcraft prior to the property exchange.

At the same time the business between Henry Smith and Colonel Stevens was being transacted, one John Evans was involved in a lawsuit against the executor of Robert Cager's estate.[22] Evans had obtained leave from Cager to plant crops at Cager's plantation in exchange for accommodations for himself, his wife, and one negro man. The plaintiff sought payment; a jury was called and found in Evans's favor.

Public records show that Evans and John Tyler, a carpenter, were living on Smith Island before 1686. For nine thousand pounds of tobacco, Tyler bought two hundred acres, part in Virginia, part in Maryland, and built a home at Horse Hammock.[23] His son, Thomas, was born there in 1688. John Evans bought another parcel out of Pittcraft, and gradually the population of Smith Island began to grow. Other public records show more early island names in Accomack as indentured servants who had sold their services to pay their passage across the Atlantic.[24]

As Lord Baltimore continued to encourage settlement of Somerset County, more people moved up from Virginia, and Henry Smith sold off his island in parcels of various sizes. The new landowners registered their properties and cattle marks in either state, and sometimes in both.

In the Archives of Maryland and at the county seats of Somerset and Accomack are the records of property transactions, births, deaths, and marriages. But most of the information about the "old days" on Smith Island has been handed down by word of mouth in the form of tales told by the old-timers, tales told to them by their own parents and grandparents. Many of the old-timers are gone now, but their stories linger on.[25]

These stories give a fairly good idea of what life must have been like for the early settlers. They say that the first islanders noted the patches of forest, and called their new home "Woodlands." Wildflowers and sassafras sprinkled the high ground beyond stretches of marsh grass. The soil on the ridges was rich; the little creeks and coves provided excellent harbors.

Like the tidewater Indians who had used the islands before them, the first islanders depended upon their knowledge of the land and the resources available to them. Furnishing food for immediate and future use was a constant concern, and a never-ending process. But nearly everything they needed was right at hand. The fertile ridges, acres of grazing land, and miles

27

of surrounding water promised a steady and healthful means of subsistence.

Providing their food meant plenty of hard work for the settlers. They had brought with them to the island seeds and seedlings and farm animals—sheep, pigs, and cattle. But first the fields had to be cleared and the soil prepared with heavy, hand-drawn or pushed plows, and hoes and rakes. Day after day they toiled, tilling the soil and planting crops.

But even after a crop had been produced, the work had just begun. For then, the stockpiling of winter food really began. White potatoes, sweet potatoes, and turnips were dug and carefully stored in shallow pits. The pits were lined with dried grass and the tangled flax fibers they called "tow." The tubers were laid in padded rows, then covered with a layer of padding and topped with soil. A low roof over the storage pit gave added protection against rain and snow. Beans and peas were dried in the sun; peppers and onions hung from the rafters.

Day after day, hours were spent in paring, coring, and slicing fruits: apples, peaches, and pears. There were also cherries, figs, and pomegranates to be picked and processed. In those days, very little canning was done; most of the fruits were dried on racks. The few jars that were available were used to put up pickles and relishes, jellies and preserves. The jars were boiled over an open fire, then filled and sealed with a mixture of tallow and lard.

When the corn crop was ripe, it had to be harvested, husked, dried, and part of it ground into meal. Smith Island had one of the few sail-driven gristmills in Maryland.[26] Construction of the mill was simple: sails were mounted on a wooden frame that was connected to a shaft made from the trunk of a tree; the gear and pinion were attached to a shaft that ran down through the centers of a pair of millstones.

Because it rotated, the top stone was called a runner. The other, the bedstone, was mounted solidly so it would remain stationary. The surfaces of both stones were furrowed with rows of grooves running outward from the center. The grooves on the runner were cut in the opposite direction from those on the bedstone.

When the wind set the sails in motion, the gear, pinion, and shaft forced the huge top stone to turn. Grain was poured through the hopper, and the weight of the mighty runner

28

ground the kernels against the bedstone. One of these mill-stones has been found and pieced together. It rests in the yard of a Tylerton waterman.

Sometimes the early islanders combined their work with pleasure. The early days of spring, for instance, were the time for shearing, when neighboring families got together to share the work, the fun, and the feasting.

In the warm weather, the sheep were ready to shed their winter coats. Young boys rounded up the herd and chased the sheep into a holding pen. Then, one by one, they were separated from the herd and divested of their wool. Two men worked together, using a process called ruing to pluck the loose wool that they piled into great mounds that looked like piles of dirty snow. As the men worked, the children played, and the women visited together while they prepared the feast that all would enjoy when the work was finished.

Another busy day came in late November, when the weather was frosty, and the moon just right for butchering. Butchering was an unpleasant job that took much work and many hands. Early in the morning, huge pots of water were set to boil over open fires. After the hog was killed, the scalding water loosened the hair so the hide could be scraped clean. Then the carcass was strung up to a tree, and as the men went to work cleaning and trimming, the air would be full of steam. Even the women helped to prepare the cuts of meat for smok-ing, salting, or drying.

As everyone worked, the pots on the open fires were filled again. One became a sausage pot to be filled with scraps of fat, trimmings of lean meat, and savory spices. The other was filled with fat to be rendered into lard. Once again, the families worked together, then gave thanks and ate together before poling their boats back through the guts toward home.

What the land could not provide for the islanders' use, the Bay waters did. Just like the land, the water was there to be used, a vast sweep of water given to them by God as an extra resource. They treated this water as a continuation of their own pieces of property, and harvested it just as they did their fields.

Although the small farms were isolated from each other, the shallow waterways that laced them together were easily navigated. The early settlers had observed the native Indians' use of the log canoe and adapted it for their own use. The log canoe was made simply by felling a large tree, then shaping and trimming the trunk, and hollowing or burning out its insides. The canoe, or ka'noo, could be rowed, poled, or rigged with sail. It was an ideal vessel to be used in the shallow waters that separated the islands.

Besides the canoe, the islanders experimented with their own type of boat. The Smith Island skiff, with its low sides rounding to a moderately pointed bow and a blunt stern, was used for many chores: hauling firewood and water, gathering sea'ors, or simply for getting from one part of the island to another. Even women and children became adept at poling a canoe or skiff up and down the guts and marshy inlets.

Those early islanders, like the Indians, made good use of all the resources and materials at hand. One example is their use of sea'ors. The natural die-off of grasses washed up by the tide, sea'ors made good winter forage for their animals. Packed around the foundation of the house, the grass gave added protection against the cold wind. Dried out, it made stuffing for cushions and bedding, and seasoned blocks of sea'ors mixed with a little marsh mud resembled peat; it burned easily and made a hot cooking fire.

In the spring, new grass grew to replace the sea'ors. Molting crabs hid in the new growth to shed their old backs, and emerge soft and succulent. An islander, standing in his skiff with a net woven onto a long-handled rim, could catch and dip up enough of this delicacy for a good meal. There was an abundance of fish and terrapin, as well as hard-backed jimmy crabs.

When winter came, the islander took out his nippers to pinch off a mess of oysters for supper. Ducks and geese hung by their feet in the smokehouse, and a barrel of herring soaked in brine stood in the corner of the kitchen. A wild goose, complete with potatoes, onions, turnips, and dumplings, served with corn pudding and sweet potato pie, graced the islander's table; while outside, the wild winter wind played havoc with the Bay.

Observation and experience taught the early islanders respect for the elements. They weathered severe winter storms with gales of wind that lasted for days, high tides that threatened to inundate their homes, freeze-ups that kept them isolated for weeks, and quickly rising summer squalls that could change the placid water into a witch's cauldron. Of necessity, they became naturalists, observers of nature, and

30

A Smith Island crabber rests on an up-ended crate as he sorts his catch. (Photograph by Marion E. Warren.)

from their experiences, seasoned to their new environment. As the secrets of the sea life they had begun to live were unfolded to them, they became at home in their surroundings and gained a healthy respect for the dangers the Bay represented.

They also learned to use all their senses to foretell the weather: the taste of foul weather (the bitter, coppery tang that comes from the marsh in late fall, leaving its warning of unsettled conditions), the smell of rain on the way, the sound of thunder in the distance, the sight of a blue rim on the horizon, or the heavy feeling of lowering pressure that comes before a storm.

An eastern sky, dead gray and flecked with low white clouds, foretold that soon the wind would be driving tidal waters far inland, while late fall's high blue sky with puffs of fluffy white clouds scudding before a breeze meant a few more days of good sailing. But as winter put its first chill in the air and flood tides crept higher and higher, that last, highest tidemark, along with a sudden calm and a gray-blue sky, spoke of a powerful nor'wester, when the beautiful glistening Bay turned into an awesome, terrifying turbulence.

By learning to recognize the weather signs that told of the possibility of danger or discomfort, those first islanders acquired a system of self defense against the elements and a healthy respect for the laws of nature. And by adapting to their environment, each generation has passed on the knowledge gleaned from those experiences and observations.

In both work and recreation, family life was the nucleus of island living. Each family member had his or her own special place in meeting the needs of the whole. Girl children learned early how to tend the garden and help with the many household chores, chores like carding wool, sewing, soapmaking, and candlemaking.

On soapmaking day, mother and daughters cut up chunks of fat, and added them to leftover grease, then boiled the mixture in a huge iron pot over an open fire. It was long, hot work to stir wood ashes into the boiling mixture until it reached the proper consistency to be dipped out into containers, cooled, and stored.

To make candles, they cooked sheep tallow and hunks of suet in stale pot liquor until the mixture was ready to be poured into molds that hung from a rack. To make the wicks for their homemade candles, they twisted cornhusks to be tied on the rack and suspended through the molds.

The list of chores in a pioneer home was never-ending, and there was little or no waste. Leftover bits of fabric and the still-strong pieces of outgrown garments were sewn into quilts and comforters that were packed with goose feathers. Other outgrown clothing was turned inside out, taken apart, and recut to fashion garments for a smaller member of the family.

Making fabric was another important project shared by mother and daughters. The early islanders grew their own flax and extracted linseed oil from the seeds. The stems of the plants were field dried, then retted and skutched. The women soaked the fibrous stems until the woody outside covering was rotted away from the inside fibers. Then, alternately crushing and scraping, they separated the long inside fibers. The fibers were then spun into a fine linen thread.

On cold winter days, they worked with sheep's wool, carding it into webs, then twisting and spinning it into woolen thread. To make a coarse cloth for sturdy clothing, they carded pieces of old red flannel into webs of blue-dyed wool, then spun it into a thread called lustre, which was then woven into a fabric called "fustian," or home-up.

All fabrics (wool, linen, and fustian) were woven on hand looms, some on easels or frames, others suspended from the ceiling beams.

The daylight hours were busy ones for all family members. Little boys learned how to fish and catch crabs, how to gather sea'ors and mix them with mud to make blocks of fuel for the cooking fire. They helped in the fields, sharpened tools, and chopped wood. On stormy days, they watched and learned, as the skillful hands of their fathers carved household utensils—spoons, ladles, bowls, and butter presses—from pieces of wood or bone.

From tending the animals to tanning hides, from planting gardens to washing dishes, each had his or her share in the chores. The family struggled together to provide for themselves and to maintain their health and well-being.

Although a few stands of pine, a few cedar trees and fruit trees remained by the end of the colonial period, Smith Island could no longer be called Woodlands. The hardwoods had been used up in the building of boats and houses.

Smith Island, Chesapeake Bay

The first island homes were small, but solidly built one- or two-room cabins. Each house was built on a frame of well-seasoned timbers, strongly braced and pegged together. The roofs were made of split-log shingles that overlapped on a gentle slope. To prevent loss of heat, most homes had only one or two small windows. Some were paned with glass brought from the mainland, but most were merely square openings with shutters that could be opened or closed as needed. Since there were no stones and no clay for brickmaking on the island, those used for fireplaces were brought over by boat.

More recent island homes consisted of two rooms, one downstairs and one up, with rooms added on as needed. To keep the main dwelling safe from fire and confine the heat of cooking to the smaller building, a summer kitchen stood a little distance from the house. Later, colonnades, or "colonnettes," were built to connect the two.

Each house had its separate outhouses, milk house, and storage sheds. For some reason—the old-timers say it is the marsh grass and brackish water—horses did not live long on the island. For this reason and the convenience of travel by water, few stables were needed.

Milk houses, or dairies, were built low and squatty, with an extended roof to shade the building and keep the climate inside cool and moist. Smokehouses were built high off the ground, and had raised roofs and slatted sides.

Away from the dwelling house, usually in the farthest corner of the garden, was a tiny building placed over a shallow ditch—the "necessary," or the "toilette." This little building was always kept as neat and clean as the other outhouses. There are still a few milk houses and a few necessaries behind Smith Island homes, their old siding silvered with sea air and age.

Inside the big house, most of the living was done in the large downstairs room. It was the only room that was heated, and it was lighted only when absolutely necessary. Except for a few pieces brought from "home," the furniture was rough-hewn, but sturdily built: strong cross-buck table and benches, a heavy sideboard, storage chests and wall cupboards, and the ever-present spinning wheel. Each piece of furniture was designed for a specific purpose and built to last a lifetime or more.

Many island homes still proudly display pieces of furniture from the colonial period. There are drop-leaf china closets and sideboards, gateleg tables, high, heavy oak or cedar wardrobes, and pie safes. There are trestle tables and round dining tables on pedestals. Most homes possess pieces of fine china and silver, pieces that have been passed down from mother to daughter through generations.

Those things are cherished by the islanders as part of their heritage, as are the stories they tell about the old days. It used to be hard, they say, but homelife might have been better then. An elderly lady who lived almost at the tip of Rhodes Point said, "Everybody worked hard back then, but when the husband come home, the family was together. When it became time, they'd all go to bed together. It was just a good homelife."

But with all the hard work needed to maintain home and farm, beauty and pleasure were not forgotten by the islanders. There was beauty in the handcrafted furniture and the flower gardens, in gaily colored yarn, and intricate handwork. Dull work became pleasant fellowship when shared with friends and neighbors. Quilting and spinning bees were frequent; shearing days and a "butcherin' " were occasions of shared work and feasting.

There was beauty, too, in music. Islanders have always loved music and dancing. In the old days, a long week of hard work was often followed by a weekend of frolic: dancing, singing, and games, when families would all gather at one of the homes.

After Saturday morning chores were finished, boats laden with quilts, children, and pots of food began to tie up down at the landing. They brought cakes and tarts, sweet biscuits, nutty breads and muffins, preserves and pies, and plenty of hearty food like stewed jimmies with dumplings, or oyster pie, or duck simmered down with potatoes and onions, succotash, sweet potatoes, corn pudding, pickles and relishes, and cakes filled with figs and nuts.

While the women visited, the men played marbles and pitched quoits and the children played games of tag, tic-tac, or hide the switch. In the game of tic-tac, lengths of cord were attached to various objects. When the cord was plucked, it made noise. In a variation on this game, later generations of island children attached the string to the shingles of a house and vibrated the string to make a horrendous noise. In one islander's recollection, "It sounded like the house was comin' apart."

Smith Island, Chesapeake Bay

After an afternoon full of fellowship and feasting, the little ones were put to bed in the big room upstairs, and the grown-ups enjoyed a night of frolic, dancing to the music of fiddles and pipes. In the small hours of the morning, pallets were made up on the floor for the weary dancers. By early Sunday afternoon, the boats began to head for home; the weekend of frolic was over; it was time to rest and prepare for the next week's work.

Island living suited these people. They lived well in their snug homes; their children grew strong and sturdy in the combination of land and sea. They enjoyed their semi-isolation; it was an idyllic existence, charmingly simple, rustic but secure, with enough contact with their neighbors to satisfy an occasional desire to mingle with other people.

A large family of island people has descended from the first few families who chose a secluded bit of land for their frontier home. All are related, not only by blood, but by their kinship with the sea. It is a bond that has been strengthened by three centuries of life on what has often been called "the last frontier of Maryland."[27]

III

The Islanders Meet the Enemy

Sure they was pirates out here. Not in my granddaddy's
lifetime; way back there in his daddy's time, I guess.
Used to tell yarns about 'em. Why, Rhodes Point used to
be Rogue's Point afore they changed it, you know.
—Capt. Winfred Evans

WHILE the first few island families were adjusting to their environment, traffic on the highway of the Chesapeake was increasing. Ships from the mother country were bringing more settlers to the shores of the Bay, and ports like Oxford, Chester, and Annapolis began to bustle with activity. As ships, big and small, plied the waters, the islanders added their own craft to the traffic flowing by.

The settlers along the Bay's shore lived in harmony with their surroundings, but far away in Europe, trouble was brewing. When William of Orange came to the English throne in the late seventeenth century, a series of French and English wars broke out, and when the British and Dutch tried to prevent the succession of a French prince to the Spanish throne, the War of the Spanish Succession began.

Fighting between the European powers was to last nearly seventy years, and the conflict spread to the New World. It wasn't very long before Spanish and French privateers were cruising the highway of the Chesapeake.

According to the "Old Accomack Records" at Eastville, Virginia, lookouts were stationed on Smith Island in that county to watch for alien ships. Posted on the far reaches of the island, the sentinels lived in crude camps set up in the marsh, barely existing on the supplies they had brought with

37

them. Exposed as they were to wind and weather, their lives were miserable, their duties harsh, and their living conditions poor. Their pay for a six-month period of duty was a pittance.[1]

The lookouts were also necessary to protect the Bay trade from pirates. Unlike the privateers, who were licensed to prey on enemy ships, pirates were lawless adventurers, sea robbers who committed crimes against vessels of all nations.

Infamous pirates like Blackbeard, Captain Kidd, and Stede Bonnett harassed merchantmen carrying cargo to and from Bay ports. Lesser pirates, like Edward Davis and Captain Cook, troubled Eastern Shoremen, and as the colonies prospered, pirate activity escalated.

Prominent Virginians reported that "pirates swarm in this part of the world." They considered it "a most egregious shame that so fine a colony should be exposed to depredation by every picayune rogue."[2]

One of those rogues was Bartholomew Roberts, Black Bart, whose great ship carried 240 men and half-a-hundred guns. Another was Roger Makeele, a small-time pirate whose base of operations was tiny Watts Island at the lower end of the Russell Isles. In the Archives of Maryland, there are affidavits with long and explicit accounts of Makeele's violence and malicious thievery.[3]

The inhabitants of Smith Island, only a short distance from Watts, were aware of the pirate activity so close to home. But today, only a few islanders can remember the stories passed down by their ancestors. These old islanders say that picayunes haunted the island's secluded coves and inlets, and that "sometimes you could hear them partyin' on other people's stuff." But they also say that they "never heard of our folks havin' trouble with 'em. They just let 'em alone."[4]

Perhaps these picayunes did conduct their wicked business without bothering the islanders, but before long, there would be another species of pirate to worry about, a different kind of pirate who would put the islanders in the position of having to defend themselves with almost no help from the outside.

Far away in Europe, England had made peace with France and Spain, but only a few years after the Treaty of Paris was signed in 1763, the colonies were quarreling with England. For the time being, the islanders had little cause for unrest or rebellion, but on the mainland, dissatisfaction with English rule was growing. Relations between the colonies and the mother country continued to deteriorate until finally, the Americans banded together to stand up for their rights.[5]

At the beginning of the Revolution, confusion concerning loyalties was widespread on Maryland's Eastern Shore. Inhabitants of the islands were primarily Loyalists; after all, most of them were direct descendants of the first English colonists. England was their home country, and loyalty to the king was a tradition that was hard to break.

But that loyalty was soon shaken by the tribulation the islanders were forced to endure. Early in the war, British men-of-war appeared in the Bay, and the island farms were vulnerable from the onset. The enemy relied on plundering for their food, and sent out tenders to forage. Islanders watched anxiously to sea, fearing for their property and their lives. The isolation that had always been in their favor now alienated them from the rest of the world.

The British in the Bay were encouraged by communication with the Loyalists, and messages flew back and forth advising the Maryland Council of Tory activities. Orders went out to the militia to distress or check the enemy by cutting off the tenders. The Somerset militia was encouraged to put a stop to all kinds of intercourse between the people and the men-of-war. Their orders were to "find any persons carrying on correspondence with the enemy, secure such and their vessels if you can . . . secure those who may be suspected of corresponding with the enemy."[6]

As always, in wartime or in peace, there are those who are tempted to make their fortunes from the misfortunes of others under the guise of loyalty to a cause. Most islanders wanted a quick end to the war; others, through greed or loyalty to the Crown, carried on a treacherous type of guerrilla warfare.

With its many hidden harbors, Smith Island soon became a way station for escapees, refugees, and Tories.[7] Unscrupulous men, among them the Tory, Joseph Whayland, brought their small boats to the shallow water surrounding the island. They were soon joined by island men whose loyalties belonged to the Crown.

Under cover of night, raiding parties sailed out from their island bases to plunder Eastern Shore farms, and capture their neighbors' vessels, then dart back by the light of dawn to their convenient hiding places.[8]

These thieves earned for themselves the title of "picaroon," a name derived from a Spanish word meaning rogue or brigand. To the rest of the islanders, they were just more of the picayunes—the small-time pirates who had plagued their fathers.

But the islanders who did not go along with the picaroons had not one enemy, but three. British ships sent tenders to raid them, and the Patriots also needed supplies. They, too, demanded produce and other provisions. The islanders planted and harvested, fed their animals and butchered them, and made their clothing, only to have most of it taken from them. The enemy within, the traitorous picaroon, who sold his loot to the British, only added to their misery.[9]

Island-based rogues continued to harass the Shore, looting, plundering, and burning. Men wanted for crimes against the new nation found an avenue of escape by hiding on the far reaches of the island until they could be picked up by the British. In March of 1777, two notorious Tories, called only by their last names, Callalo and Moore, hid out on Smith Island.[10]

In a ruse designed to lure the traitors off the island, Captain James Campbell, the commander of Maryland's naval forces in Tangier Sound, was ordered to hang out British colors and cruise the sound. Campbell reported that several Tories had escaped through the sound three days before he arrived, but he sent his captain, Stewart, to search the island.

Neither Stewart nor Campbell was able to find the Tories on the island, so the ship left the sound. Governor Smallwood later learned that the fugitives returned to the island about two hours after Campbell left, and that a British ship had anchored off to pick them up. He called Smith Island a "place of reception of deserters and escaping prisoners." Captain Campbell returned to search for the offenders; he repeatedly warned the islanders that he would hang any person he caught giving aid to the enemy.[11]

People on the mainland declared the islands a hotbed of illicit activity, a den of rogues and thieves, but it is unfair to say that all island men were Tories or rogues. Most were honest, God-fearing men. The presence of the picaroons was a dreadful imposition that had to be tolerated. It would take generations to overcome this lawless reputation, and, as time would tell, it played an important part in shaping the character of the future island waterman.

The Islanders Meet the Enemy

But in the meantime, the situation in Tangier Sound grew progressively worse as the picaroons grew bolder. Joseph Whayland, from Garden Island, was one of the picaroon leaders. A Smith Islander, Marmaduke Mister, was one of his captains, and among his crew were Marmaduke's nephew Stephen, John Evans, and Basil Clarkson.[12]

Whayland's gang found secluded coves and inlets where they could scud in and lie in wait for unsuspecting vessels sailing through the sound and Kedges Straits. From their hidden harbors, they could steal silently from cover, attack their prey, then return to their marshy hideaways.

Captain Joseph Yell and Joseph Mariman were among Whayland's victims. Mariman and Yell had left the Hungar River bound for the Potomac with a load of "Plank and tar." Turned back by the sight of Lord Dunmore's fleet of British men-of-war, they stood for "Smith's Island," where they were captured by Whayland and "one Lazarus, a mulatto."[13]

Mariman and Yell were taken aboard a schooner, where they saw about twenty men sharing plunder. Yell requested that they be allowed to go ashore to find food, and after taking their money and most of their clothes, Whayland allowed them to do so.

They found the home of Richard Evans, who fed them, but after a while, Marmaduke Mister came and forced them to go back to the schooner, where they were questioned about their loyalties. Then, Whayland informed his prisoners that he was under orders from Lord Dunmore to take away any vessels belonging to rebels, to destroy such as he thought proper and carry the rest to the fleet.

As Captain Yell was pleading for the return of his vessel, Whayland received a message from the British demanding his services at once. He ordered two vessels in the harbor burned, but had Yell's cargo removed, set the crew on shore, and gave them permission to leave. Men of the island helped them free their boat, and Mariman and Yell departed, feeling lucky to have escaped with their lives and their vessel.

A short time later, Whayland and several of his men were captured. John Evans and two others named Price and Howith gave bond and were set free.[14] Whayland must have been considered dangerous or desperate, for at the time he was seized, all his clothes were taken from him. He petitioned the Maryland Council to grant him an order for the return of his clothes:

Smith Island, Chesapeake Bay

> The petition of Joseph Whayland, jr., a languishing
> prisoner in the jail at Annapolis, humbly showeth, that
> at the time your petitioner was taken by Maj. Fallin's
> guard he had all his clothes taken from him, and that
> he is now naked and has been so ever since his confine-
> ment and has not wherewithal to purchase any clothes;
> he therefore humbly prays your honors would be
> pleased to grant him an order on Maj. Fallin for the
> delivery of his clothes and your petitioner as in duty
> bound shall forever pray.
>
> [Signed]
> Joseph Whayland

His petition was granted, and shortly afterward, Whayland was
free again, turned loose to plunder and burn.[15]

Plagued continually by the British, deviled from within by
the picaroons, Smith Islanders feared for their very lives. One
young rogue was heard to say that he was determined to have
several of the principal people on the island dead or alive, or at
least get some of their negroes.[16]

As the picaroons and the men of the British cruisers
continued to torment their victims, orders came down from the
Maryland Council to remove all stock of any kind from the
Eastern Shore and adjacent islands to prevent its falling into
the hands of the enemy.[17] Every vessel that could be had was
pressed into service, and to make matters worse, American
boats returned time and again to search for picaroons. Armed
boats were ordered to Tangier Sound to prevent any trading
with the inhabitants of the islands.[18]

Finally, Governor Jefferson extended the provision law to
cover the Virginia portion of the offshore islands. He ordered
Commodore Barron to the Tangiers to slaughter and salt the
cattle there, to take all surplus provisions, and leave the
islanders only what was absolutely required for their subsistence. Jefferson also wrote to the governor of Maryland advising him to do the same on the Maryland section of Smith
Island.

In his orders to the commodore, Governor Jefferson included depositions "which will inform you of reason to believe
inhabitants of the Tangier Islands supply the enemy's cruisers
in the bay with provisions . . . Execute this business principal-
ly by deputy, and as to the mode of getting the cattle which we
are told are nearly wild, we leave it to yourself to contrive."[19]

42

A Smith Island waterman and his crab shanty with its wooden
walkway built on pilings driven into the marsh. (Photograph by
Marion E. Warren.)

The official letters to the governors reveal the depth of feeling against the islands. Joseph Dashiel of the Somerset Militia wrote his opinion to Governor Lee. He said, "I consider them (the people of the islands) the most dangerous enemy we have to watch."[20]

As the situation worsened, the Maryland Council felt that evacuation of the islands was imperative. Instructions were sent to the county commanders; their orders were to remove immediately all inhabitants, their stock, and all other movable property to some part of the mainland, to seize and sell all boats or cannon belonging to them.[21]

No person was to be permitted to live on any of the islands. Able men were to be deemed enlisted soldiers for the war, or forced into service on the barges; old men, women, and children were to be quartered at public expense.[22]

Captain Alexander Trueman was sent to the island with the state boat *Plator*, the armed vessel *Decoy*, and the state barge. Although several boats and other valuable items were taken and sent to Annapolis for public sale, the mission was never completed. The *Plator* was ordered elsewhere with provisions for the army.[23]

At the same time orders were sent to Captain Trueman, like orders were sent to Commodore Grayson. The commodore had been to Smith Island several times and had earned the reputation of being a cruel, vindictive officer. Stories of Grayson's cruelty and the circumstances surrounding his death have been passed down from generation to generation on the island.[24]

Island old-timers say that Commodore Grayson was a cold man who was given to tantrums. He raided island homes, and was wont to remove anything that struck his fancy. Shortly before he encountered the British and met his death, an island woman came to him begging for the return of her children's clothing that his men had taken from her home.

The commodore was in a bad temper, and stalked away, but the woman continued to plead for her children's clothing. As she followed him, pleading her case, Grayson suddenly turned and struck her with the flat of his sword. Hurt and angry, the woman fell to her knees and prayed to God that a ball might go through Grayson's heart before the same time the next day.

The Islanders Meet the Enemy

Grayson had been ordered to depopulate Smith Island, but the help he had been promised was not available. He left island waters and took his barge to the mouth of the Potomac, where he made an attempt to capture enemy vessels. Grayson and his men fought bravely against the British, but lost the battle. Commodore Grayson was killed instantly and horribly, with a ball through his heart.[25]

Grayson's barge, the *Revenge*, was one of the vessels that had been built especially to combat the type of warfare being waged against the residents of the Eastern Shore. The shoal water, shifting bottoms, and sandbars of that area created a unique situation as far as defense was concerned.

The small, shallow-draft boats used by the picaroons could maneuver easily through the maze of channels that intersected the marshy islands. Even the British were using small barges to rob the islanders and the people who lived along the Bay shore. When parties of militia were sent in pursuit of the smaller vessels, their own boats could not navigate the waters.

The citizens of Somerset wrote to the Maryland Council pleading for help.[26] But in spite of "some profitable captures down the bay and among the islands by the Philadelphia barges,"[27] the picaroon activity continued. Finally, in 1780, the Maryland Council was authorized to purchase or cause to be built a fleet of barges or rowboats capable of carrying swivels and a minimum of twenty-five men.[28]

Following the design of the watermen's boats, the barges sat low in the water. Rigged with both sail and oars, the shallow-draft vessels could go anyplace the picaroons could go, and carried enough guns and men to wage war on their own home ground.[29]

All details were taken care of, including a magazine of provisions at Snow Hill, a supply boat, a doctor and paymaster, and commanding officers who were well acquainted with the Bay and the hiding places to which the picaroons usually resorted.

After Commodore Grayson's death, Zedikiah Whaley was commissioned as commanding officer of the barges. On July 31, 1782, the Maryland Council decreed that "the Rank of the Captains be as follows, Walley, Dashiell, Frazier, Spedding."[30] A commission was issued to Levin Handy to serve as captain of the marines on board the command barge, the *Protector*.

Smith Island, Chesapeake Bay

Whaley was put under the command of the French Marine at York with specific instructions that if particular circumstances should require separate activities, he would be in sole command of the barge fleet. Operations were to be restricted to the Bay area, to protect the Bay trade, and to defend the citizens of the state and cover such of their property as was exposed.

As the barge fleet was being made ready, the picaroons were becoming bolder, striking indiscriminately at their help-less victims. In September of 1782, Whaley received a message from the Maryland Council that the enemy's privateers were committing depredations as high as the Patuxent.

The council's message expressed urgency. It said: "It is our desire that you proceed down the bay immediately with the barges under your command . . . to put a stop to their depreda-tions and to protect the citizens of the shore."[31] The stage was being set for the bloodiest naval battle of the Revolution.

On the twenty-second of November Commodore Whaley wrote to Governor Paca. He said that on the twelfth, when the barges were at Onancock in Virginia, he had learned of five British barges heading for Gwynn's Island. On the morning of the fifteenth, his fleet sighted the enemy barges, chased them, and captured one, the *Jolly Tar*. They pursued the others until they chased them out to sea from Wreck Island Inlet, then returned to Onancock.

The commodore informed the governor that he was deter-mined to continue his defense of the shore as long as he possibly could, and that he had not the least doubt of frustrat-ing any attempt the enemy might make on the Bay. Less than a week later, Whaley and his men met the enemy again.

Several accounts of the Battle of the Barges have been faithfully recorded in the Old Accomack County records at Eastville, Virginia, and in the Archives of Maryland.[32] One of these accounts was written by Captain Frazier of the barge *Defence* a few days after the battle.

In his account, Frazier said that on the twenty-seventh of November, the fleet observed "seven sail" coming up the Bay, and gave chase. Night came on, and they stood into Watts Island to wait for dawn.

By morning the British were anchored off Tangier Island. There were seven of them, and only four American barges. Whaley's barge was the *Protector*; Solomon Frazier captained

46

the *Defence*; Robert Dashiell, the *Terrible*; and Levin Speddin, with Zadock Botfield his lieutenant, the *Fearnaught*.

It was agreed, because of the uneven odds, to dispatch an express to the lieutenant of Accomack County to fit out a barge lying at Onancock, and raise volunteers to man her and the *Langodoc*, a barge that had been taken from the British a few days earlier.

By the time these arrangements were made, the British fleet was nowhere in sight. Captain Frazier was ordered to proceed to Tangier Island to reconnoiter the enemy. Flying British colors, he sailed into the harbor at Tangier. There was no sight of the British, so he landed at the home of "one Crocket" to ask if he had seen the American barges. He was informed that although no one had seen the Americans, six of the British barges had just left for Fox's Island up Tangier Sound. The British intended to lay over that night in Kedges Straits at Smith Island.

Frazier returned to the fleet to make his report. With the information he had been given, he was able to inform Commodore Whaley of the enemy's strength and number. By then, the Onancock barge and the *Langodoc* had joined the group, but the Onancock barge could not keep up with the others, and Whaley ordered her back. The Virginia volunteers who had manned that barge went on board the other vessels. Colonel John Cropper, the commanding officer of Accomack County, and several other Virginia gentlemen joined Whaley on the *Protector*.

The barge fleet set out for Fox's Island, where they anchored off and sent Lieutenant Samuel Handy in the *Langodoc* to inquire of the enemy. Handy was told that the British were already headed for Kedges Straits. As night came on again, the British huddled in the shadow of the island; the Americans anchored off a little south and west of Kedges.

In the early light of dawn on the thirtieth, the bargemen drew their rations from the supply ship *Flying Fish*, while the officers met to plan their strategy. In his account, Levin Handy, who would become the only survivor of the *Protector*'s officers, wrote that Commodore Whaley believed the enemy's push would be at the command barge. He requested the support of his officers, and received their declaration that "this they would do, or all sink together."[33] Reassured, his men rested

47

and fed, the commodore gave orders to make sail and give chase.

By nine, the enemy hove to and formed a line, rowing slowly but steadily toward the barge fleet. In bare semblance of order, the Americans faced the British bearing down upon them. At half past the hour, the action began; a brisk fire from both sides was kept up, although it was said that Captain Dashiell lagged a little astern of the other barges. The *Flying Fish* and the *Langodoc* kept themselves well astern, never catching up to participate in the action.

The enemy's fire was concentrated on the *Protector*, and was answered just as briskly. But in the heat of action, the *Protector*'s magazine was blown up.[34] All bedlam broke loose when a trickle of powder from a broken cartridge spilled across the deck. The six enemy barges were now less than fifty yards away, and the commodore shouted orders to wet the powder.

Suddenly, a flash from a nearby musket ignited the trickle of powder; a horrible explosion ripped through the vessel. Bodies hurtled through the air; men with their clothes afire leaped into the water, while others jumped overboard to escape the flames.

Commodore John Kidd, who had been using tiny Watts Island as his base of operations, commanded the British barge, the *Kidnapper*. Now, the *Kidnapper* closed in for the kill as a second explosion rent the air.

In a continuous shower of musket balls, the men on the *Protector* fought bravely. With fire all around, they struck out with anything at hand: cutlasses, daggers, boarding spikes, and iron rods.

Greatly overpowered by the British, brave Commodore Whaley fought to the finish. Captain Joseph Handy lost an arm, but fought nobly with the one remaining. Both Whaley and Handy were shot down, killed at nearly the same time. Levin Handy received seven wounds, and nearly lost his life; Colonel Cropper, the valiant Virginian, was gravely wounded. Finally, with all of her officers killed or wounded, the *Protector* struck her colors and surrendered to the British.

According to Colonel Cropper's letter to Governor Paca, of the sixty-five men on the *Protector*, twenty-five were killed or drowned, twenty-nine were wounded, some of whom later died. Only eleven escaped with their lives. But the sixty-five gave good account of themselves. British Commodore Kidd was badly wounded, several of his officers were injured or killed, along with fifteen of the *Kidnapper*'s crew.

In the heat of battle, where were the rest of the American barges? On December 6, Colonel Cropper wrote a narrative of the action. In his letter, he said, "There never was before upon a like occasion so much cowardice exhibited." The commodore's orders were for all the barges to support him, but, according to Cropper, Frazier and Speddin fired a few round shot at a long distance, rowed about, then ran away. Dashiell kept his distance; Samuel Handy never fired a shot and ran off before the other two, and Bryant never got up at all.

The barges *Defense*, *Terrible*, and *Fearnaught* bore away up the sound with the enemy after them; the *Langodoc* and the *Flying Fish* stood toward the main.[35] At the upper end of Hooper Straits, the enemy gave up the chase and the barges managed to make safe harbor in the Choptank. The supply boat and the small barge made it to Annemessex, where Captain Bryant stripped his supply vessel, and landed his sails and provisions on shore.

In his report, Colonel Dashiell told the governor that none of the dead was carried ashore except the commodore and Lieutenant Handy. The rest were fished from the water by Smith Islanders.

In horror, residents of the island watched the bloody battle. Solomon Evans, who lived near Kedges Straits, climbed a tree, and clung to its branches throughout the fight.[36] The cries of the wounded and dying rang in his ears, along with the clang of steel and the explosions of gunpowder. Through the wavering smoke, he watched as the blood of brave men mingled with the waters of Kedges Straits, and the wounded were gathered up to be taken to Onancock. As the smoke of the awful explosions drifted away, and the echoes of the struggle faded, Evans climbed down from the tree. With other island men, he buried the bodies of the enlisted men on Bayside.

Shortly after the battle, Levin Handy and the Virginia volunteers who were on board the *Protector* accused some of the other officers of cowardice, of deserting them after their promise to fight together to the end.[37] Dashiell and Botfield were charged with highly unbecoming and improper conduct, and were suspended.[38] The others were ordered to answer for their actions.

In self-defense, the officers wrote their reports, excusing themselves wherever possible. Solomon Frazier claimed confusion as to whether to stand or retreat. Speddin and Botfield, after losing one of their big guns, saw Frazier being chased by the enemy, and went to his aid.

In the confusion, their barge was being rowed around in circles, part of the men rowing ahead, the others backing water. Speddin claimed that his men were confused, and would not follow orders. Dashiell's excuse was that he found it necessary to secure a retreat.

But these officers had exhibited bravery and patriotism on previous occasions; none was known to be cowardly. It could have been that they were merely honest victims of confusion and disorder, men who believed themselves without a leader and outnumbered. There is also the possibility that they fled hoping for another opportunity to return and fight under more favorable circumstances. Even Levin Handy came to the defense of Samuel Handy, and captains Bryant, Frazier, and Speddin.

After careful consideration, the council and the governor decided that the previous records of the officers of the barges overcame any doubts about their conduct. All but Dashiell were reinstated and returned to duty.[39]

Encouraged by the defeat of the barges, the picaroons were soon back in the Bay, flaunting their ability to rob and plunder without fear of capture.[40] The enemy barges hovered constantly in Kedges Straits. While they were recovering from their wounds, the men from the commodore's barge told that while they were being kept prisoner on a barge in Kedges, the inhabitants of the Maryland and Virginia islands voluntarily came on board to give information to the enemy.[41]

The situation in Somerset rapidly worsened. By February, there were eleven barges, a sloop, and two schooners loose on the waters. Manned by Tories and picaroons, rogues who looted and burned homes and vessels, they made passage on the Bay and sound hazardous.[42]

Plagued by a lack of funds and the refusal of a good many of the bargemen to reenlist, the small Maryland navy continued its operations in the Bay and sound.[43] Believing that all the islanders were active in the piracy, the officers of the barges raided Smith island to search out the culprits. They left behind bitterness and a hatred of intruders.

The winter of '83 was an especially hard one, and that old pirate, Joseph Whayland, added to the islanders' misery by "taking post with a considerable force," and boldly constructing barracks for his crew at Kedges Straits.[44] It was necessary for the islanders to be constantly on the watch against raids.

Finally, the war dragged to an end, and the picaroons disbanded. Whayland was captured several times, but he never really paid for his crimes. However, the rogue Marmaduke Mister reformed and gained the confidence of the Maryland Council, who decreed: "Marmaduke Mister has permission to return home, he having brought some American prisoners from the Tangier Islands."[45] The council paid him nine pounds for this service.

Commodore John Kidd abandoned his base of operations on tiny Watts Island. The enemy's ships sailed out of the Bay, but the southern tip of Smith Island was dubbed "Rogue's Point," a place of ill repute, named for the sea bandits who had kept the islanders in virtual captivity for nearly a decade.

Peace was welcomed, but the war had changed the islanders' lives. Wartime hardships caused them to turn inward, to learn to depend almost entirely upon themselves for their wants and needs. As if in self-defense, the islanders built a tough outer shell around themselves; they no longer trusted outsiders.

But outsiders did not include the neighboring Tangiermen. Separated only by a narrow sheet of water, the two islands rejoiced together in their deliverance from the enemy. Along with the people of Tangier, the people of Smith Island were stronger and wiser for their wartime experiences. They were knit together with a common bond of self-preservation. Endurance had become the key to survival. They had endured, and they had survived.

Commodore Whaley now sleeps in a private graveyard in Onancock, Virginia. A simple stone marks his final resting place in the Corbin plot at Scott Hall, where his grave is carefully tended by those who revere his memory.[46] On Smith Island, the waters of Kedges Straits flow peacefully past the shores of the Glenn L. Martin Wildlife Refuge, where the marshland is carefully managed to ensure the preservation of a natural habitat for wildlife. This refuge seems to be a fitting memorial to the men who fought and died in Kedges Straits.

But even today, Smith Islanders are reminded of the days when their ancestors faced wartime hardships. A twentieth century islander wrote:

Smith Island, Chesapeake Bay

The early development of Maryland with all of its
problems has never passed over this community lightly.
They endured hardships beyond description that faced
them during all our wars. Often ships sought harbor
and the atrocities of the warriors were known to those
early settlers. Houses were sacked, animals butchered,
most of their food supplies carried aboard ship . . .
These hardships left the little group with the knowledge
that they must always lend a hand whenever a neighbor
needed one. No greater brotherhood can be found today
anywhere in Maryland.[47]

IV

The Enemy Tests a New Faith

The memory of the just is blessed to generations following; and it becomes a grateful, and a useful task to per-
petuate the influence and example of a good life—such a
life as that of Joshua Thomas.
                                    —The Rev. James A. Massey

DURING the Revolution, there were still only a few widely
scattered farms on Smith Island, but by the turn of the
century, there were nearly a hundred people, most of them
related to each other. Nearly all bore the names of Marsh,
Evans, Bradshaw, Tyler, or Thomas. At Rogue's Point, there
were four families and four more at Drum Point; at North End,
there were five, and on that part known as "Over the Thorofare,"
lived six families.[1]

There had never been a set method of worship on Smith
Island or Tangier, no church building or regular services. Each
family was responsible for its own spiritual and educational
needs, usually following the pattern set by its forebears. Among
those families, there were those who lived by a rigid moral code,
others who were less strict, and those who chose not to obey
the rules of God or man.

On Smith Island, there are no legends concerning the
actual religious customs of the earliest settlers. It is known that
they possessed prayer books, but the earliest Bibles on the
island date from the midnineteenth century.[2]

However, on Tangier Island there is a recorded legend
concerning the religious habits of the earliest settlers there. In
Something Fishy From Tangier, E. Frank Dize says that the first

53

permanent settler on that island was John Crockett, who took up land there in 1686. He was "a very pious and believing man, and must have set a good example for his entire household to abide by." When he came to Tangier, Mr. Crockett brought with him a small book that contained just one prayer.

In his booklet, Mr. Dize also says:

> They were happy people and lived simple, God fearing and worshipping lives even though they did not have the spiritual guidance of a church or a Bible. By today's standards, that might seem pretty dull, but John Crockett continued to read his one prayer all of his days, and his children followed his example.

Later, in 1755, Thomas Crockett became the recipient of the first Bible on Tangier. In gratitude for his kindness in directing them to safe harbor, two men on a strange boat gave him the Bible. That same night, "Tom Crockett sat up very late and by the light of pine knots, tried reading and spelling the words, as he found great comfort in them. The next day, news flew all over the island that Tom Crockett had a Bible, and people came to gaze at it, wondering at the words that Tom read and spelled from it."[3]

Shortly after the Revolution, the new evangelical religion, The New Society, or Wesleyanism, spread through Accomack-Northampton in Virginia, and more traffic was added to the highway of the Chesapeake—vessels carrying people to the camp meeting revivals of the Methodists. A resident of both Tangier and Smith Island was to play a significant role in the tremendous revival that swept the Eastern Shore. Joshua Thomas was to become known as the immortal "Parson of the Islands."

No one community can claim Joshua Thomas, who has his own special place in the history of Methodism. He belongs to the Eastern Shore. Born in Potato Neck in Somerset County, Joshua was the son of John Thomas, a schoolteacher who later became a sailor.[4] After his father died, Joshua lived for a time on Tangier Island with his mother and stepfather. As a result of the war, the stepfather became a drunkard:

> "He used us very well for a time, and having some property of his own added to mother's, he appeared to have good management, and was steady and kind. But the refugees came along and burned our house down, and destroyed nearly everything we had in the world. This had such a bad effect on him, that he became

54

Buy boats, like the *Katie S* and *Grover G* pictured in the boat basin at Ewell, Smith Island, purchase seafood from island watermen and transport it to markets on the mainland. The back of Miss Willie's store and the Ewell United Methodist Church and parsonage are in the background. (Photograph by Marion E. Warren.)

harsh to us, and took to hard drinking, and never done much for us afterward."

—Joshua Thomas, in *Parson of the Islands*

When the stepfather drowned, the already destitute family was left to fend for itself, and when Joshua became old enough to think of his future, he was apprenticed to Captain David Tyler, a Smith Islander who followed the water.[5] Captain Tyler was a morally strict man, and as Joshua Thomas said later, "as far as he knew in what religion consisted, he practiced it, and taught it to me. I learned a great many good things from him." The Tylers grew to love Joshua as one of their own, and raised him to be a hardworking, industrious young waterman.

As a small boy, Joshua had harvested Bay waters to provide food for his mother and family; through his work with Captain Tyler, his skill as a waterman increased, and he became one of the first of that unique breed that has developed into a special class of man, separated from the rest of humanity by his very existence. His work on the water groomed him for his years of service as parson to the islands; the storms he faced at sea prepared him for the spiritual battles that lay ahead of him.

At twenty-three, Joshua chose a bride, an island girl named Rachel Evans.[6] After their marriage, the couple continued to live with Captain Tyler until they had saved enough money to build their own small house at Tangier.

As a youth, Joshua Thomas was considered to be the best dancer on Smith island; he played just as hard as he worked. As a family man, he settled down, and began to consider the state of his soul. He had always been grateful for his blessings and had been taught to worship God, but questions remained in his heart. He sought answers, continually talking to island elders about God and those things spiritual. Attending divine service in island homes, using his prayer book, and lifting his voice in hymns of praise was not enough for him.

As the new religion spread, Methodist evangelists were holding bush meetings all over the region. Because of his knowledge of the water, Joshua was often asked to act as pilot to the groups of vessels carrying people to the meetings.[7]

He usually kept his distance at the bush meetings, observing, but not participating. Like the other islanders, he was skeptical of this holy spirit that could make its converts faint, then pick them up laughing and shouting. And he remained suspicious, but still searching, until the day finally came when he gave himself over to God completely. Then, for the first time, he prayed aloud without a prayer book, and lifted his voice in public testimony.

Through the prayers and efforts of Joshua Thomas, Methodism was established on the Chesapeake Bay islands, welding a holy chain that remains unbroken to this day. In his log canoe, the *Methodist*, he visited the islands, where he held prayer meetings during which he urged his listeners to fast and pray for a revival of pure religion.

His canoe, the *Methodist*, was said to be the largest canoe afloat. It was built from a tree so large that when it was felled, its fall was "like the roar and reverberation of heavy ordnance, and shook the ground for many miles around."[8] In fact, it was so large that two canoes were hewed from its mammoth trunk. The length of the *Methodist* was between twenty and thirty feet; her beam was five feet. She was rigged with raking masts and triangular sails. With these sails unfurled to catch the breeze, Joshua Thomas sailed to every island home, bringing God's message to every heart until, one by one, the islanders came to believe.

Two prominent landowners were considered the wisest among the islanders. They were looked to for counsel and leadership. These brothers became the leaders of the community and church, and became known as King Solomon and King Richard.[9] King Richard's home had once been used as the social center where great balls, or frolics, were held; now his home was to be used as a place of worship, for the first organized prayer meeting on Smith Island.[10]

On an island, the wind and the tide often determine important events. At low tide, vessels cannot always navigate the shoals, and sailing depends upon the wind. When the time, the tide, and other conditions were right for a call to worship, a flag was hoisted to signal the people that meeting was about to begin, and a horn was blown to signal those close enough to hear. With the *Methodist* leading the way, the waters of the sound would soon be white with sail.

While the people of the Tangier Islands were experiencing a religious awakening, the waterway to Maryland harbors was busier than ever before. Baltimore City had grown into a sprawling industrial metropolis with mills, factories, lumberyards, and a bustling port where oceangoing vessels sailed in to load up with lumber, pitch and tar, cotton and paper goods. Cambridge on the Choptank and Annapolis on the Severn were thriving with trade. Farmers carried wagonloads of grain to Chestertown to be stored while awaiting shipment; Bay shipyards were busy turning out vessels to carry American products to other nations.

Young America was busy, but while America was growing and trying to build a stable government, war between France and England was renewed. England destroyed the French and Spanish fleets, and became queen of the seas again, while Napoleon Bonaparte was rapidly becoming the conqueror of Europe.

The American nation was at peace with the nations of Europe, but as tension grew between France and England, America's foreign commerce was threatened. Great Britain issued orders against ships from neutral countries who were trading with ports under Napoleon's control; Napoleon retaliated by authorizing the seizure of neutral ships that dared to trade with the British Isles. He seized American ships and sold their cargo.

To make matters worse, the British overhauled American ships to search for deserters. Although the laws of England did not allow her citizens the right to transfer allegiance to another country, hundreds of British sailors had come to the United States to become naturalized citizens. On American ships, they earned better pay and received more humane treatment.

British captains made a habit of boarding American ships, and refused to recognize naturalization papers. Often, they seized American seamen as well as Britons who had jumped ship. American shipping concerns seethed with indignation.

An incident in American waters roused a raging fury. The American frigate, *Chesapeake*, left Norfolk in June of 1807. Just outside the capes, she was overtaken by the British warship, *Leopard*, whose captain ordered her to stop and be searched for British deserters. The commander of the *Chesapeake*, Captain Barron, was not prepared to put up a fight, but the *Leopard* attacked, killing three seamen and injuring nearly a score. After taking off four men that they claimed were British deserters, the *Leopard* sped away out to sea, leaving the *Chesapeake* to limp back to Norfolk.

When news of the *Chesapeake* incident reached the president, he was angered by the attack, and issued a proclamation forbidding British warships to enter American waters. He also ordered an apology from Great Britain and an end to impressment. The apology came quickly, but the search and seizure continued.[11]

If the people of Smith Island were aware of the strained relationship between the two nations and the possibility of a new war, there was not too much concern. Their population, too, had grown, expanded with more branches of the same families, to nearly one hundred people. As they worked their little ridges of farmland, tended their sheep, gathered oysters and crabs, and organized their church, Smith Islanders thought England and the problems of the new nation seemed far away.

But it wasn't long before the nation's problems were brought to their own back door. Soon, they would need all of their newfound faith, for in June of 1812, Congress declared war on Great Britain, and by midwinter, the British were in the Bay. Once again, war was carried to the islands via the highway of the Chesapeake.

The United States was hardly prepared for war. Its naval forces numbered less than twenty frigates and sloops, all built in the days of Washington and Adams, and just over a hundred small boats intended only for coastal defense.[12] England, with her superiority in numbers, was mistress of the seas. Soon, British cruisers were crippling the nation's foreign trade by keeping a tight blockade along the East Coast.

By late December, the Chesapeake was in a state of blockade, with trade and transportation disrupted. Admiral Sir John Warren ordered the blockade and sent Admiral Sir George Cockburn to carry out his orders. Sir George sailed into the Bay with four ships of the line, eight smaller vessels, and nearly two thousand troops. The Chesapeake campaign had begun.[13]

The British fleet bypassed Norfolk for Hampton Roads; from there, they sailed up the Bay, creating alarm along its shores. As they had during the Revolution, the British relied on sacking farms and homes to feed their men. They sailed in and out of the Bay at will, harassing the coasts of the Carolinas as well as Maryland and Virginia shores.[14]

Cockburn and his men soon gained a reputation of wanton destruction of property. Farmers on the Eastern Shore and the islanders lived in constant dread of the enemy. Cockburn seemed to have a grudge against Americans; he vented his spleen against the shores of the Bay with cruelty and bloodshed. His large warships could not navigate the little creeks and inlets, so he sent out tenders to forage for fresh water and provisions. Stealing, looting, and burning, he and his men ravished the Shore.

Intent as he was on ridding the waters of all American vessels, Cockburn did not overlook even the smallest, meanest of boats. His tactics were to seek out and destroy. Squadrons of men went out on patrol; oyster boats, crabbing skiffs, any waterman's boat left unhidden, fell victim, burned to the waterline. Sir George was especially eager to steal away slaves from farms and plantations. To persuade them to join the British troops, he promised them freedom and arms.

Admiral Sir Alexander Cochrane had ordered Cockburn to recruit blacks to the British cause. Cockburn had planned to take his army to New Hampshire, leaving only a few of his men in the South. As part of the scheme Cockburn intended to seize Tangier Island. "When fortified," Sir Alexander said, "it will be a place of refuge for the blacks to fly to."[15]

That summer, a frigate and four smaller boats came up the Bay and anchored right off Smith Point.[16] In the fall, *Niles Weekly Register* reported another frigate off the mouth of the Potomac, at Smith Island's back door, committing the usual depredations on the farms and Bay craft. Admiral Cockburn went hunting again on the rivers and creeks of the Chesapeake; even the most miserable craft he burned or otherwise destroyed.[17]

Island homes were not safe from the foraging parties. Enemy cruisers hovered in Kedges Straits and Tangier Sound, boldly helping themselves to island produce. Once again, islanders watched anxiously to sea, dreading enemy intrusion into their homeland.

To make matters worse, British warships sailed into the harbor at Tangier, where they anchored off and sent troops on shore to take possession of that tiny island. Tangier was to be used for the base of their operations while they ravaged the Bay shores.

As enemy soldiers marched across the beach on Tangier, they were met by a group of islanders who feared for their lives and property. The islanders were informed that they were now prisoners of war, and were to furnish the troops with meat and produce, for which they would be paid a price set by their captors.[18]

The officers requisitioned island homes for their headquarters, while their troops began to clear ground for the construction of two forts. In Joshua Thomas's own words, "They still went on with their buildings and walks; and when they were finished, it was a most beautiful place. The two forts were erected a little to the south of the camp ground, east and west from each other, and about three hundred yards apart. The tents of the army were pitched in a semicircular form, extending about half round on the north side, and a very pleasant summer house was built in the centre."[19]

By late June, the fort was almost finished; three sides, each 250 yards long, were completed and the soldiers were building a hospital large enough to accommodate one hundred sick or wounded. Twenty houses, all laid out in streets, were built for the officers.

Although the people of Tangier were prisoners of the British, and their movements were restricted, they did not fare too badly. For the most part, they were treated with courtesy and respect. They accepted pay, such as it was, for their supplies, and were grateful that their belongings were not stolen outright. The only real damage done on Tangier during the occupation was the destruction of the beautiful trees that were cut down to furnish lumber for the enemy forts.

The prayer grove at Tangier, site of the conversion of many souls, and therefore, sacred ground to Tangiermen, was spared through the intervention of Joshua Thomas. The parson approached the admiral himself to plead for the preservation of the grove where the camp meetings were held. The hardened commander of the British navy solemnly gave his word that not one of the trees in that sacred place would be touched.

Reverend Thomas found that many of the British soldiers respected the Tangier beliefs and were eager to join with the islanders in worship and fellowship. He was allowed to minister to the troops in the role of chaplain, and held services for them, as well as for his own people.

The British made Tangier their center of operations while they continued to plunder the Maryland and Virginia shoreline. The pickings were so good that Admiral Cockburn sent a message saying: "The only difficulty I have now is how to dispose of the prize goods after we get them. I believe you must convert some of the barracks on Tangier into store houses till the Admiral sends us a transport to take away our riches."[20]

61

Smith Island, Chesapeake Bay

Tangier was used, not only as a base of operations by the British, but also as a training center.[21] Slaves, stolen or lured away from their masters, had been promised new lives. They were brought to Tangier by foraging parties. An encampment was prepared for them on the beach, where about eighty slaves, both men and women, were kept while the Englishmen drilled them and tried to shape them into a fighting squadron. All this activity seemed strange to the people of Tangier; they waited patiently for deliverance.

But peace was not to come for a time. On April 16, enemy barges landed on Sharps Island, where the troops stole stock and slaves, looted, plundered, and went on to harass farms and plantations along the river banks.[22] Shortly after, a squadron from the fleet searched out and burned seven vessels in the Little Annemessex. The depredations continued.

Finally, in May, Commodore Joshua Barney, intent upon attacking the encampment on Tangier, led sixteen vessels down the Bay. But Barney was greatly outnumbered and was compelled to retreat.[23] For the people of the Eastern Shore, the situation was serious, almost desperate.

The Tangiermen tried to keep their friends and relatives on Smith Island aware of the movements of the enemy, warning them of danger whenever possible. Risking their own safety, they slipped quietly away from the harbor at Tangier to take news to their neighbors. Time and again, couriers poled boats across the stretch of water between the two islands to take messages from friends and information concerning the British troops.

This close communication is part of a Smith Island legend:

> During the War of 1812, there was only one supply store on Smith Island. It was built at the edge of the marsh, on a pile of oyster shells eight feet high, and was appropriately named, "Shell Pile." Toward the end of the war, the supply of stores was getting extremely low when the storekeeper, Alex Tyler, received news from a Tangierman that the enemy fleet had sailed away on maneuvers and was not expected back at Tangier for several days.[24]
>
> Alex decided to take a chance on running the blockade, to try to reach Baltimore in his boat, and pick up enough supplies to replenish the store, then hurry back before the battleships returned. He left his young wife, Sarah, in charge of the family and store.
>
> Before Alex could get back, news arrived from Tangier that the British fleet had been sighted. Quickly, Sarah

gathered up her children, locked up the store, and fled to the refuge of her brother's house. But Sarah was troubled. In her rush to get her children safely away from the isolated store, she had forgotten a sacred trust.

Alex was the church treasurer; the money chest was hidden in the potato house back at Shell Pile. Sarah had been left in charge, not only of the family and the business, but of the church treasury as well. Determined to retrieve the box, Sarah left her children in bed and her brother on his knees praying for her protection, and began the long trek across the marsh by moonlight.

There were no bridges across the marshy inlets and ditches, and the way was hard. At each ditch, she had to lug a long tree trunk that had been cut for that purpose. After finding the log, she had to push it over the ditch to make a bridge to walk on. This she did six times, each time pulling the log away from the ditch and hiding it in the rushes to discourage pursuit. Although Sarah weighed little more than a hundred pounds, she was young and strong, and sheer courage and determination kept her going. Finally clear of the marsh, she ran to the potato house at Shell Pile to find the money chest.

The young island girl began her trek back through the marsh carrying her precious burden, once more lugging the bridge logs across the ditches. Once again, she hid them to be sure no enemy soldier could find his way across the marshy inlets. She made her slow way back to the safety of her brother's house.

Exhausted from her ordeal, she trudged silently up the path. Then, from inside the house came the deep tones of a man's voice. Cautiously, Sarah crept nearer the house, fearful that the soldiers had arrived and had captured her family. Then, she realized that the voice was that of her own brother, still on his knees praying for her safe return. Throughout that long night, the brother and sister kept watch, and for one more night, they were safe from the enemy.

To Sarah, her husband's position as church treasurer was a sacred honor; the treasury, a sacred fortune. The money, all fifty-six dollars of it, was safe in Sarah's keeping until Alex returned.

In August of 1814, a large British force under the command of Admiral Sir George Cockburn sailed up the Bay toward the Patuxent, where Major General Robert Ross landed his troops for the march on Washington. The British set fire to the Capitol and the White House; President Madison and his cabinet fled to Virginia for refuge.[25]

Far off on the Canadian border, the Americans forced the British to retreat, and in the Southwest, General Jackson gained victory over the Creek Indians and forced them to sign the treaty of Fort Jackson, then marched into Mobile and Pensacola. In the Great Lakes region, U.S. naval vessels were prevailing over British ships, but the islanders knew nothing of these victories.

What they did know was that the enemy was right at hand, hovering in Kedges Straits and off Smith Point, burning boats and plundering.[26] And at Tangier, the citizens became aware of a new excitement among the troops quartered there. Preparations were being made to move out for an attack on Baltimore.

It was here at Tangier that Joshua Thomas gave the British a fiery sermon with his warning that the troops would be defeated.[27] As bands played on the decks of ships lying offshore, the British gathered for religious services before their assault on Baltimore.

The parson stood on a little platform in the prayer grove to give an emotional exhortation; he emphasized the evils of war and warned the troops of the dangers that awaited them. Without fear, he predicted the defeat of the expedition to Fort McHenry:

> "I warned them of the danger and distress they would bring upon themselves and others by going to Baltimore with the object they had in view. I told them of the great wickedness of war, and that God said, '*Thou shalt not kill!*' If you do, he will judge you at the last day, or before then, he will cause you to 'perish by the sword.'
>
> "I told them it was given me from the Almighty that they *could* not take Baltimore, and *would not succeed in their expedition.*
>
> "I exhorted them to prepare for death, for many of them would, in all likelihood die soon, and I should see them no more till we met at the sound of the great trumpet before our final Judge."

Respectfully, the English listened, but they refused to believe. Up to now, their troops had met with little resistance on the Bay. The seat of American government lay in smoking ruins; they were confident of victory. The fleet weighed anchor and stood up the Bay.

Throughout the night of the thirteenth of September, the people of the islands heard the far-off booming of heavy artillery, and waited anxiously for news of the battle. When the ships returned, the Tangiermen learned that the British had not been able to take Baltimore. Hundreds of troops lost their lives, including Major General Ross. The parson's prediction had been fulfilled, and it was remembered by the defeated soldiers as they came ashore to nurse their wounded and bury their dead.

In January of 1815, peace came once more to the nation and to the Bay islands. Because of the fort on Tangier, the islands were among the first to hear the news. As Joshua Thomas told Adam Wallace:

> "We perceived a mighty stir in the camp one day; and witnessed signals flying, and great commotion of ships and shore. We could not tell what it meant for some time. By and by, one of the officers came riding up to my house as hard as he could gallop, crying out, 'Oh, Parson Thomas! Parson Thomas! *There's peace*, THERE'S PEACE!!' I inquired, 'How do you know?' 'Oh,' said he, 'yonder is the ship,' pointing down the bay to where a large vessel was seen coming up, 'and she has a *white flag* at her mast head. That signal means peace, and now we know the war is over!'"

One British soldier is buried on the grounds of Pittcraft, the oldest plantation on Smith Island. For many years, a British flag flew over the grave of the unknown soldier. But it is at Tangier that the bodies of many British soldiers lie in unmarked graves south of the prayer grove. The waters of the Chesapeake now cover the sleeping British, and there is nothing left of the forts they constructed on Tangier Island.[28]

As swelling tides began their work of washing away the signs of occupation, the islanders turned once more to their routine of plowing and fishing. And once more, they rebuilt their ruined boats, uncovered the hidden ones, and went about their business.

Joshua Thomas lived on Tangier Island until he was nearly fifty; then he moved his family to Deal Island and became a minister of the local church. He continued to travel his circuit of the islands, preaching to his people, until he grew old and became a helpless cripple. Even then, his family and friends built a special carriage to transport him back and forth to church.

65

Smith Island, Chesapeake Bay

He died on Deal Island at the age of seventy-seven. His tomb is in the churchyard of the chapel on the island, where visitors can read the following inscription:

> Come all my friends, as you pass by,
> Behold the place where I do lie
> As you are now, so once was I,
> Remember, you are born to die.

Down through the ages, the life of Joshua Thomas has been a living guide for his people—as they say on Smith island—a light to go by. Like his watermen friends, he was not endowed with the social graces, or an overabundance of culture. He had no formal education, no great vocabulary. He was a simple, faithful, holy man of God.

In his voyage through life, he touched every island home and heart, leaving behind a legacy of God's love and reverence. To others beyond the islands, Joshua Thomas may be only a long-ago preacher of Methodism, but on Smith Island, he is still the "Parson of the Islands."

V

On the Border of Rebellion

I hold, that in contemplation of universal law, and of the Constitution, the Union of these States is perpetual . . . no state upon its own mere motivation, can lawfully get out of the Union.

—Abraham Lincoln
March 4, 1861

WHEN the War of 1812 ended, America was already beginning to divide itself into sections. The area north and east of the Potomac quickly became the center of industrialism; the South developed its plantation system, and the western frontier with its rich expanse of farmland drew settlers toward the Mississippi.

Each section of the country had different types of people with different occupations and traditions, and each had different problems. Now that the war was over, the nation was able to turn back to dealing with the problems associated with its rapid growth and the ensuing sectionalism.

But on Smith Island, where life was quickly returning to normal, the people were not concerned with the nation's difficulties. They were concerned only with their own immediate problems.

To feed their families and replenish their storehouses, they plowed their fields and planted Indian corn, sweet potatoes, melons, and garden vegetables. They retrieved their boats from their hiding places, and went to work repairing them or building new ones.

Smith Island, Chesapeake Bay

Now that the enemy ships had sailed away, the islanders were once more able to enjoy the freedom of their watery world. Once more, they were able to fish and crab, and to visit their neighbors without fear of the enemy.

Their boats were a vital part of their lives, and they were master boatbuilders. The early islanders had developed a unique vessel, one adapted to their specific needs—the Smith Island crabbing skiff. This small but seaworthy craft had a full, V-shaped bottom, was planked fore and aft, and was built with a square stern and just one mast. Other island skiffs were flat bottomed to enable them to skim across shoal water.

They became adept at building larger boats, too: the log canoe, the brogan, and the bugeye. But eventually, the two-masted pungy became the favorite vessel of island captains. This sturdy, schooner-rigged boat could be used for both fishing and oystering, or to carry cargo from one Bay port to another.

During the cold winter months, farmer and boatbuilder turned to harvesting muskrat, wildfowl, and oysters. The islanders tramped the marshland, setting traps for the small beaverlike animal that built its winter home in the marsh. Called marsh rabbit by some of the islanders, the muskrat was a welcome addition to the table. So were the ducks and geese that migrated from colder climates. The islanders set up duck blinds to conceal themselves as they brought down wildfowl to add to their food supply.

Hunting for muskrat and shooting ducks and geese were as much sport as work. But oystering was, and still is, cold grueling work. Such hard work and constant exposure to raw weather have always been a part of the islander's life; he's learned to live with sore knees, aching back, and freezing hands that sometimes break open and bleed.

Shaft tonging is the oldest method of gathering oysters. The hand tongs consist of two iron rakes mounted on the ends of a pair of long wooden handles that are riveted together or fastened with a wooden plug. Standing on the washboard of his low-sided boat, the tonger grasps the handles of his tongs and allows the heavy iron to slide down into the water. Then, opening and closing his tongs with a pincerslike movement, he feels for oysters. He works his tongs until he feels that he has a good catch, then he pinches the oysters away from their bed and carefully raises the shafts and dumps his catch on the culling board.

68

Aerial view of a portion of Smith Island as it was in 1969. In the right foreground are shanties and pounds that contain overboard floats. Pounds like these are no longer in use; they have been replaced by a more modern system. The pounds were connected by plank walkways and surrounded by wooden frames. When the floats became crusty with barnacles and moss, they were dragged up on the frames for cleaning and repair. (Photograph by Marion E. Warren.)

When his board is full, he drops to his knees and begins the task of breaking the clusters of oysters apart with a culling hammer. Those oysters that are too small to keep are tossed overboard, where they will catch on a rock and continue growing. Slowly, his baskets fill with legal-sized oysters, and as the wintry sun begins to slide down the western sky, he turns his boat toward home.

The islanders first heard of the growing market for oysters from "foreigners," who traveled to the Chesapeake from the northeast coast in search of a new source of supply when their own oyster beds could not keep up with the increasing demands of the northern market. The strangers who introduced the dredge to the Bay area were dubbed "Nordmen" by the islanders. Since the Nordmen were prevented by law from taking seafood away from Bay waters, large processing plants were set up in Baltimore, and a new industry opened up on the shores of the Bay.[1]

Then, as now, buy boats met the oystermen to unload their catch and haul the oysters to market. However, it wasn't very long before a few observant islanders realized that freighting the oysters themselves would be even more profitable.

Other island captains turned to freighting cargoes of local produce up to the long dock at Baltimore. Or they sailed across to the western shore of the Bay to pick up cordwood, lumber, or grain. Some ventured as far as the West Indies to trade for tropical fruits, sugar, and molasses.

Usually, Smith Island freighters were gone for months at a time; they sailed from port to port, loading and unloading, then moved on to repeat the process. Traveling the Chesapeake highway became a profitable venture, and it made little difference to the island men that some of the ports they visited were in Virginia and some in Maryland.

Although these islanders had always enjoyed free use of the water surrounding their home, they had always been aware that a dividing line did exist. They knew the locations of the stones that marked the boundary between the two states. They did not know exactly when, or by whom, the markers had been placed, but they believed that the stones had been sunk long before the first settler made his home on Smith Island. These ancient stones were a part of island tradition.

Stories are told of island fathers making a ritual of impressing on the minds of their young sons the fact that the island sat on the line that divided the two states. As a reminder to the next generation that the line must be observed, boy children were taken to one of the stones and whipped, or rowed out to one just offshore and dunked.[2]

This ceremony was reminiscent of a feast day observed by their ancestors in old England. Processional Day was a ceremonial day, the day when the elders assembled to parade through the town, walk off its boundaries, and record exactly the land belonging to the people. Paper could not be used for the recording, for paper was easily destroyed or lost; markers could be moved or stolen away. Instead, they used boy children to pass on the boundary limits.

To ensure that territorial bounds would be remembered, each boy was taken to a landmark and severely whipped. If the boundary crossed a pond or river, he was picked up and held under the water until he emerged, gasping for breath, the location of the boundary indelibly etched on his memory.

In the early nineteenth century, only a few stones remained to mark the line across the island, but where the line was clearly indicated it was strictly observed. Some island landowners paid taxes in Virginia, others in Maryland, and some in both states. Most had their property recorded in the county seat of Somerset County, Maryland; some recorded their property in Accomac, Virginia. Several recorded it in both places because they were not absolutely sure just where Virginia left off and Maryland began.

Island oystermen obtained licenses from either state or both, and voters registered in the state they called their home state. Until a separate and additional election district was laid out in 1835, a few voted at different times in each state. But after that, voters whose homes were not designated as being in the new Maryland district sailed to Accomac to cast their votes; the rest were able to stay at home and vote at the Methodist meeting house.[3]

Sometimes it was even convenient for the island to be part in Virginia and part in Maryland. For instance, on the southwest shore of Smith Island there is a place called Hog Neck. Marshy now and long since eaten away from the rest of the island by erosion, Hog Neck once sustained homes and farms. The house of John Parks was at Hog Neck. The greater part of his house was in Maryland, but his kitchen and outbuildings were considered to be over the line in Virginia.

71

This provided a unique situation for couples who wanted to elope. They could run away from their Virginia parents and be married in John Parks's Maryland parlor, or cross the line from Maryland and be wed in John's kitchen.

Sometimes the ceremonies were conducted by the local justice of the peace, but according to testimony given to the Arbitration Commission in 1872, Tangier's Joshua Thomas presided over most island ceremonies. When Maryland couples desired to wed, the Parson of the Islands met them in John Parks's dwelling house. When a couple from Virginia wished to marry, he took them to the kitchen, "that part of the house being considered in Virginia."[4]

Another boundary legend concerns Cow Ridge, close to Pittcraft. In 1877, there were seven homes on Cow Ridge, all complete with gardens and orchards. Long ago, the houses were moved inland, and a herd of wild goats now inhabits part of the ridge. It is now an island called simply, Cross the Creek. Shortly after the turn of the century, a ditch was dug across the ridge; that ditch is now the channel that brings boats into the harbor at Ewell.

A huge gum tree once stood on Cow Ridge, a tree whose branches shaded nearly half an acre. On one of its enormous boughs hung a rope swing. Children were taught that the gum was a line tree; they were told to remember that when swinging high out over the ground, they were flying over Virginia. When the swing flew backwards, they soared back over Maryland. In this way, the children were taught that the line that divided the two states went straight across Smith Island.

By midcentury, the islanders were beginning to realize the very real significance of that line. For as the demand for oysters increased, so did the harvesting of oyster beds in the Potomac River and the Pocomoke and Tangier sounds. Oystermen became greedy, and Marylanders and Virginians began to argue over the oyster beds they had been sharing.

In the confusion over the exact location of the boundary, several Smith Island vessels were arrested for dredging in Maryland waters. The *Edington* and the *Amelia Ann* were condemned, but the captain of the island vessel, *Fashion*, won his case against the state of Maryland, and also won a judgment against his arresting officer.

John Cullen, an officer of Somerset County, arrested Captain John Tyler, who lived at Horse Hammock on Smith Island.

On the Border of Rebellion

Although Captain Tyler was charged with being a Virginian caught oystering in Maryland waters, his attorney was a Marylander. Mr. Crisfield, for whom the town of Crisfield was named, won a judgment of one thousand dollars against Mr. Cullen.[5]

Marylanders and Virginians continued to argue with each other, but before the controversy over oysters had a chance to grow into a full-fledged war, Smith Island finally became involved again in the nation's problems.

The differences between the North and South were leading to the War Between the States. Shortly after Abraham Lincoln won the presidency, the animosity between the industrial north and the slavery-dependent south came to a head. South Carolina severed its ties with the Union, and six other states quickly followed suit. In April of 1861, Virginia seceded from the Union, but Maryland cast her votes against secession. And Smith Island, part in Maryland and part in Virginia, was truly on the border of rebellion.

The Eastern Shore of Maryland, especially the southern counties, held strong sympathies with the South, and it was the same on Smith Island. In spite of their differences over oysters, the islanders had strong ties with family and friends in Virginia. There were only a handful of slaves on the island, but the islanders resented the authority of the Union, and feared the limitations that might be imposed on them. They wanted nothing more than to be allowed to live in peace, to remain isolated from the conflict, and to follow the water.

But they were not to be let alone. In the same month that Virginia seceded from the Union, President Lincoln declared a blockade of the Confederate States. His proclamation commanded that "any vessels attempting to enter or leave ports would be warned first; if further attempt was made, the vessel would be captured and confiscated."[6]

Since 1852, steamboats had been running regularly between Washington and Virginia, and between Baltimore and Norfolk, and by 1860, service to Eastern Shore communities had been increased. Then the steamboats were pressed into service by the government, converted for use as naval warfare vessels.[7]

Before long, when it became imperative to keep the Potomac River open, the Federal forces began to use some of these vessels to patrol the waters close to Smith Island. The capital city of Washington is on the northern shore of the Potomac;

73

just across the river is Virginia. Along the Virginia shore of the river, Confederates began erecting batteries to prevent the safe passage of Union vessels.

The Potomac Flotilla was established and set aside as an independent command to provide security for the capital, to keep the Potomac clear, and to help prevent smuggling of contraband to the Confederacy.[8]

After his first blockade proclamation, the president issued a second command to appoint Flag Officer Stringham, United States Navy, as commander of the squadron that would "carry into effect the proclamations at all the ports and the capes from the Chesapeake to the southern extremity of Florida Key West, including the ports, rivers, and inlets of the Chesapeake Bay."[9] Stringham's ship, the *Minnesota*, was dispatched to Hampton Roads at the lower end of the Bay, where a considerable force gathered to ensure the blockade.

But in spite of the blockade, supplies were reaching the Confederates. Naval Secretary Gideon Welles sent messages to the Potomac Flotilla, warning the officers that since the president's proclamation had been issued, there had been hostile and insurrectionary movements of a threatening character in and near the waters of the Chesapeake.[10] Armed rebel vessels roamed the waters; small boats loaded with contraband from Maryland sympathizers scuttled across the line. Cargo supposedly bound for southern Maryland counties was being unloaded just below the boundary, or in those Eastern Shore towns where willing hands received it and smuggled it on to the rebels.

Instead of putting into Eastern Shore harbors, other small craft loaded with supplies headed for rendezvous among the Tangier Islands. Once more, the hidden harbors of the offshore Bay islands became hiding places for boats being used for illicit activities.

From secluded island coves, rebel sympathizers watched for opportunities to cross the Bay and sail to the Rappahannock on Virginia's western shore. Secretary Welles sent instructions to his officers that they were to take measures to prevent these violations of the blockade and to vindicate the authority of the government.[11]

The elusive rebels continued to capture small steamers to try to get supplies through to Virginia. The *Hurl*, a steamer plying between Baltimore and the Pocomoke River, was reported to be laden with contraband. Her destination was to be

Smith Island, where the articles were to be hidden until they could be sent across the Bay and into the Confederacy. D. L. Braine, commander of the USS *Monticello* was dispatched to the island to intercept the *Hurl*, to seize the steamer and question the island people.[12]

Early in the morning of June 24, the *Monticello* started for Tangier Sound. Following blockade instructions, Braine steered up the Chesapeake from Hampton Roads, stopping all vessels on his way. From a captain of a small boat, Braine received information concerning the whereabouts of a steamer loaded with contraband a short distance from the mouth of the Rappahannock.

The commander changed course for the western shore. Not seeing any sign of a steamer, he ran a short distance up the river to the plantation of a man reputed to have strong Union sentiments. There, he hoped to get information. A squadron of men rowed into shore in a launch, while the lieutenant stood watch.

The master of the house gave the men a cordial welcome, then stepped back. Almost immediately, Braine's men were fired upon from the surrounding trees. Braine opened fire with the ship's artillery, and demolished the house. In his own words, "killing and wounding many, completely silencing their fire." Several of Braine's men were wounded; the excursion to Smith Island was aborted.[13]

The *Hurl* continued to smuggle contraband across the Chesapeake, and again, Lieutenant Braine was ordered to cruise in the vicinity of the islands. Other steamers, the *Daylight*, the *Mt. Vernon*, the *Penguin*, and the *Albatross*, were sent to keep vigil between the islands and the shore.[14] The *Penguin* cruised Tangier Sound, boarding all vessels to check for contraband.

On one of his cruises, the ship's officer sighted the American flag flying over Tangier Island. He sailed into the harbor and hoisted a jack to induce the islanders to come off. Soon, three men rowed out to tell of a Confederate plot to take over the island.[15] One islander, a secessionist, was planning to raise a rebel flag on Independence Day. When Confederates at Accomac saw the signal, they intended to send over a force to occupy the island.

They also reported that the steamboat *Wilson Small* had been down from Baltimore with a load of goods to take through to Chincoteague. The *Penguin* stayed for a while at Tangier, to discourage the confederate plot and to try to seize the *Wilson Small*. The steamboat made another appearance, but fled at the sight of the Union ship in Tangier harbor.

Nearly a month later, the sloop *Jane Wright* became the first war casualty on the Bay. She was sunk by the USS *Yankee*, just off Smith Point, the first victim of the "scorched earth policy."[16] As part of this policy, all boats operated by southern Marylanders on the lower Bay, on or near the Potomac, were to be seized or destroyed. Secretary Welles sent orders to the Potomac Flotilla to "be vigilant and not to hesitate to seize all vessels about whose movements you have the least suspicions, particularly the craft called pungies."[17]

Once more, pressure from outside forces interfered with the islander's ability to support his family. No license to fish, no permit to travel or operate a boat, to ship produce, carry freight, or even to catch oysters, was to be granted without the oath of allegiance to the Union. Without the proper papers, no boat—large or small—was to be allowed to operate on the Bay or its tributaries.

Late in the first year of the war, Federal troops invaded Virginia's Eastern Shore; Accomac and Northampton surrendered. By then, Confederate authorities had moved their capital from Montgomery to the city of Richmond, across the Potomac from Washington. Less than a hundred miles separated the two seats of government, and soon, Maryland's next door neighbor, Virginia, became the major battleground of the Civil War.

As the war escalated, small steamers like the *Wilson Small* continued to slip through the waters between northern Maryland and the southern counties, and the Potomac Flotilla was kept busy. Some flotilla vessels searched for privateers off the Carolina coast; others were sent to guard the harbors and islands of the Chesapeake.

The captain of the port at Fort Monroe took two steamers up the Bay to overhaul and search the *Wilson Small*. He overtook her in Kedges Straits and hove her to, but found nothing illegal aboard. Later, it was reported that arms and ammunition bound for the South had been removed and hidden. But after a thorough search of barns and outbuildings, the officers reported that they had found nothing.[18]

After this incident, Captain of the Port Lieutenant Pierce Cosby paid a visit to Tangier. He called all the men together and administered the oath of allegiance to them. The islanders were warned not to hold any communication with the shores of Virginia and were threatened with imprisonment and confiscation of their vessels. Since the Tangiermen's licenses came from Accomac, they were prohibited from engaging in any trade.[19]

In fact, no vessel was allowed to trade in any part of the blockaded area. When the Lieutenant Commander of the USS *Freeborn* asked for specific instructions, Secretary Welles replied that "no vessels except such that are in the government service will be permitted to pass in or out of the waters of Virginia without special permit of the Sec. of Treasury, or of the War or Navy Dept."[20]

Smith Island could not help but be affected by the rigid enforcement of the blockade. Many small incidents kept the islanders in a state of suspense. Gunboats cruised constantly, capturing or destroying small vessels suspected of aiding in smuggling operations.[21] Seine boats, crabbing skiffs, even oyster boats were destroyed.

Off Smith Point, a sloop was captured for not having legal papers and carrying on trade with the blockaded country. Among the prisoners taken was one Solomon Evans. The cargo? Old rags, oysters, pieces of iron, raw hides, and some old copper. The sloop was confiscated, her crew kept prisoner for a few days, then given the oath of allegiance and released.[22]

Conditions were nearly the same as they had been during the Revolution and the War of 1812. The islands were ideally situated to become way stations for refugees escaping the conflict. The coves and tiny inlets in the marsh made convenient hiding places for smugglers' boats, and vessels captured by the rebels could easily hide in a secluded gut and wait for an opportunity to sneak across the Bay.

It was in one of these secluded guts that the smuggling boat, *Titan*, hid from the Potomac Flotilla.[23] Before they were captured by the rebels, the Union army tug and her sister ship, the *Aeolus*, had been laying telegraph cable just off Cherrystone on the Eastern Shore of Virginia. When the *Aeolus* put in at the Cherrystone wharf, she was boarded by a band of guerrillas.

Disguised in their captives' clothes, the rebels waited for the *Titan*, and captured her, too. They disabled the *Aeolus*, robbed her crew, and sailed off in the *Titan*. But before leaving Cherrystone, they cut the telegraph wires, killed all the horses they could find, and burned the Union guardhouse and commissaries.

Union gunboats visited the islands frequently to question the islanders about the *Titan*'s whereabouts. Two steamers were detailed to search for the *Titan* and the *McClellan*, an armed steamer that had also been captured. A tug and two heavily armed schooners were stationed at Pt. Lookout; the rest of the command's vessels, except for two small tugs, cruised between the Piankatank River and Smith Point.

Under cover of a dense haze, the *Titan* sailed out of hiding, and reached the Piankatank, but she was found a few days later, burned to the waterline.

Although Union forces were unable to verify the identity of the leader of the guerrilla band that caused the *Titan*'s destruction, they suspected the notorious rebel, John Taylor Wood. Wood, grandson of President Zachary Taylor, was only one of the dashing young men willing to take desperate chances to aid the Confederacy.[24]

Among the most famous were Colonel John S. Mosby, the legendary "Gray Ghost," and the infamous W. C. Quantrill. Colonel Mosby led a band of irregulars on daring raids; they harassed Yankee supply lines, raided their outposts, and burned their wagons. Quantrill, more an outlaw than a soldier, led a band of desperados who spread terror throughout Kansas. The South also had its blockade runners, daring men who risked their ships and their lives to smuggle arms, munitions, and other desperately needed supplies to the Confederacy.

The Chesapeake had its own brand of guerrilla. There was Rice Airs, who headed a band of 150 guerrillas who were described as "a most desperate set of thieves, robbers, and murderers, who use the cloth of the rebel flag to cover their crimes."[25]

In addition to Captain John Taylor Wood and Rice Airs, there was Captain Webb, of the rebel ship *Banshee*, who was captured just off the Eastern Shore of Virginia. Webb and his men had been engaged in the plundering and burning of vessels in the Bay, and when they were caught, they admitted that they had been planning to capture a schooner with the intent of using her to board the first transport they came across and commence privateering.[26]

Men like these were often called pirates, or marauding robbers. Using hit-and-run tactics, they wrecked lighthouse facilities, disabled Yankee vessels, and raided storehouses for supplies to smuggle to the South. Basically, they were watermen who knew the tidewater rivers, the creeks and guts, and the hidden coves as well as they knew the marsh and the woods. They hid their small boats up the creeks, or drew them up into the bushes by day, then left under cover of darkness or fog to carry out their raids.[27]

Some of the guerrillas, like Captain Wood, were members of the Confederate military forces. Another was Hunter Lewis, a naval lieutenant who hatched a plot to steal a Baltimore steamer and convert it to rebel use.[28] The steamer, *St. Nicholas*, made a regular run from Baltimore to Pt. Lookout; from there she ran up the Potomac. As part of the plan, three of Lewis's collaborators would board the steamer at Baltimore; Lewis and a crew of men would wait on the Virginia side of the Potomac, and after the *St. Nicholas* left Pt. Lookout, they would take the steamer.

Disguised as a French modiste, one of the men who boarded at Baltimore charmed the other passengers until they reached Pt. Lookout. But when the French lady retired for the night, she soon reappeared, dressed in uniform and "armed to the teeth." With the aid of the other gentlemen, Richard Thomas, the French lady, captured the *St. Nicholas*.

The steamer sailed out of the Potomac and around Smith Point, where the rebels captured the coffee-laden brig, *Monticello*, the schooner *Mary Pierce*, and the coal carrier, *Margaret*. Lieutenant Lewis's plot was a complete success.

Another member of the Confederate military was John Yates Beall, a gentleman farmer who earned for himself the name of "the Mosby of the Chesapeake." Beall had served in the army under Stonewall Jackson until he received a wound that ended his army career. After recovering from his wound, he left the army and began a new career as a Confederate agent.

In 1863, Beall accepted an appointment as acting master in the Confederate navy.[29] His job was to harass the enemy by using guerrilla strategy in the Chesapeake Bay, to impede Union shipping, to destroy lighthouses and lightboats, and to make raids on the Eastern Shore, wrecking as far as possible any Union installations. The Mosby of the Chesapeake acquired two boats, one painted black and called the *Raven*, the other painted white and named the *Swan*. A considerable force of men joined him to form the Confederate Volunteer Coast Guard.

In early fall, Beall's coast guard began their destructive work of stripping the lighthouses along the coast of Virginia.[30] After gutting the facility at Smith Island, Virginia, the guard began capturing schooners and smaller vessels. The captain and crew would be sent on shore, the cargo sent to rebels in Virginia, and the vessels burned or converted to Confederate use.

Lieutenant Beall was destined for a daring, but short, period of glory. In November, he and his band captured a schooner in Tangier Sound. The guerrillas were overconfident, and didn't burn this vessel; part of the crew of raiders was sent toward Virginia with the prize. A Federal gunboat overtook them, and one frightened crew member was persuaded to talk. Beall and fourteen of his men were captured by the First Regiment of Eastern Shore, Maryland Volunteers.[31] Beall and his men were not in uniform and possessed no official orders. Therefore, they were held, not as prisoners of war, but as pirates. They were sent in irons to Fort McHenry. When the Confederate government protested this treatment, Beall was sent on to Fort Monroe to await an investigation.[32]

Eventually, Beall was released; he shifted his activities to the Great Lakes area, where he was captured again and tried as a spy. Protesting to the end that he was not a spy or a guerrilla, but a true Confederate, the dashing Mosby of the Chesapeake was hanged.[33]

The South mourned its hero, but other rebels stayed busy in the Bay, plundering and burning, risking their lives to smuggle contraband to their friends across the line. Numerous small boats hid in the creeks and swamps, ready to pounce on any unsuspecting captain who was brave enough to venture out on the water.

The highway of the Chesapeake was also being used to shuttle troops to and from battle sites. Other transports, loaded with wounded soldiers, sailed toward northern hospitals, and some carried captured rebels headed for prison camps.

One of those camps was at Pt. Lookout. Nine miles southwest of Smith Island is Smith Point, where the *St. Nicholas* captured her prizes; less than twenty miles northwest of the island, on the very tip of the northern bank of the Potomac, is Pt. Lookout, where Hammond General Hospital was located. In 1863, a small number of Confederate prisoners, most of whom were southern

80

Marylanders under suspicion of giving aid to the rebels, were sent there. After that, Pt. Lookout was designated as a depot for captured rebel soldiers. A camp with a capacity of 10,000 prisoners was constructed and named Camp Hoffman.

The number of rebel prisoners at Pt. Lookout swelled to far past its capacity, and living conditions there were wretched.[34] The prisoners suffered from the lack of proper food, fresh water, and sanitation facilities. To add to their misery, their camp was almost completely surrounded by water; severe storms battered the point, and high tides frequently inundated the camp. Exposure to freezing wind and rain weakened the men, leaving them susceptible to disease.

Southerners were aware of the miserable situation at Camp Hoffman, and attempts were made to free the prisoners. Confederate boats, launched from the Piankatank or the Rappahannock, made excursions to harass the naval vessels and the army transports that were shuttling up and down the channel between Smith Island and Pt. Lookout.

A naval force sufficient to protect the prison camp was directed to be always in close vicinity.[35] And also for the camp's protection, no expeditions were allowed up the Potomac. Then, after the light at Blakistone was destroyed by rebels, the naval force around the point was increased even more.[36]

The people of Smith Island, already aware of increased military activity so close to their home, were made even more uneasy when lookouts were posted on their land. According to island legend, these lookouts perched on rooftops to keep watch with spy glasses.[37]

Early in July of 1864, Gideon Welles sent a telegram to Admiral S. P. Lee. The telegram warned the admiral that rebels planned an attack on the prison camp at Pt. Lookout. Information had been received from a group of refugees that Captain Wood of the Confederate navy had left Richmond with eight hundred men and two armed blockade runners. Captain Wood was planning to release the prisoners and arm them for a march on Washington.[38]

The Potomac Flotilla increased its vigilance; the *Roanoke* was sent to help guard the prisoners, and all available vessels from the North Atlantic Squadron were sent to patrol the waters between the mouth of the Chesapeake and Pt. Lookout.

The plot to liberate the prison camp was part of a larger Confederate plan. While Captain Wood was preparing to free

81

the prisoners, Confederate General Jubal Early was marching from Martinsburg into Maryland with fifteen thousand infantry troops and five thousand cavalry. The plan was to seize Baltimore, and to hold that city with the foot soldiers, while the cavalry proceeded to Pt. Lookout.[39]

In the meantime, Captain Wood had reached Wilmington, and was headed for the same point by water. The two forces were to meet, attack the camp, liberate the thirty thousand prisoners and arm them. The combined forces were to meet General Early for the proposed assault on Washington. In a letter to Major General Price (Confederate Army), the Honorable John Tyler described the plan and said that he regarded it as "decidedly the most brilliant idea of the war."

On July 10, Confederate President Jefferson Davis sent a telegram to his officers in the field. The object and destination of the expedition had become so widely known that he feared the operation would be met with too many obstacles. President Davis clearly indicated his belief that Captain Wood's attempt to take the prisoners and join General Early would now be fruitless.[40] Although General Early continued with his attempt to take Washington, the plot to liberate Pt. Lookout was abandoned.

In spite of the attempts to free the prisoners, few escapes from Pt. Lookout are documented. But there is a Smith Island legend concerning a prisoner who did manage to gain his freedom. The young rebel slipped away from the camp and hid in the bushes of a nearby farm. Under cover of night, he launched a crude raft, and floated across the channel. His little craft came ashore on Smith Island, where the people took him in and cared for him.

The prisoner of war changed his name, adapted well to island life, and fell in love with an island girl. In the 1870 census, he gave his new name and listed his new occupation as sailor. Carlos and his bride, Hester, produced a large family; their descendants proudly repeat the legend of their prisoner of war ancestor. They tell of his daring escape, his perilous journey from Pt. Lookout, and his love for the beautiful island girl.[41]

By 1864, oyster boats with the proper papers were allowed to work. The flotilla was still keeping careful watch over their activities, but at least the watermen were permitted to fish and oyster and carry their catch to market. But attempts were still

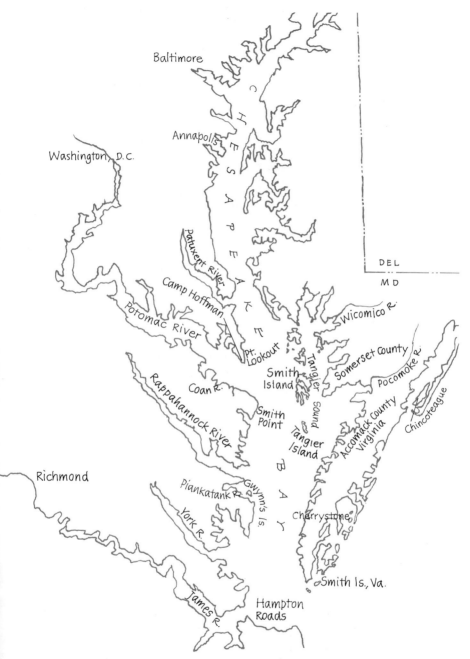

During the Civil War, the Potomac Flotilla patrolled the waters from the Patuxent River to Hampton Roads. Confederate sympathizers smuggled contraband to rebel forces along the western shore rivers and used the Tangier Islands as way stations.

83

being made to smuggle supplies to the South, and Smith Islanders were still under suspicion.

The office of the provost marshall at Onancock issued an order to arrest anyone found running the blockade and to seize any goods that looked suspicious.[42] Union officers from the troops occupying the Virginia peninsula were sent to the island to administer the oath of allegiance.

The islanders were now faring quite well, though, except for their constant fear of raids. Just as in the previous conflicts, their position in the Bay made them especially vulnerable to attack by the guerrillas searching for supplies.

One incident occurred when a refugee from the western shore reported to authorities that three hundred guerrillas were planning to leave the Coan or Yeocomico River for Maryland.[43] Their destination was to be Smith Island. The gunboat *Fuschia* was sent to the island to question the people and try to protect them, while the *Mercury* was sent to cruise the Bay. The islanders had already heard about the proposed raid and were very much alarmed.

At the same time, another expedition was forming on the Piankatank.[44] Flotilla officers suspected that this band of guerrillas intended to join the first group to cross the Bay in small boats and canoes. The object of the raid was to capture boats and use them for transportation into eastern Virginia and the lower Bay.

Union gunboats cruised the waters surrounding the island, keeping watch day and night. Their vigilance foiled the plans of the raiders, but it was a season of anxiety for the island people, who could stand in their fields and observe the patrolling gunboats. From their doorsteps, they heard the sounds of warfare—the shouts of men and the rumbling of guns.

Early in January of 1865, rebels managed to capture the Smith Point lightship.[45] Although cruise operations were often hindered by storms, ice, and breakdowns, security was increased. Then, close to Smith Point, guerrillas burned the steamer *Knickerbocker*, and warnings were issued that they were collecting men and boats with the intention of increasing guerrilla warfare on the Bay.[46]

Thomas Nelson, ensign in charge of the *Mercury*, sent a message to Commander Hooker that he had just learned from a reliable source that 154 guerrillas "at the head of whom is Rice Airs, the person who captured Capt. McDonald of the light vessel off Smith's Point, and the same that shot Capt. Dungan," had left Little River, and were bound for Smith Island. In his message, Ensign Nelson described the guerrilla band:

> The whole party is a most desperate set of thieves, robbers, and murderers who use the cloth of the rebel flag to cover their crimes. Their design on the island is to rob the stores, capture and bring back the numerous refugees and deserters who have gone there from Virginia, and to capture some steamers, with which they intend to attack and destroy the light vessels and even surprise the blockading vessels. The force is now on the eastern shore, with orders to visit the light house, Smith's Island, etc., and gain all the information they can concerning the whereabouts of the guerrilas.

Lieutenant Hooker then reported that he had sent a vessel to the island and had found that the people there were very much alarmed.

As gunboats cruised between them and Smith Point, the islanders steeled themselves against the anticipated raid. While they waited, Lieutenant Commander Hooker received a report that the guerrilla force had swelled to four hundred, and that "they had fifteen large boats and a number of canoes . . . and intended depredations on the bay."[47]

Two gunboats were sent to watch Smith Point; the *Anacostia* was sent to Tangier Sound, where it was reported that the rebels had two tugs. Commander Parker, of the USS *Commodore Read*, requested that more boats be added to the flotilla. He wrote to Secretary Welles that he frequently heard of guerrillas, carrying with them boats on wheels, preparing for raids. He asked that two hundred men be detailed to help him capture the guerrillas.[48]

Finally, Commander Hooker sent a message that he had received a report that the party of rebels had become aware of the increased security and of the people's awareness of their intentions. The guerrillas returned to the creeks along the Rappahannock.[49]

On the heels of this aborted raid, another plot was uncovered.[50] Information was received by Navy Secretary Welles that a group of rebels dressed as females intended to decoy a steamer by flying a white flag at the Wicomico River. Using the ruse that they were women in distress, they planned to board the steamer and capture it, then use it to seize the new Smith Point lightboat. After that, they were to go to Smith Island and Tangier to steal provisions and run the blockade. Once again, advance information enabled the Union navy to intercept the rebels and save Smith Island from a guerrilla raid.

The war finally dragged to an end. Robert E. Lee surrendered to General Grant, and two weeks later, General Johnston handed his sword to Sherman. But in that same month, President Lincoln was assassinated. His murderer escaped, and alarm spread across the Eastern Shore.

The commanding officer of the *Freeborn*, a Union ship stationed off Pt. Lookout, received this message:

April 17, 1865

Sir:
In consequence of information having been received that the murderer of the President has been seen in this vicinity, I would request that you patrol the bay from Lookout to Patuxent, keeping strict watch on movements of all vessels and on any small boats that may attempt to leave the western shore of the Bay. Hail all steamers bound down the Bay. Order them to proceed to Point Lookout and remain there until further orders.[51]

—J. H. Eldridge, Acting Master,
commanding USS *Delaware*

Gideon Welles sent a telegram to the commander at Hampton Roads:

Booth is endeavoring to escape by water. Send a gunboat or tugs to examine the shores and islands of the Eastern Shore and all vessels in that direction. Arrest and seize all suspicious parties.[52]

Rear Admiral Porter was ordered to exercise the utmost vigilance over all vessels departing from the limits of his command; the gunboats *Pontoosuc* and *Osceola* were sent to the Eastern Shore. The *Osceola* was ordered to proceed to Pocomoke Sound to make a thorough search of all the shoals and islands, and on board all vessels between that place and Chincoteague Inlet.[53] The navy sent another telegram to Hampton Roads, commanding the naval force there to send any unemployed vessels to blockade the Eastern Shore of Virginia and the Maryland coast from Pt. Lookout to Baltimore.[54]

But John Wilkes Booth had not tried to escape by water; instead, he had hidden in a barn near Bowling Green, Virginia. When word came that the president's assassin had been killed, security around the mouth of the Potomac relaxed, and by July, the Potomac Flotilla no longer existed.

With the dissolution of the Potomac Flotilla, the waters surrounding Smith Island returned to normal. Some island captains set sail to pick up the business of carrying cargo from port to port on the Bay, and crabbing skiffs and fishing boats took the place of patrolling gunboats. Once more, the nation— and Smith Island—was at peace.

VI

The Dividing Line

On the eleventh of September last, a party of citizens of
this state, understood to be the posse of an inspector, arrested several citizens of Maryland on Pocomoke Sound,
on the charge of taking oysters therein, in violation of
the laws of Virginia. In connection with the arrest, a
citizen of Maryland was shot, and he has since died of
the wounds then received. The circumstance is on all accounts deeply to be deplored, the more because it is al-
leged that the unfortunate man was unresisting when
fired upon, and was left to drift, wounded and bleeding,
at the mercy of the wind and waves.
—Governor James L. Kemper, Virginia, 1874[1]

WHEN the Civil War came to an end, the rest of the nation
concentrated on reconstruction of the South and expan-
sion of the western frontier. Smith Island struggled with the
return to the day-to-day problems of making a living.

But this time, their problems were not as simple as they
had been after the War of 1812. The island's population had
grown to over three hundred.[2] There were more people to feed
and, because of encroaching marshland and erosion, less
arable land to provide that food.

Even before the war, many of the islanders had turned to
oystering to support their families. In the census of 1860, only
eight of the island men had listed their occupation as
farmers. Of the sixty-nine heads of households, four were
merchants and their clerks; one kept the lighthouse; one was
a carpenter, another a brickmason. The others worked on the
water.

88

Oystering had become a profitable industry. A network of railroads enabled packinghouses to ship their product to inland cities and as far away as the Midwest. But, as the demand for oysters had increased, so had the disagreements as to which state had legal rights to the valuable oyster beds in the vicinity of Smith Island.

With the outbreak of the Civil War, that controversy had dimmed, and now that it was safe to go back out on the water, Marylanders and Virginians went back to work. Some of the island oystermen continued their use of shaft tongs to work the shallow bottoms close to home. Others equipped their boats with dredges and set out for deeper water.

The oyster industry continued to grow, and Smith Island's nearest mainland neighbor, Crisfield, became the "seafood capital of the world." Oyster marketing became a multi-million-dollar industry, and oyster catchers became greedy and quarrelsome.

Even the shaft tongers and dredgers quarrelled with each other. Shaft tongers worked in small boats; they could operate only in shallow water. The dredgers worked from larger vessels carrying two or more dredges made up of large bars with iron teeth. As the teeth scraped the oyster beds, oysters collected in rope-net bags attached to the dredges. Not only could the dredgers catch more oysters than the tongers, they could do it faster and make more money.

They also poached on the tongers' territory. Although the practice was prohibited by law, the dredgers scooped oysters from designated tonging beds anyway. Tempers flared, and before long, the quarrelling led to open warfare between the tongers and the dredgers.

In 1868, the legislature established the Maryland State Fishery Force—the Oyster Navy—to protect the tonging beds. But the oystermen were so greedy that dredgers raided the tonging beds at night. To protect their beds from poachers, the tongers built crude shacks on stilts and hired watchmen to guard their territory. The watermen fought and sometimes killed each other over the valuable oyster.[3]

Added to the conflict among the oystermen was the lack of a securely established boundary. Virginia oystermen poached the Maryland beds; Marylanders retaliated by crossing over the line into Virginia. As the value of the oyster beds grew, the number of incidents escalated, and people began to look more closely at the line that separated the two states.[4]

For nearly two centuries, both states had shared riparian rights in the Potomac River, but it wasn't the waters of rivers that were now in question. At stake were 150 square miles of water in the Bay and Tangier and Pocomoke sounds, including the seedbeds of oysters in the waters off the Eastern Shore. Also at stake were the rights to forty square miles of territory on the mainland between the Little Annemessex River and the head of Pocomoke Sound and on Smith Island, as well as all the isles, all water power, all alluvium, and all rights of jurisdiction, all of no less value than twenty million dollars.[5]

Once more, a joint commission was appointed to adjust the boundary. But before arbitration could begin, commissioners from both states found that it would require many months of research and study before they could adequately prepare the statements upon which the negotiations would be based.

The Maryland commissioners were able to begin their study immediately, but the Virginians found their way impeded by unforeseen problems. It was difficult to get all of the commissioners together for a successful conference, the weather refused to cooperate, and to make matters worse, they found that some of the former reports concerning the boundary had been mutilated.[6]

There had been nine volumes of manuscripts with forty-six copies of maps and other evidence in the state archives. Some vouchers and copies had been destroyed or almost completely ruined; other valuable papers were missing. Six of the volumes had been taken; pages containing valuable information had been cut from the three remaining volumes, making the whole lot useless to the commissioners. Commissioner Wise called this, "a felonious act by some interested party." In a letter to Governor Gilbert C. Walker, he said:

> This motive is too apparent for the act to be mistaken, and it is so effectual to prevent or obstruct a correct investigation of the boundary on the Eastern Shore, involving not only the oyster fisheries of the Tangier Sound, but the terminus of the railroad at Crisfield, that the present commissioners who have examined the records, concur in the conviction that these missing papers must be recopied in England and be restored, before it will be safe to meet the Maryland commissioners, or to try the title of boundary.[7]

Before the war, Colonel Angus McDonald had gone to London to make copies of valuable papers; it was these copies that had been ruined. In another letter, William Watts wrote: "The fact that the McDonald papers have been stolen and mutilated shows that somebody interested against us regarded them as important."[8]

Arrangements were made to send D. C. DeJarnette to England to make copies of colonial papers. In his search, DeJarnette uncovered a plot by Lord Baltimore with his brother-in-law, a man named Peasley, who had been secretary to the king. DeJarnette believed that Peasley had attempted to conceal the original Maryland charter, and had altered the published charter to please Lord Baltimore.[9] DeJarnette was thwarted in efforts to gain access to Peasley's department, and was unable to obtain definite proof of any complicity on Maryland's part. In one of his letters, he complained that it would take years to perfect this case and get all that related to it. He returned to Virginia with his papers.

Henry Wise and his fellow commissioners studied and worked for almost three years to "ascertain the truth of history, find the original muniments of title, prove and test the evidence of boundary, and construct fair arguments and conclusions."

Among the documents they collected was a copy of the London Company's second charter issued in 1609. This amended charter had given the company all those lands in Virginia "from the point of land called Pt. Comfort, all along the seacoast to the northward 200 miles; and from the said Pt. Comfort all along the seacoast to the southward 200 miles; all that space of land lying from the seacoast . . . up into the land from sea to sea, west and northwest, and also all the islands lying within 100 miles along the coast . . ."[10]

The commissioners noted that enormous area and made a list of all the factors that had contributed to its dismemberment.[11] Among those that affected the present dispute were the granting of Lord Baltimore's charter, the grant of the Northern Neck of Virginia, the Treaty of Paris in 1763, Virginia's State Constitution, and the Compact of 1785. One by one, they examined these factors.

They found that Lord Baltimore's charter had cut drastically into territory already granted by James I. The Pt. Comfort on Virginia's charter was, and still is, at the northern headland of the mouth of the James River. A two-hundred-mile radius from that point encompassed the entire Chesapeake as well as the peninsula that separates the Bay from the Atlantic. According to Lord Baltimore's charter, a dividing line was to run from Cinquack, a point just below the mouth of the Potomac, to Watkins Point near the River of Wighco on the Eastern Shore, and from there across the peninsula to the ocean.

From the very beginning, Virginia had objected to this encroachment on her territory. Three years before the first Maryland settlers had arrived in the Bay, William Claiborne had settled Kent and Palmers islands, and it was his rebellion against Lord Baltimore's authority that had led to the first battle between the two provinces.

That first battle was fought in Pocomoke Sound, not far from Smith Island. Although Claiborne's men lost the battle, he continued to occupy the Isle of Kent until 1638, when Governor Leonard Calvert led an expedition to Claiborne's headquarters, captured his fort, and claimed the Isle of Kent for Maryland.[12] The Kent Islanders continued to rebel against Calvert, but lost their claim to the island when the lords commissioners gave all rights to Lord Baltimore.

While Maryland and Virginia were feuding over the Isle of Kent, the monarchy was overthrown, and Oliver Cromwell became Lord Protector of England. Shortly afterward, William Claiborne had his revenge. He became one of the commissioners who were sent to demand the surrender of Maryland to the commonwealth. He also served on the parliamentary commission that governed the province from 1652 to 1657. But finally, the government of Maryland was returned to Lord Baltimore, and William Claiborne returned to Virginia.

Although the furor over Kent subsided, it wasn't long before the peninsular line on Maryland's charter caught the attention of Virginians. The population of the peninsula had been growing and spreading northward, and Lord Baltimore had become aware of his need to encourage settlement of his territory near the boundary. Even as he was negotiating for the reacknowledgement of the proprietary government, he was busily writing letters urging that "special care be taken that no encroachment be made by any upon any part of his lordship's province."[13]

More than two centuries later, the Virginia commissioners examined Baltimore's letters and proclamations, and studied reports and depositions pertaining to the events that led to the first attempt to settle the boundary question by negotiation—the Calvert-Scarborough Agreement of 1668.

The controversy over the peninsular line began when the governor of Maryland appointed commissioners to grant land to religious nonconformists who were fleeing Virginia. Certain Virginians, among them Colonel Edmund Scarborough, were convinced that Baltimore planned to acquire a thirty-mile section of Virginia territory by settlement. They claimed that the land being granted by Maryland rightfully belonged to Virginia.

As the basis for their claim, they used the location of Watkins Point. At that time, the map of Captain John Smith was the only source of information concerning the geography of the area, and Smith's map gave the location of the promontory called Watkins Point as a neck of land situated at the north headland of the River Wighco where it discharged into the Chesapeake.

Maryland claimed that the Pocomoke was the river that Smith had called Wighco, and that a point of land that projected into Pocomoke Sound was Watkins Point.[14] Virginia, and especially Colonel Scarborough, disagreed with that location of the point.

In a maneuver designed to force the Eastern Shore settlers to submit to Virginia authority, the colonel arrested one of the governor's commissioners.[15] In a letter to the Maryland Council, John Elzey of Manokin wrote, "My business drew me down to Accomack, where Cl. Scarborough arrested me at his Majestie's suit, and made a demand for Obedience and Right for land . . ."

Immediately, the council sent a letter of protest to Sir William Berkely, and requested a commission from Virginia to meet with Maryland commissioners to "determine that place which shall be accounted Watkins Point according to His Lordship's Patent for Maryland."[16]

Then Scarborough invaded the Eastern Shore. With five other prominent Virginians and a band of forty horsemen, he rode to Annemessex and Manokin "to repel yt contempt w'ch I was informed some Quakers and a foole in Office had threatened to obtrude."[17] On the doors of some households, he put the broad arrow, a mark designating those households to be Royal Goods. As an excuse for his invasion, the colonel used an act that had recently been passed by the Virginia Assembly.

"An Act Concerning the Bounds of this Collony on the Eastern Shore" authorized Colonel Scarborough to post orders commanding the residents from Watkins Point southward to render obedience to Virginia and make payment of His Majesty's rents and public dues to that colony.[18] That act stated that the assembly had concluded that Watkins Point was on the north side of the Wicomico River opposite the Patuxent, and not at the mouth of the River Wighco, as named on John Smith's map.

This time, Charles Calvert went in person to Virginia, where Governor Berkely denied any responsibility in the affair. Colonel Scarborough had been authorized to publish the orders, but he had not been ordered to proceed by force.[19] The act clearly stated that the surveyor-general would meet with Lord Baltimore's representatives; it had not given him the authority to enforce the proclamation.[20]

In March of 1664, Governor Berkely ordered Scarborough to meet with the Maryland commissioners at Manokin on the tenth of May. The king's surveyor-general did not keep that appointment, but Scarborough was there on May 16th.[21]

Again, an irate Governor Calvert protested the colonel's audacity. He appointed Phillip Calvert to go to Virginia and demand justice against Edmund Scarborough for "entering the province in a hostile manner and by blows and imprisonment outraging the inhabitants of Manokin and Annamessex without commission, and also for attempting to mark a tree upon a point of land above thirty miles to the Northward of Watkins Point in Maryland."[22]

Scarborough was ordered to meet Phillip Calvert at the place called Watkins Point, and in June of 1668, they signed an agreement designating the point of land made by the north side of Pocomoke Bay and the south side of Annemessex Bay to be the true Watkins Point. From there, a line was run eastward to the ocean.[23]

After studying all the Calvert-Scarborough documents, the Virginia commissioners agreed that although Colonel Scarborough had been a man of great ability and much energy, his actions were "characteristic of the man, of the times, of the people of Annamessex, and of the nature of the controversy."[24] Then they turned their attention to the grant of the Northern Neck of Virginia.

The Hopton grant, as it came to be known, was awarded while Charles II was in exile during the years of the commonwealth. When the monarchy was restored, the king notified Virginia that he had granted to Henry, Lord Jermine, and to Ralph, Lord Hopton, and to others:

> all that tract, territory, or portion of land in America
> bounded by and within the heads of Tappahannock,
> alias Rappahannock, and Quiriough or Potomack
> Rivers, the courses of these rivers and Chesapeake Bay,
> together with all the Islands within the banks of said
> rivers.[25]

In 1667, when the patent was registered in the Public Record Office of England, it was amended. The original grantees were all dead; the new letters of patent gave the Northern Neck to the gentlemen's heirs. Eventually, Lord Thomas Fairfax inherited the estate, and in 1733, he petitioned the king for a determination of his boundaries.

At that time, the Hopton grant seemingly did not affect the Eastern Shore. The Northern Neck of Virginia is a wide tract of land that stretches down the western shore of the Bay from the Potomac to the mouth of the Rappahannock River, approximately fifty miles northwest of the entrance to the Bay. The wide neck narrows between the courses of the rivers, then fans out far inland.

Since the grant called for land lying south of the Potomac, Charles, Lord Baltimore, believed that none of his territory was at stake. Therefore, when commissioners were appointed to represent Virginia and the Crown, Maryland did not send a representative. But Baltimore's territory was at stake. That commission's final determination gave Virginia, through Lord Fairfax, a sizable amount of land on the northern bank of the Potomac, and relocated Maryland's southern boundary.

The Hopton grant had specified the territory between the heads of the two rivers. There was no question about the location of the head of the Rappahannock, but two branches of the Potomac come together to form that river. The commission determined that the Cohongaroota, the northern branch, was the longer. Therefore, they declared that this branch was the headspring of the Potomac, and Lord Fairfax fixed the initial mark of his boundary at this headspring.

The Hopton grant also claimed the courses of the rivers and all the islands within their banks. The surveyors ran their line, not to Cinquack, several miles south of the Potomac, but to Pt. Lookout on the very tip of the north bank of the river.[26]

In the meantime, Virginia continued to grant lands high up on Smith Island, and Maryland made grants of her own in the same region. The lines of these grants were vague; in some instances, they intersected each other. Two land grants, one by each state, called for the divisional line, and were separated by that line without a description of where the line was located.

A line drawn from Pt. Lookout to Watkins Point did not correspond with the Calvert-Scarborough line that had left all the island to Maryland. Instead, it left the island unequally divided between the two provinces. Because of confusion over this line, titles were also confused and ownership disputed.[27]

At that time, Smith Island did not concern Frederick, the sixth Lord Baltimore, but when Lord Fairfax opened an office for the sale of his newly acquired lands, Frederick ordered his governor to look into this invasion of his territory. By then, however, war between England and France had spread to the New World, and although Maryland representatives began a survey, the outbreak of the French and Indian War made it impractical and dangerous to attempt a survey of the land north and west of the Potomac.

When that war came to an end, the Treaty of Paris called for the fixation and description of the provinces of the respective sovereignties in America. His Majesty, George III, ordered his geographer to fix the boundaries of the various provinces. The boundary of the Potomac was set to Pt. Lookout and across the Bay to the sea.[28]

The last points on the commissioners' list of factors that had affected the dismemberment of Virginia's territory were the State Constitution and the Compact of 1785. After the Treaty of Paris in 1763, Virginia could no longer claim to the extent of her original grant, and in the twenty-first clause of her constitution, she ceded all rights to territory claimed with the charters of Maryland, Pennsylvania, North Carolina, and South Carolina. She retained only the rights of free navigation and use of the rivers Potomac and Pocomoke.[29]

Maryland, in her own first constitutional convention, passed a unanimous resolution that the state of Virginia had no right or title to any of the territory, bays, rivers, or waters included in Lord Baltimore's charter.[30]

When the nation was united under one government, neither state was satisfied with its limits. Congress left the question of boundary to the states, and some of the most prominent men of Virginia and Maryland agreed to meet with George Washington to settle the dispute.

In the Compact of 1785, Maryland yielded the line from Cinquack and accepted Smith Point, six miles farther north, as the starting point of the boundary across the Bay. The seventh article of the compact provided that the citizens of both states should have full property rights on the shores of the Potomac, and the rights of fishing in that river were to be common to the citizens of both states, with free navigation and use of the river.[31] Because it was ratified by both legislatures and declared to be obligatory except if superseded by the constitution, this compact should have quieted the arguments. But it had not: both states had continued to pass acts and resolutions designed to settle the ongoing dissension.[32]

With the study of the Compact of 1785, the commissioners ended their review of the history of the boundary disputes, and journeyed to Annapolis for an informal meeting with the Maryland commissioners.

In May of 1872, the joint commission met at Crisfield to take depositions of witnesses. By this time, Crisfield had the largest oyster trade in the state. At least 250 vessels unloaded their catch here; the fifteen packinghouses employed over fifteen hundred shuckers and packers, and shipped more than a million gallons of oysters.

The trade at this little town was estimated to be worth three to four million dollars per year. Commissioner Wise wrote to his governor that the stakes in the boundary question were worth too many millions to be lightly relinquished. Virginia controlled seventeen hundred square miles in the Chesapeake; Maryland controlled only seven hundred, but as the commissioner said, "If Maryland acquires the seed beds of Tangier and Pocomoke Sounds, her lesser domain will be as valuable as the greater owned by Virginia."[33]

At Crisfield, several Smith Islanders testified about the tradition that a divisional line crossed the lower end of the island. John Cullen, a Crisfielder, testified that he had gone to the island with the Maryland commission who had been sent there in 1835. These commissioners had based the limits of the

Smith Island election district on verbal descriptions of the boundary as given by elderly residents. They had not searched out the line for themselves, but had taken the description at a meeting at the church.[34]

The commissioners made a trip to Smith Island to investigate the tradition. Commissioner Wise wanted to see the exact line by which the voters were separated. He also wanted to see if the location of the stones he'd heard about corresponded to a line of marks and monuments east of the Pocomoke. Smith Islanders Johnson Evans and John Marshall took him by canoe to the site of the ancient stones.[35]

The men landed close to a stone sunk in the marsh just north of Horse Hammock, and the commissioner sighted the marker's bearing by compass. He found that this ancient stone corresponded remarkably to a line he called the Michler line, a line that ended at Crisfield and cut the terminus of the railroad at the end of the barrel wharf.

The commissioner had been told that no one on the island knew the origin of the markers, and the mystery of the stones deepened when he was taken to the location of another one. This stone was near Troy Island in the island's main thoroughfare. It was too far north to correspond with the line that ended at Crisfield. In fact, a line drawn from Troy Island to the mainland and back to Horse Hammock would make an acute angle.

Later, the puzzle deepened even further when the joint commission met to visit the sites of two more stones, one at the mouth of the "Creek" just off the "Barn," the other on the island's west side. Two more islanders testified that they had

———Opposite:

The approximate locations of ancient boundary stones in the vicinity of Smith Island, as related by Smith Islanders in 1872: (1) in the marsh, three-quarters to one mile north of Horse Hammock; (2) at the mouth of the Big Thorofare off Orchard Ridge, north of Hog Neck (stone is four to five feet across, six to eight feet long); (3) at Hog Neck, on a west line from the site of John Parks's house; (4) at the south end of Troy Island, seventy yards from shore (approximately one ton); (5) one-third to one-half mile southeast of Troy Island, one hundred yards south of Beaver Hammock in the "Bottom" (one ton, in two pieces); (6) at upper end of Otter Island (shaped like a "Ridged Coffin"); (7) one hundred yards southeast of Barne's Point, forty feet from shore, knee deep (diamond-shaped, about three feet in size). (Adapted from the Lake, Griffing, Stevenson Map, 1877.)

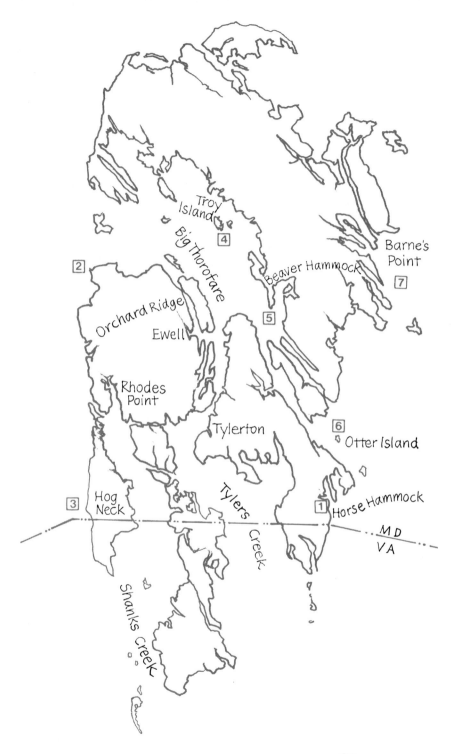

Troy
Island

Big Thorofare

4

Beaver Hammock

Barne's
Point

2

7

Orchard Ridge

Ewell

5

Rhodes
Point

Tylerton

6 Otter Island

3 Hog
Neck

Tylers Creek

1 Horse Hammock

M D
V A

Shanks Creek

99

found a stone at Beaver Hammock, a half-mile southeast of Troy Island in the Big Thorofare.[36]

The commissioners came to no conclusion about the origin of the markers, but in a letter concerning the mystery, Commissioner Wise agreed with Maryland's Isaac Jones that the representatives ought to meet again and try to agree on a compromise line.[37]

In a series of meetings at Baltimore, the commissioners presented their arguments and proposals. In their statement, the Maryland commissioners cited an error made by surveyors more than two hundred years earlier.[38] That error had been found by Lieutenant Michler of the U.S. Engineers, who had done the preliminary survey for the joint commission of 1858. When Lieutenant Michler was assigned the task of tracing the Calvert-Scarborough line, he found that instead of an east line, as called for in the agreement, the course of the line had been run more than five degrees north of east. In his report to the commission, Michler had concluded that the line had been run by compass without allowing for the standard variation of the needle.

The commissioners claimed that this mistake had given Virginia twenty-three square miles of Maryland territory in the northern part of Virginia. They described a line that would correct this error and restore Maryland's lost territory, but were willing to concede that line and negotiate for a compromise line across the peninsula.

The Marylanders were also willing to admit that in the Compact of 1785, Maryland had agreed to common fishing rights in the Potomac, but had failed to secure reciprocal rights in the Pocomoke. They gave Virginia credit for her policy of allowing Marylanders equal privileges in both rivers "until recently," but they declared that they were "compelled to say that the attempt of late to exclude Maryland from equal privileges in Pocomoke Sound is a departure from that reciprocity."[39]

One of their proposals was a compromise line from Smith Point across the lower end of Smith Island, then on to the middle of Cedar Straits, and from there to the channel of Pocomoke Bay, then up the river, with the right of taking oysters to be common to the citizens of both states.[40]

Virginia countered this proposal by citing the records of the circuit court of Maryland in 1854.[41] That court had already

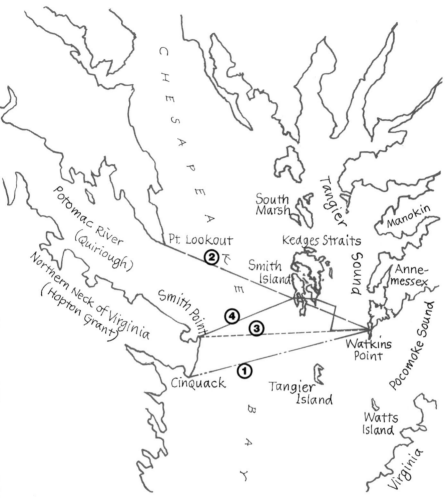

The four boundary lines that have separated Maryland and Virginia:
(1) Lord Baltimore's charter, 1632; (2) The Treaty of Paris, 1763; (3)
The Compact of 1785; (4) The Black and Jenkins Award, 1877 (present
line). *Note*: The position of Cinquack is approximated; according to
the *Report and Journal of Proceedings of the Joint Commission to
Adjust the Boundary of the States of Maryland and Virginia, 1872*,
Cinquack is located five to ten miles south of the Potomac River.

101

decided that the territory Maryland was now negotiating for was not within the limits of their state. This court action had taken place after two Smith Island vessels were seized for violating Maryland's law against oystering in her waters. The Virginians also noted the irony of the fact that the Honorable I. D. Jones, a current commissioner for Maryland, had been the attorney for John Cullen in the case of *John Tyler v. Cullen,* and that Cullen had lost his case. They rejected Maryland's proposal.

While these negotiations were going on, the mystery of the missing volumes resurfaced in Virginia. It was discovered that part of the manuscript records were in the possession of a Mr. Thomas Wynne, a member of a senate committee concerning the boundary.[42] Mr. Wynne had never disclosed to the commissioners that he had the missing papers. Now he admitted possession of the volumes, but refused the use of them by the commission.

Mr. Wynne released two of the volumes, and returned one more to the state library, but he was evasive about his reasons for the theft of the papers. After his questioning, he took the remaining books away with him, saying that he would return them to their rightful place in the library. As a member of the library committee, Mr. Wynne negotiated with the commission to allow the papers to be reprinted, but Commissioner Wise refused to accept any further responsibility in the matter.

Eventually, Mr. Wynne released two more of the volumes. There were now five of the missing volumes in the hands of the commissioners but the cost of sending DeJarnette to London for replacements had already taken a large part of the money appropriated for commission expenses.

In spite of the amount of time and money involved, the Joint Commission of 1872 failed to reach an agreement. In their final report, the Maryland commissioners suggested that it might be necessary for the governors to "call in an umpire," whose decision would be final. The whole matter was submitted to arbitration when the legislatures of both states appointed J. S. Black and Charles Jenkins to determine the true line of boundary.

These arbitrators also examined the voluminous evidence and delved into the mystery of the markers that crossed Smith Island. They, too, came to no conclusion about the ancient stones. In their report of 1877, Black and Jenkins said, "If ever it (a divisional line) was run, it cannot now be told by whom, when, for what purpose, by what authority, or precisely where. It dates back to what may be called the pre-historic times of the island."[43]

The true boundary, as described by the Black and Jenkins award, begins at Smith Point and runs north by east to Sassafras Hammock on the western shore of Smith Island, thence across the island to Horse Hammock on the eastern side, then to the middle of Tangier Sound. This line divides the waters of the sound southward, then north by east to Watkins Point. From there, it runs due east to the middle of Pocomoke River by a line of irregular curves until it intersects the Calvert-Scarborough line. These acts of arbitration and the award were approved by both states, and Congress gave its consent to the award.

In their explanation of their judgment, Black and Jenkins confined Maryland everywhere within the original limits of her charter. She was:

> allowed to go to it nowhere except on the short line run-
> ning east from Watkins Point to the middle of the
> Pocomoke. At that place, Virginia never crossed the
> charter to make a claim. What territory we adjudge to
> Virginia north of the charter line, she has acquired
> either by compacts fairly made or else by a long and un-
> disturbed possession.[44]

Thus, Virginia gained prescriptive rights to the southern portion of Smith Island.

Apparently, Maryland didn't place much value on that portion of the island, for in their report of 1872, her commissioners had described it as "only a few miles of salt marshes with the exception of four or five acres of firm ground, mere sites for rude fishermen's huts."[45]

As the oyster industry continued to grow, watermen from both states ignored the restrictions placed on them by the award of 1877. Virginia oystermen crossed the line to fish Maryland waters, and Maryland watermen were equally guilty. Armed men patrolled the water; shooting incidents, even deaths, occurred. And the proud, independent watermen of Smith Island were very much a part of the fracas.

By 1880, there were almost five hundred people living on the island, and most of the men made their living on the water.[46] In the census for that year, only twelve listed farming as their occupation. In schooners, pungies, and bugeyes, the island fleet ranged far and wide to harvest oysters.

Island old-timers still talk about those violent years.[47] They talk about the time when Virginia dredgers were met with a volley of bullets from angry Somerset County watermen. And the time when the Virginia police boat chased island oystermen back home, only to be met by a salvo of five hundred rounds of shot or more. They still talk about the fifteen-year-old island boy who was shot and killed while on his way to Crisfield. They say that John T. Evans was a crabber, but he wasn't working the day he was shot; he just happened to stray across the line.

These old-timers, and some not so old, remember hearing their fathers talk of the time when Smith Island became an armed camp because the islanders feared an invasion by the Virginia oyster police. A retired dredge boat captain remembers his own father's story like this:

> They'd go over the line; the Virginia boats'd shoot and the islanders shot back. They kept guns aboard, you see. The Virgina boat had a cannon. Dad said they stuffed bed clothes in the holes to keep from sinkin'.
>
> My dad, at the time of the squabbles, was twenty-five years old. The law was so rough and working conditions so dangerous, that his chin whiskers turned white from one weekend to the next. You see, the captain of the boat in them days as well as these—that law has never been changed—has full authority on his boat. But he also—now get this—has full responsibility for observing the law and for the safety of his crew. That's why his chin whiskers turned white. Too much on his mind. With the police boats a'watchin' and the drudgers tryin' to work the tonger's beds, it was all a-squabble. The bullets from the police boat busted the spokes on the steering wheel in my daddy's hands. The splinters flew.[48]

Another islander lost his boat when it was rammed by a Virginia tug.[49] In November of 1889, Maryland Governor Jackson released a proclamation concerning the location of the boundary near Hog Island in the lower Potomac. Application had been made by both states for the U.S. Coast and Geodetic Survey to determine the exact location of the line.

In question were oyster beds claimed by a Charles Lewis, under a lease from the state of Virginia. Using Surveyor Whit-

104

ing's decision that the line followed the low water mark of the Potomac and around the north side of Hog Island, Governor Jackson proclaimed that the beds leased by Mr. Lewis were within the bounds of Maryland, and declared them open to the free use of the citizens of Maryland and Virginia.

A few days later, while dredging oysters at Hog Island flats, the Smith Island schooner *Lawson* was rammed and sunk. The captain of the tug said, "Mr. Lewis directed me to sink any boat I found there. The Lawson was the only boat on the reserve grounds, and I sunk her."

There were many incidents of armed conflict between island oystermen and the Virginia or Maryland police. There was at least one battle involving all three: the battle of Woman's Marsh in 1895. Rival oystermen were battling each other until a Virginia police boat arrived on the scene. When a Maryland boat joined the fray, open warfare broke out. There were casualties on both sides, and one island captain received a wound that prevented him from working for the rest of his life.[50]

It isn't surprising that with the ever-increasing number of boats working the Chesapeake and the lack of conservation efforts, that the supply of oysters was steadily decreasing. However, another Bay industry was rising. The Chesapeake Bay blue crab was becoming as valuable as the oyster.

With this in mind, the Maryland-Virginia legislatures once more appointed committees to argue the case concerning concurrent legislation by the two states for the protection of oysters, fish, and crabs in the common waters of the Potomac and the Pocomoke Sound. Maryland asked for a uniform culling law and the right to oyster in the sound. Virginia conceded the propriety of the culling law, but denied that Maryland should have any rights in the sound.

Maryland claimed that from time immemorial, the citizens of both states had exercised the common right to take oysters in the sound, both north and south of the boundary, until 1884, when Virginia had, by her oyster police, deprived Marylanders of these rights.

In his closing remarks Senator Stubbs of Virginia admitted that Maryland had made a splendid appeal to her sister state. He said, "I had rather retain good feeling and brotherly love between Maryland and Virginia than have all the wealth of the Indies. I had rather Virginia should give up all the oysters than sever the claim of friendship which now binds us together." Senator Hayes from Maryland replied that he would go back home and tell his people that Virginians could still lay claim to having among them giants as men, and women as lovely as any that were ever born of women.[51] In spite of this rhetoric the oyster conference ended in a stalemate. The only agreement made was to appoint subcommittees for further investigation and negotiation.

Finally, the United States Supreme Court ruled in the case of a Somerset County waterman against the Sheriff of Accomack County, Virginia, that Maryland had no right to oyster in the Virginia section of Pocomoke Sound.[52] Officially, the oyster war was over.

For the watermen of the lower Eastern Shore, however, the controversy was far from over. Armed patrol boats from both states continued to roam the waters close to the line, and watermen from both states continued to stray beyond that line.

By now, the economy of Smith Island depended completely on commercial fishing. The farmland on the outer reaches of the island was no longer arable. Spreading marshland had forced the islanders to abandon their farms and move inland to the higher ridges of the main portion of the island. Their homes crowded the ridges; there was no room for farms. In the census for 1900, none of the island men listed their occupations as farmers.

In the fall, most of the men left home to dredge for oysters. In the spring, they fished the rich crabbing bottoms that surround the island. Along with their crabs, they sent large quantities of shad, rock, and herring to the packinghouses in Crisfield.

With their livelihood depending upon their freedom from restriction, island watermen paid little attention to the invisible line that divided the waters. Along with other Maryland watermen, they were arrested for taking Virginia oysters. In one incident, a Virginia patrol fired on their boats. The islanders returned the fire, then tried to escape, but they were caught and arrested.

In another incident, the Virginia police boat, *Marguerite*, challenged a group of island crabbers. The *Marguerite* took five rounds of shot as she chased the crabbers back to Smith Island.[53] Virginia then authorized machine guns for her patrol boats, and both states ordered armed patrols to cruise Tangier Sound.

With Virginia and Maryland constantly on the alert, the number of hostile incidents decreased, but as late as 1949, a Crisfield crabber was shot and killed by a Virginia fisheries officer.[54] And some of the younger island men still talk about the winter that the Virginia police chased Smith Island dredgers back to the southern tip of the island, where armed men hid behind poles to defend themselves.

Although the shooting incidents finally ceased, the patrol boats continued to cruise the sounds. If caught fishing over the line, Maryland boats were towed to Virginia; their captains faced stiff penalties for illegal shellfishing.

Virginia was well within her rights to make the arrests, but Marylanders continued to challenge those rights. They soon found that by forming an organization to represent them, they could make the changes for which generations of individuals had fought.

In 1971, three members of the Tangier Sound Watermen's Association filed a suit against their own state to open the shellfishing grounds of Maryland to all Maryland watermen regardless of county lines. They claimed that county residency requirements violated the Fourteenth Amendment to the Constitution. The court ruled that shellfish in tidal waters are the common property of all the citizens in the state of Maryland.[55]

After winning that suit, members of the association filed a lawsuit in the U.S. District Court in Richmond against the Virginia Marine Resources Commission, that agency's commissioner, and the state of Virginia. The suit contested Virginia's law that prohibited the catching of fish or crabs in that state's tidal waters by nonresidents.

Because their workboats are federally licensed and documented by the United States government, the watermen based their claims on the supremacy of the United States Constitution, that constitutional provisions concerning interstate commerce hold precedence over state law. The ensuing court ruling invalidated the Virginia residency requirement; Virginia opened her waters to any shellfisher who pays an annual license fee and abides by the laws that govern that state's fishing industry.

The boundary disputes are over, but Smith Island's "tail" still hangs over the dividing line that makes a hump across the island's bottom. The desire to change that line no longer exists, but islanders still like to spin yarns about how it came to be.

They tell the story of an island ancestor who had a store just north of South Point marsh. He figured he could make more money in Virginia, so, since he was "a man with considerable influence," he exerted pressure to have the line drawn so his store would be in Virginia.

Another yarn concerns a man who deliberately built his house so it straddled the line. By doing so, he became eligible to fish and vote in both states. The islanders still speak of the old days when couples could elope to Hog Neck and be married in the state of their choice.

But the story most often told is the tale of the Smith Island preacher who ended the despicable activities of a man who lived in a house that was built so part of it was in each state.[56] They say that the man sold illegal whisky, and when the Virginia officers came to investigate, he moved across the line to another room; when Maryland officers visited him, he moved back into the Virginia side of his house.

The Smith Island preacher decided that something needed to be done, so he prayed for an end to this man's devilish ways. "Now, Lord," he prayed, "we got a man in our community that's working for the devil. Destroying our young people. Leading them astray. Now, Lord, if you really aim and intend for this man to quit his meanness, make him do it, and do it soon. But if you don't have that in mind, then take him away, and don't wait too long to do it."

As the story goes, the man was taken away—and soon. Only a few days later, he shot himself and died.

These yarns, and others like them, are a part of island heritage, and telling them is a favorite pastime of retired watermen. Their sons and grandsons have a few of their own to tell, and although the boundary war is finally over, it will live on in legend as long as there is a Smith Islander left to tell the story.

VII

Smith Island: Then and Now

Here, if anywhere, can be found old ways preserved
without being fossilized and new ways adopted and
adapted without being idolized. An archipelago; . . . a
region laced and threaded with numerous waterways:
thoroughfares, creeks, runs, and guts, and indented
with coves; a place of few trees; an all but submerged
mite of terrain unsheltered against the whims of winds
and waters alike. Smith Island supports a hardy, self-
reliant, unspoiled, generous natured, and sincere people
whose cultural contributions will yet be felt and ap-
preciated.

—Blanche H. Phillips[1]

T RAVEL writers often call Smith Island a place that time
has not touched. But time has touched the island in many
ways. Throughout more than three centuries of island living,
many changes have taken place. Gradually, historical events
and the forces of nature have altered the character and life-
style of the islanders and, in the process, have created a unique
culture.

The handful of farmers who first settled on the island,
gradually grew into a large community.[2] In 1808, there were
nineteen families, but by the end of the Civil War, the population had grown to three hundred, with only eight of the men
still actively working their farms.[3] The others listed their
occupation as sailor. In the true sense of the word, however,
they had not yet become watermen.

On Smith Island, a man does not learn to be a waterman. In
his infancy, he begins to assimilate knowledge of water lore, to

absorb wisdom and intuition from his environment and his association with his extended family, the island elders whose fathers and grandfathers were as much at home on the water as they were in their own backyards.

Long ago, the first island watermen learned that with the first full moon of spring, when the snowball bushes bloomed and grass was growing on the bottom of the crabbing grounds, young crabs would be hiding in that grass, waiting to be caught on a knotted line. They learned that fall rains fattened the oysters that covered the floor of the Bay and sound. They recognized the subtle changes of color that marked the difference between shoal water and deep. Each generation of island sailor passed on to the next generation an accumulation of learning experiences, and the waterman gradually evolved.

Another change that took place was also a gradual change. It, too, came from learning experiences. The wars that touched Smith Island left the islanders deeply scarred. Wartime hardships wrought changes in the personality of the Smith Islander, characteristics that were intensified by succeeding experiences, and are recognizable to this day.

The islander learned to be secretive and crafty; he hid his supplies and vessels. He watched carefully for an opportunity to take his boat out on the water; he dared to defy the enemy, to use his watery backyard as he felt God had intended him to. He became thrifty in times of plenty to save against hard times to come. And he learned to treasure his little bit of land, to guard his inheritance from a real or suspected enemy. This self-reliance, suspicion of strangers, fierce pride, and tenacity were passed on to his children.

Through the three major wars that touched the Eastern Shore, islanders struggled long and hard to maintain their homes; time and again they were denied the right to harvest seafood, not only by the enemy, but by their own countrymen. Wartime restrictions interfered with what they felt was their right to use their surroundings to provide for their families.

During the Revolution, they were threatened by the British, their stores were confiscated by their own countrymen, and they were robbed by bandits from their own community. The islanders also had to contend with public opinion on the mainland. The people of Somerset County believed that all the islanders were working against the patriotic cause, and considered Smith Island a hotbed of traitors and Tories. By the

110

end of that war, the island had acquired a reputation for lawlessness that had to be faced and lived down.

Nursing their wounded pride, and economically shattered, the islanders were ready for the religious reformation that swept the Eastern Shore at the turn of the century. They needed the comfort and discipline offered by this new and drastically different religion. And by then, there was also a real need for community organization. Methodism became the answer to personal, emotional, and community needs. As the islanders banded together in common worship and adopted religious law as their guidelines, their society grew around the church.

Two elderly men, considered wise enough to be called King, became the community leaders. With their leadership, the new religion became the means for a firm foundation of self-organization and self-government that has survived for almost two centuries.

The new rules were strict; the islanders became almost puritanical. Observance of the Sabbath was mandatory; Sunday was spent only in rest and religious pursuits (worship, study, and discussion of the scripture), a tradition that is still maintained by most of the islanders. Always a musical people and accustomed to frolics, they turned to worship in singing and praising the Lord, and declared fiddle playing and dancing the devil's work. Liquor was considered an abomination. Exhorters sternly commanded them to "serve the Lord and keep His commandments."

The first religious service on the island was held at the home of King Richard on "Fogg's Point" in the year 1808.[4] The following year, a three-day bush meeting was held on the upper end of the island at a place called Old Orchard, or Kizzie's, where the first church building was erected. For many years, religious services were held in the home of Marmaduke Mister, the same Marmaduke who had been a leader of the picaroons.

In an old manuscript found on Smith Island are these words, "King Solomon lived on Solomon's Lump. The brothers, Solomon and Richard Evans, were found in every good work from the time they espoused the cause of Christ until they finished their courses, respectfully, at or near the age of a hundred years."[5] And, more than a century ago, Adam Wallace described a typical Smith Island meeting day:

111

Smith Island, Chesapeake Bay

> Soon we cross the Sound channel, and stretch down towards Kedge's Straits, taking care, if the tide is not full, to clear the Musclehole Bar, and make a landing at the Light House on Fogg's Point . . .
>
> The arrival of the preachers, and the hour for public worship, is made known on Smith's as on Tangier Island, by hoisting a flag at the little church. The signal flag was procured by the Sons of Temperance, who have a flourishing division there. It bears their motto—"Union Band," and when unfurled to the breeze, may be seen from every part of the Island.
>
> The people mostly come to meeting in canoes, and a more picturesque sight cannot well be imagined, than that witnessed about the time of service. From every point they come, some careering before the breeze, boomed out, and almost smothered in the spray; others close hauled on the wind, holding their course for the landing, and some expertly tacking against the wind, to reach their destination.[6]

During that same period, the island people began to realize that another enemy was working against them. Their friend and daily companion, the Chesapeake Bay, was making claim to their homes. Changes in the land were becoming increasingly evident. Ground that had been firm, was now soggy; ridges that had supported crops of corn and potatoes now grew marshy grass. Good rich soil had become salty. This invasion of the Bay waters could not be stopped, nor even fought.

One by one, as erosion ate away at the shoreline, and encroaching marshland took over their farms, the islanders moved inland.[7] They lifted their houses onto logs, rolled them down to the landing, loaded them onto scows, and poled across the water to more protected parts of the island. With great labor, they made trip after trip, moving houses and furniture, outhouses, sheds, and dairies, dismantling them when necessary, to relocate on firmer ground, the higher ridges that run through the communities that are now called Rhodes Point, Tylerton, and Ewell.

Each chose as many acres as possible on the high ground, and as youngsters grew up and began to start their own families, lots were parceled out from the parents' acreage. New dwelling places were erected for the new families. This practice continued until the houses were close to each other in the three distinctly outlined communities.

112

More often now, islanders were coming in contact with modern "civilization." Boat captains were ranging farther away from home, to the big port cities of Baltimore, Annapolis, and Philadelphia, and some even farther. They brought back newspapers and magazines, news about modern fashions and new products. Visitors from the outside became more frequent and occasionally an entire family went for an excursion on a steamboat.

As the population increased, the local supply of wood diminished, until today there are only a few small stands of woods; the trees that remain are old and cherished. Eventually, it became necessary to import firewood from the western shore of the Bay. Later, as oil-burning heaters became popular, oil barges began making regular stops to fill dockside holding tanks.

There have been many times when fuel has had to be rationed because the oil barge was unable to make a delivery. For instance, during the severe winter of 1976-77, the Chesapeake was frozen solid for three months.[8] In spite of dangerous conditions, the oil barge attempted delivery to the nearly desperate islanders. The barge struggled through masses of ice until it became stuck fast, unable to move with its load of oil. Finally, the Maryland National Guard helicopters airlifted the fuel, drum by drum, shuttling back and forth between frozen-in island and icebound barge. Although it was good experience for the guardsmen, it was a tedious, dangerous procedure.

That freeze-up reminded islanders of the winter of 1917-18, when snow fell steadily for four days and nights, and "the snow froze to the upstairs windows."[9] Lickin' Billy Bradshaw is a character from the last century, who has become the hero of many island legends. Lickin' Billy's grandson was only fourteen in 1917, but he remembers that the supply of food ran out, and three young men rigged a sail onto a skiff, put on their ice skates, and set out for Crisfield to bring back food. It was a perilous journey, for even when the Bay seems to be frozen over completely, treacherous air holes can turn solid ice into slush. To stumble into one of these air holes would mean almost certain death. These young men, Otis, Willie, and Asbury, made the trip safely, and won the gratitude of the people of Rhodes Point.

In 1936, during another long, bitter freeze-up, a party of courageous men attempted to take supplies over the ice from

113

Crisfield to Tangier Island.[10] They had not gone far when two of them fell through the ice. They were pulled out and sent back to Crisfield, and survived the ordeal.

The rest of the party pushed on toward an open channel, where a Coast Guard cutter was waiting to take on the food. Then, another man fell through the ice. Although his comrades managed to pull him out of the frigid water, Sergeant Hunter froze to death, and the expedition was aborted.

Another tragedy occurred during the same winter, when transportation by water was virtually impossible.[11] A young island wife went into labor, and when the birth became complicated by the mother's convulsions, a desperate attempt was made to save her life and that of her child. Down in the cabin of the packet boat, *Island Belle*, the mother fought for her life, while outside in the frigid air, the crew aimed the boat toward Crisfield and medical help. Armed with axes and hatchets, they hacked away at the ice to cut their way through. With the men spelling each other, the work went on throughout the long day and night. Finally, the *Island Belle* and her half-frozen crew reached the harbor at Crisfield—too late for both mother and child.

Today, most expectant mothers are able to reach Crisfield with time to spare. Some install themselves in the mainland homes of relatives to await birth, and in an extreme emergency, helicopter service is now available. But, as recently as 1974, during a vicious winter storm when no boat could leave the dock, and no helicopter could chance a landing, a Christmas baby was born. Islanders know how to cope with almost any emergency.

In severe freeze-ups, Coast Guard ice cutters and the state boat do their best to cut through the ice so that islanders can get food and supplies. But nearly every winter, there is a period of two weeks to two months when the island is nearly inaccessible. This is a condition of island living, however, that the hardy people have endured since the first freeze-up that their ancestors were forced to endure.

As the old-timers are fond of saying, "We fare better than them as is on the mainland—we're used to it, you see. Ain't nobody as has starved yet."[12] A freeze-up is a time of conservation, planned for in advance. It is a time when folks use stores held in reserve for just such an emergency. They conserve on food and fuel, and help each other.

Wooden Coast Guard cutters similar to those used during the freeze-up of 1936 when State Police Sergeant Wilbert Hunter died of exertion and exposure after falling through the ice. (Photograph courtesy of John Thomas, Fruitland, Maryland.)

The deep freeze is usually welcomed by the high school students, the youngsters who make the trip over the water daily to school on the mainland. For a few days, they have a vacation, but the school system always finds a way to send books and lessons over or through the ice. They are brought over by the ice cutter or sent by helicopter. When the books arrive, the kids congregate in the church basement and, monitored by volunteer mothers, do their lessons.

Smith Island has an unusual school system. In the 1790s old King Solomon began the first school, using the Bible, *Pilgrim's Progress*, a hymn book, and the works of Shakespeare as textbooks.[13] That first school was at Fog Point. Since then, there have been a series of tiny, one-room buildings where the children were all taught together. Some of the buildings were built on puncheons in the marsh. As better schoolhouses were built, these little buildings were incorporated into houses, and used as kitchen additions. Some are still in existence. Today, Rhodes Point has no school, but there are modern facilities at Ewell and Tylerton.

In 1959, the state provided a school bus route that runs between Tylerton, Rhodes Point, Ewell, and Crisfield. Route #53 included a boat that ferried junior high students from Tylerton to Rhodes Point, then bused them to school at Ewell, and the *Island Star* was authorized to carry high school students to Crisfield, where they boarded by the week in mainland homes.

Ewell School is a modern building where classes from kindergarten to the eighth grade are taught, while Tylerton boasts a classic one-rooom edifice where children are taught through the sixth grade. This up-to-date building stands on the site of the old sail-powered gristmill.

Island high school students no longer have to board in Crisfield. The only school boat in the state of Maryland, the *Betty Jo Tyler*, complete with a double row of bus seats, a tiny restroom, and life preservers, makes the trip each day with students bound for Crisfield Senior High School.

During the last few generations, island families have come to realize the importance of higher education. They are uncertain about the island's future, and realize that there is a world outside their own. Some young islanders have gone away to work in professional fields—medicine, law enforcement, or teaching. Others have found careers in various branches of state and federal government.

116

Smith Island: Then and Now

Traditionally, young boys dropped out of school, some as early as the fourth or fifth grade, to work on the water with their fathers. The girls usually finished only the amount of schooling available on the island. Only a handful, mostly girls, elected to leave their homes every week to continue their education.

Today, even some of the young men who choose to follow their father's occupation are preparing themselves for the future by graduating from high school. Each senior class is larger than the preceding one, and more and more island young people are going on to technical schools or college.

The school boat is only one example of the modern vessels used by the islanders. Besides their low-sided scraping boats and the round- or square-sterned hydraulic tonging boats, many of the islanders own speedboats that can make a trip to the mainland in less than thirty minutes. And then there are the large, sleek, fully equipped tour boats that bring passengers from Crisfield and the western shore to spend a few hours touring the island and feasting on island home-cooking. These vessels are a far cry from the boats used at the turn of the century.

By 1910, the island population had grown to eight hundred, and for ten years, packet boats had been delivering mail, although stormy weather or ice often interfered with the regularity of service.[14] More recently, boats like the *Miss Whitelock*, the *Island Star*, and the old *Island Belle*, began providing passenger service and the freighting of necessities to the island.

In those days, however, the trip to Crisfield usually took over two hours. The boat left home port at eight in the morning and began its return trip shortly after noon. Any passenger who could not complete his mainland business in time to catch the boat was left behind to spend the night in Crisfield or to catch a ride with a crabber.

Today, modern, high-powered fiberglass boats make the trip twice daily. They return laden with freight, for Smith Island is no longer self-sufficient, or self-contained, nor can it be for longer than a few weeks of winter isolation. Islanders cannot grow enough food to sustain themselves; in fact, they are almost completely dependent upon the supplies and services they purchase from the mainland. The boats come back home laden with groceries, hardware, parts needed for boat repairs, furniture, and island housewives who've been off shopping.

117

The islanders' boats are considered part of their equipment, one of the tools of their trade. Although they are often used for transportation, they are seldom used for recreational purposes. However, the islanders' work is time consuming, and they have very little time for recreation. But they take great pleasure in the simplest forms of entertainment, such as church socials, community dinners, and the annual firemen's "show."

The early islanders also had little time for recreation. They were content with their family life, and with an occasional frolic, or dance, that gave youngsters an opportunity to select mates and do their courting. These frolics became a thing of the past when the islanders accepted Methodism, and the newly devout islanders were more than content with their work, their prayer meetings, and their Bible study.

Over the years, this strict control has gradually relaxed, and islanders have learned to entertain themselves. For the women, a visit with a neighbor of an evening, and for the men, a round of talk at the general store, a cup of coffee with a friend, or a few hours of television constitute after-work relaxation.

For the youngsters, cars have the most appeal. They ride up and down the less than five miles of narrow, one-lane roads in old junkers, crowded in together, making their own fun. They laugh and joke and flirt, just like teenagers everywhere. The kids stop to party a while at the little wooden bridge that crosses the gut between Ewell and Rhodes Point, or drop in at the store for a sandwich and a game of pool.

It is a far cry from the old days of the last generation, when young people "walked out" on a Saturday night.[15] Then, there was a jukebox at the old store, the store that one old-timer says was held together by "two termites shaking hands." Then, the kids danced, played jokes on each other, and shared a can of potted meat and a bottle of pop. Walking out together was a courting custom, and many a young man married the "first girl he ever walked out with."

Smith Island youngsters are genuinely fond of each other; they behave like brothers and sisters. They are all members of the island family; they have lived together, or at least their family groups have, for many generations. These kids have a touching gesture that even the tourists notice. It is a meaningful gesture that seems to take the place of words. They scratch each other's backs; it is a gentle way of expressing quiet approval and affection.

118

Smith Island: Then and Now

There are three very special times of the year for Smith Islanders. The first of these is Christmas week. Even the early converts to Methodism celebrated Christmas by ceasing all work for the entire week. The week is planned well in advance and is eagerly anticipated. For this week, the people are reminded of the time long ago, when the entire island fleet sailed away in late fall, and returned home just in time for Christmas. They celebrate the tradition.

On Christmas Eve, the children's program is held, and every island child takes part in the pageantry of the Christmas story. On the Christ-child's birthday, there are church services and quiet family dinners. But something special is planned for every evening thereafter, until New Year's.

Although dances are the big events, with bands and entertainment brought over from the mainland, there are also children's parties, gospel singing, and organ recitals. Christmas is a time of festival, a break in the year's work routine.

Springtime brings a festival, too, when May Day is celebrated much as it has been celebrated in England since medieval times. The long winter is over, and it is time to celebrate the renewal of life.

For weeks, children and their teachers plan for this event. Craft booths are set up at the school, and all islanders come to admire their children's work and to be the audience for the class plays, the singing, and the dance around the maypole. The May king and his queen reign over the festivities.

Christmas is pageantry and frolic; May Day is a traditional festival, but the highlight of the island's year is camp meeting, a whole week of work stopped early, soul-satisfying evangelism, rededication, and reunion. The traditional camp meeting began in the early 1800s; the first one was a three-day meeting held in the center of a pine grove. According to Adam Wallace, "sinners quaked and ran, and got the spirit." It was a time when Tangier Sound was white with the sails of boats from other islands and the mainland, all coming to hear the preaching.

The camp meetings grew until they became weeklong revivals, and a large tabernacle was built at North End (the part of the island that is now called Ewell) to house the meeting. Hundreds of visitors came to stay the week; a large boarding-house was built at the edge of the campground to accommodate the overflow of visitors. There was a cook tent where meals were served, and tables spread out under the trees.

119

Nowadays, the island can expect a visit from a state senator or congressman, perhaps even the governor or some other important personage during camp meeting. But more importantly, it is a time of reunion, when friends and family from faraway places come home to stay the week, to renew old relationships, and attend the services.

Months of preparation go into this special week, not only by the church leaders, but by every island family. Homes are completely housecleaned; yards are mowed and manicured; flowers and shrubs are planted in time to bloom for camp. Camp meeting dresses are ordered from the catalog, menus are planned, and sleeping arrangements made for the company that is bound to come.

The graveyard that lies between the tabernacle and the church gets special attention, too. Here are the exposed rounded tops of vaults, graves of island ancestors who were buried on top of the ground. The vaults are all given a coat of sparkling white paint, and on the Saturday before camp starts, the packet boat is laden with baskets and sprays of fresh flowers to adorn both tabernacle and graveyard. Camp meeting is a season of feasting, both spiritual and physical, a tradition since 1808, when "sinners were struck down as by lightning."

At one time, there were thirty strongly built cottages on the campground. The cottages were called tents, and were simply constructed, with a common room below and sleeping room upstairs. They were owned and erected by people from Drum Point and Rhodes Point, and others whose homes were too far away to make the daily trip to camp. Whole families camped out in the cottages for this interlude of spiritual power.

The first tabernacle, a rough-hewn building in the center of the prayer grove, was a large auditorium that seated over a thousand people. In front of the tabernacle, close to the lane, was a large boardinghouse with accommodations for at least sixty people.

In 1937, a disastrous fire that began in the new church building created havoc with the campground.[16] The new church had just been completed; the first Sunday service held there was barely over when the fire broke out. Fanned by strong northerly winds, it threatened to destroy all of North End.

Men formed bucket brigades from the water's edge, and as the men fought the fire, women and children carried furniture

A Smith Island camp meeting prior to the disastrous fire of 1937, when the church, parsonage, and all but one of the campground buildings were destroyed. The tabernacle (in background) seated one thousand people; the boardinghouse (not pictured) had sleeping accommodations for sixty guests, and there were thirty cottages which were used only during camp week. (One of a series of historic photographs published by the *Crisfield Times*, Crisfield, Maryland, on July 22, 1987, in celebration of the Centennial of the Smith Island Camp Meeting.)

121

and belongings away from their homes. Believing that evacuation was their only chance for survival, groups of people flocked to boats in the harbor, and prepared to leave.

All day and all night, the fire raged out of control. Then, well into the next day, the wind changed, the fire died out, and people moved back into their homes—grateful for deliverance, but full of sorrow. The great fire had consumed the church, the parsonage, and most of the cottages on the campground; even the tabernacle and the boardinghouse were gone. There were some who claimed that the fire was the judgment of God pronounced upon a sinful people, for all of the church property was destroyed.

Today, there is a remarkably beautiful church at Ewell and a large, gracious parsonage. There is no boardinghouse, and the only remaining camp meeting cottage now sits in a state of advanced decay "Down the Field," the northeast section of Ewell, where it was used as a home for many years. But the tabernacle has been rebuilt; it stands in charming simplicity in the center of the prayer grove.

Although fire is still a very real fear for island dwellers, the bucket brigade has been replaced by a fire department well equipped with a modern fire engine and pumper, and manned by trained volunteers who take their work very seriously. Volunteer firemen and members of the auxiliary have also become emergency medical technicians; their knowledge and lifesaving skills are invaluable in situations where immediate medical help is not available.

Medical facilities have improved, too; it is no longer necessary for islanders to rely on granny women and midwives. The first physician came to live on the island in 1890, and since then, a number of doctors and nurses have cared for the island people. Along with whatever medicines were available, the first doctors brought their own instruments and boarded in private homes during their island stay.

Today, the island has its own medical center; it is equipped with an incubator, defibrillator, lab equipment, and oxygen tanks. Stores of bandages, surgical trays, and medical supplies are kept on hand. Upstairs over the clinic, are comfortable living quarters. It is certainly not a mainland facility, but it is one that serves its purpose, and it is evidence of the changes that have taken place on the island.

The island people still have no doctor or nurse of their own, but the medical technicians are familiar with the equipment in the clinic, and there is excellent medical care available on the mainland. In extreme emergency, a telephone call can bring a medevac helicopter to the island within minutes.

Although Smith Island still has no formal governing body, no barroom or nightclub, no movie theater, and no corner drugstore, it does have some conveniences. At Ewell School there is a modern library, and the island now has its own sewer system. Every island home now has electricity and running water, and nearly everyone has a bathroom and a telephone. All of this has come about in the last fifty years.

By 1930, while people on the mainland were enjoying modern inventions like washing machines, street lights, electric fans, and vacuum cleaners, the islanders were still drawing water from shallow wells by the bucketful. Several houses shared each well, and the water was often brackish or muddy.

Some of the older generation remember when it was necessary to go by boat out to Fog Point, where there was a deep well, to get drinking water. Every pantry had a water table set up with two buckets, one kept covered with a clean white cloth, the other with a long-handled dipper hanging from its rim. Large wooden barrels stood outside to catch rainwater for household use.

The old shallow wells have been filled in, some with bright flowers, holly trees, or English ivy. Long ago, the wooden rain barrels gave way to huge round metal tanks that stood at a back corner of each house to catch water as it poured from the eaves.

Lucy, a charming lady who lives at Rhodes Point, has an old, hard-backed book, its margins filled with a handwritten record of events recorded as they happened at Rhodes Point.[17] Lucy's record says that the water pipes went through her yard on November 8, 1948.

Now, each neighborhood has its own well. Each of these artesian wells is eight to fourteen hundred feet deep, and provides nearly perfect, clear, cold water. Twice a year, the water is tested for purity, and only one island well has ever had to be chlorinated.

Each well house has a water committee; each household is held responsible for its own plumbing. The cost of maintaining the pumps and small reservoirs is shared by the families "on the well," as is the chore of periodically scrubbing down the well house, or walking the lines when a leak is suspected.

123

Lucy's book also says that the lights went on at three minutes before two on August 29, 1949. Until recently, electricity on the island was shared with Tangier. Each island had its own oil-powered generator at the electric house which was maintained by a rural electric cooperative. The islands alternated generating hours, and the current passed through a series of power poles stretched across the marshland and the shallow water that separates the two islands. Bad weather and equipment failure often disrupted the service.

Before the electric cooperative was set up, batteries provided the small amounts of electricity used by lamps, radios, and pumps. Now there are underwater cables from Smith Island to Tangier, and on to the shore of Virginia.

Even before it had electricity, Smith Island had telephone service of a sort:

> The fishermen and oystermen of Tangier and Smith had passed through several severe winters—winters that had brought freezing temperatures and ice—winters which locked in boats and cut off sources of supplies, including medicines and milk for babies. In some cases, it had been a nip and tuck battle against death and privation, with death sometimes the victor. It was realized that some form of communication was needed. Rather than let the Tangiermen and Smithmen wait until a permanent system could be installed, our C & P people in Maryland and Virginia decided to place on each of the islands a portable radio-telephone unit. This was done in the latter part of 1939, although use was restricted to emergencies only. The number of messages transmitted emphasized the need for a regular commercial type of telephone service.[18]

A year after these emergency provisions were made, a system was established to provide communication between the two islands and the mainland.[19]

The system provided for the islands was the first of its kind in the country. For over two hundred years, the only communication with the mainland had been by boat. Now, for the first time, a unique arrangement of poles and rods pointing toward each other allowed messages to flash across the water. Installed at strategic locations, four public telephones used radio equipment to connect with the operator at Crisfield, the first radiotelephone installation of this kind in the Bell System.

Smith Island: Then and Now

To provide this service, some obstacles had to be overcome, obstacles presented by the unusual terrain and the watery barricade that separates the island from the mainland. Thousands of feet of wire and cable were transported in barges and oyster boats, and the poles required for the system were floated from the mainland. To prevent them from sinking into the mucky terrain, the poles were placed with the cross beams bolted onto the bottoms instead of the tops. Because of the frequent, and often fierce, storms that batter the island, it was necessary to double secure and guy all lines and poles.

One extra pole was erected in a strategic place.[20] Out of consideration for an islander's concern for her shrubbery, a workman put up an additional pole to protect her property. One of the islanders painted the pole red, white, and blue, and "inscribed it with the telephone worker's nickname, the 'Charley Pole.'" The pole is no longer brightly painted, but it is still there, protecting the shrubbery from any vehicle that might turn the corner too closely.

To prevent damage from storm tides, the floor of the building that houses the system's equipment is elevated well above normal tide levels. The central office was named Hazel 5, in remembrance of one of the most devastating hurricanes to hit the area. Now, instead of a cable, a microwave system transmits signals between Smith Island and the rest of the world.

Island transportation has seen some changes, too. Islanders used sail power on their boats until well into the twentieth century. Variations of the two-masted schooner, a commercial boat common to the Chesapeake, were favored island boats.[21] The pungy was a broad, shallow schooner-built vessel with a large keel and a broad stern, and no center well, an option which made more room for freight. The pungy's bottom was rounded, and old sailors on the island say that when a pungy was loaded right, there was little left of her above the water.

Another favorite was the bateau, which was smaller than the schooner, but similarly built. The bateau was used for crabbing and oystering. The design of the island bugeye differed from that of the schooner and bateau. Its hull narrowed to a point at both ends, and the bugeye was fitted with masts of almost equal height. The larger bugeyes were used for freighting, the smaller ones for oyster dredging.

125

Gradually, sail power gave way to motorized power, and island sailors began adapting their own boats to engines. Islanders speak fondly of the old "chug-chugs," small gasoline engines that made the changeover from sail. The island workboats of today are strong, sturdy vessels, wooden-hulled or fiberglassed, round- or square-sterned, diesel-powered or fitted with automobile engines.

When the mainland had its horse-drawn carriages, then its horseless carriages, Smith Island had only water transportation. A few Chincoteague ponies were used to plow the gardens, and a pair of oxen helped construct the first stretch of road on the island, but as a rule, what the automobile was to the mainland, watercraft was to the island.

But even that has changed. The first motorcycle came to the island during the First World War; it came down the Bay on a steamer.[22] Since then, the vehicle population has grown. An old car or a pickup truck comes in handy for hauling wire, crab pots, and supplies. It can also provide a handy way for young people to enjoy an evening out.

Most of the cars brought over to the island had already seen their better days, and the junk cars created a minor problem. There are no service garages on the island, and very few auto mechanics, and old cars get sick; they give up and die quickly in tidewater and salt air. Removal of a dead vehicle can be an expensive operation, and for years, the island's mountain of junk cars grew higher and wider in the marsh off Rhodes Point Road. Islanders asked for help to remove the mountain. Several years ago, salvage operations began, and in spite of the difficulties presented by the narrow roads, and mucky terrain in which heavy equipment bogs down, the mountain gradually dwindled.

The cars are a mixed blessing for those who have them. They are certainly an improvement over the use of wheelbarrows and trundle carts, but islanders have seen the need for a measure of control over the quality and quantity of vehicles brought over from the mainland, and there are now strict rules governing the removal of old cars. Some islanders see the cars as a symbol of progress, or a desire to catch up with the mainland, but others see them as a sign that their island is losing its separateness from the rest of the world.

In spite of the increase of automobiles, islanders are still very much dependent upon their boats. They are still used for pleasure as well as work, or as the means of just getting from one place to another. On any summer Sunday, boatloads of young people set out for Crisfield, or to Bayside for picnics and swimming. Courting is often done by boat, and each spring, the island graduating class is treated to a midnight cruise. Boats still bring new babies home to begin their island life, and the boat also brings islanders home to their final resting place.

When a Smith Islander dies, his body is taken by boat to Crisfield for embalming, then brought back home for burial. But even the present funeral director is a part of the island family. He is a direct descendant of Uncle Haney Bradshaw, a highly esteemed gentlemen who was an elder of the church. As such, he assisted at, and sometimes presided over, island funerals. His son Aaron made the coffins, which were wide at the shoulders and narrow at the feet. They were beautiful, highly polished chestnut coffins covered with black broadcloth. Their interiors were bedded with wood wool, a finely ground excelsior-like material, and lined with Baronet silk.[23]

Each coffin was a work of art made with loving care, and each bore a nameplate that stated simply, "At Rest." Aaron was a craftsman and a businessman; he also owned and operated the general store. Both businesses were conducted in the same building. He sold supplies in one of the rooms; his other, more somber, business was conducted in a smaller room. The whole became known as the Coffin House.

In those days, when a death occurred, the island was alerted by the tolling of the church bell. According to Harvey Bradshaw of the Bradshaw Funeral Home in Crisfield, the very first thing the family did was to send someone to toll the death—one stroke of the clapper for each year of life. The bell could be heard all the way out to the cove, where men would stop their work to count the tolls, pull in their nets, and head for home.

At home, womenfolk gently and lovingly bathed and dressed the body, and waited for Aaron to come bearing the black shrouded box, which would then lie in state in the parlor and never be left alone until the burial. Each night, a midnight supper was served to the watchers, until the third day, when a solemn procession of mourners followed behind the coffin to the church.

When a death occurred "Over the Gut" or "Over the Thoro-fare," the coffin was placed in a boat and, followed by boatloads

127

of family members and neighbors, was rowed across the water to the landing closest to the church. Six, or sometimes twelve, pallbearers carried their burden up the lane to the church.

The funeral was a long, solemn service. The deeply religious islanders eulogized the departed, and there was singing and preaching. After the service, each islander viewed the body, spoke to the family, and respectfully waited outside the church to follow them to the graveyard.

Aaron and his helpers nestled the coffin inside another chestnut box, an outside case, and lowered it into a carefully prepared grave, which was often lined with bricks to keep out the water. Eventually, Aaron's son went away to a school of embalming and opened a funeral parlor in Crisfield. Then, with the funeral boat, *King Tut*, he continued to care for the island's dead.

The *King Tut*, named for King Tutankhamen, was built on Smith Island. The funeral boat was complete with a galley, two bunks, and two beds. For over thirty years, the *King Tut* made the trip across the sound at least two times for each funeral; once to pick up the body and carry it to the mainland for embalming, and once more to carry the vault and coffin back home.

The *King Tut* has long since been retired, but as Harvey Bradshaw says,

> A funeral on the island is a solemn occasion. The people there have a high regard for their dead. When I take the flowers over, the children gather to carry them to the church. On the day of the funeral, the church bell is rung, the stores close, and everyone stops their work until the service is over. It is a deeply moving experience.

In every case, the loved one is a part of the island family, a family interwoven in such a way that a death touches every home. These are homes that are closely linked by family ties to nearly every home in the community. These are homes where the elderly are respected, even revered; where fathers and sons work together, and where mothers teach daughters the ways of the island family. And these are homes where families are held together by their need for each other.

Perhaps this is the reason there has never been a need for a police department on the island. Islanders have a way of looking out for their own, and a subtle way of taking care of offenders. Ostracism, a form of shunning, is not unknown.

The funeral boat, *King Tut*, was built in 1935 by Captain Lawrence Marsh, a Smith Island boatbuilder. John A. Bradshaw, Sr. bought her, and for more than thirty years she was used to carry the dead to and from Smith Island and Tangier. The *King Tut* became known as the hearse boat of the Chesapeake Bay and John Bradshaw as the Bay-roving undertaker. (Photograph by A. Aubrey Bodine, courtesy of Bradshaw & Sons Funeral Home, Crisfield, Maryland.)

Smith Island, Chesapeake Bay

Even a slight offense brings shame or disgrace to a family—and the family takes care of its own.

There have been few crimes committed on Smith Island. For years, violent crime was something that was read about in outside papers or magazines. However, during the last big freeze-up, when helicopters were taking people to and from the mainland, someone robbed an islander's home of a safe that contained his life's savings. The safe has never been found; the crime has never been solved, but most islanders are firm in their belief that it was an outsider who committed the robbery.

Since the island has caught up with the twentieth century, there have been rumors that some of the teenagers are involved with drugs, and it is easy now to bring alcohol over home, but the islanders are proud of their hard-won reputation as a law-abiding community and want to keep that reputation. However, they abide more by the laws of God than the laws of man. The Ten Commandments and seasons of prayer for sinners, along with the belief in inevitable punishment by God Himself, is thought to be the best deterrent to crime.

Visitors from the mainland find it hard to believe that there is no police force or jail. Several years ago, a group of tourists stopped the island boatbuilder, a work-hardened, gruff-talking man with gnarled hands and a disreputable looking hat.[24] One citified young lady asked about the lack of police: "What do you do if someone commits a crime—steals something or hurts somebody?"

The boatbuilder, who was on his way to the store, paused, rocked back on his heels, and replied,

> Well, now, young lady, you see that there tree over by the tabernacle? Well, we find out who done it and tie their thumbs to a rope. See that limb way up there? Well, we slings the rope over that branch, pull it up till his toes is off the ground, and throw a half-hitch around the trunk. When we think he's good and sorry, down he comes and behaves hisself.

Respectfully, he touched his finger to his hat, and went on his way to the store. On his way back home, the boatbuilder paused once more—to watch the group of tourists busily taking pictures of each other standing under the "hanging tree."

Punishment on the island is not that extreme, but one who thinks to err against his island neighbor stops to ponder the loss of his neighbor's respect, of being the butt of slurring remarks, of being shunned, or even of exile.

Of late, there has been an increase in minor vandalism, a rash of accidents, and the one unsolved crime. All are believed to be a product of progress. But Smith Island continues to live as close to the Good Book as possible, or as close as the times will allow.

There are some things about the island that have seen little change. For instance, religion still plays a dominant role in island life; it is an ingrained component of island culture. Some older residents can boast that they have never missed a camp-meeting service. Although rigid control by the church has relaxed, the influence of Joshua Thomas persists. All life on Smith Island is in some way church oriented, just as it has been for more than two centuries. The minister, the elders of the church, and the officers of the fire company who are also church leaders, are the unmistakable leaders of the community.

The combination of church and "state" works well on Smith Island. The New Testament teachings admonish the people to care for their neighbor, and support the whole through one organized establishment. Quite unlike the absolute control and harsh treatment that made dissenters flee in the seventeenth century, the present control is gentle—firm, but loving.

Any group of people must have a leader, and for Smith Island that leader is the church, the mainstay of communal life. Here, major decisions are made. Here, projects are conceived, discussed, voted on, and instituted. And here, voices are raised in prayer and harmony.

For each new island baby, a red rose is placed on the simple wooden altar in the church. And when an islander departs this life, his remains come home to that same altar, to be prayed over as he crosses the bar.

Community projects are financed in a very simple manner. On Sunday afternoons, volunteers walk from house to house to collect the donations that pay for the recreation center, the street lights, and other public improvements. Community property is paid for or improved by the same means. The nurse's home, the parsonage, and the fire hall were built and are still maintained by the people, who feel a deep sense of responsibility toward their island family.

However, that island family is changing. As islanders grow more and more used to modern conveniences, as they see the

Smith Island, Chesapeake Bay

world on their trips to the mainland, as they view advancing technology through the media, and education becomes more and more important, they are becoming more sophisticated. The new generation is no longer satisfied with the simpler things of life. They are ranging farther afield to find a new life-style, and are bringing it home to Smith Island.

Old customs are becoming out of date. There are no more tents on the campground during the week of camp meeting; there are no more dinners on the grounds; the picnic place is rarely used. As private parties take the place of public functions, the old-time observance of Christmas week, when the entire island ceased work for the festivities, is gradually changing.

Strict adherence to the Sabbath is fading, too. Young families are off to the beach for the weekend; nearly every family has a car on the mainland, so there is no need to stay at home. Community get-togethers are less frequent now; ready-made fun is taking the place of tic-tac and tin can and hide-the-switch, and some folks think that taffy pulls are old hat.

Progress is taking its toll on Smith Island. The Reverend W. P. Taylor wrote of this very thing as long ago as 1910. He said, "There has never been a liquor saloon or licensed hotel on Smith's Island. And if a house should ever be built here for that purpose, by a mutual understanding of the people, it shall be immediately burned down."

Although there is now a small motel at Ewell, there is still no saloon, and most islanders still hold with Reverend Taylor's opinion; they resent the outside influences that exert subtle pressure to give in to progress and will resist these changes to the end.

The Smith Island of today is a study in contrasts, an odd mixture of the old and the new. There are folks here who have never been to a movie or a drive-in, and have never eaten a sandwich from a fast-food restaurant. One old-timer, when first introduced to french fries commented, "Why, these ain't nothin' but Irish taters!" One senior citizen has not made a trip to the mainland in over fifty years, while during the same time span, members of his family have had treatment in the most modern big city medical facilities available.

The parsonage that was built to replace the one that burned in 1937 provides another contrast. Recently, it was remodeled and refurbished to make it as up-to-date as any mainland manse. Its interior is a composite of twentieth-century conveniences and

132

old-world charm. Soft, inviting color enhances the beauty of modern furnishings and vintage architecture.

Across the spacious living area, huge, gleaming picture windows frame a typical Smith Island scene. Just a few yards away, a sleek, gaily colored yacht glides past the county wharf and the silvery hued shanties across the creek, to put in next to scraping boats docked behind a rustic store.

Inside the store, the sloping floor sags with the weight of boxes and barrels of foodstuffs. Off to one side is stacked a conglomeration of perfumes and cosmetics. Everything from cat food to candles is displayed along the walls on floor-to-ceiling shelves. A glass case left over from the last century displays bags of gumdrops and pocketknives; next to it, a refrigerated case contains cold cuts, pork chops, and cheeses. Pyramids of shelving down the middle of the huge room are filled with T-shirts and gloves, casserole dishes and panty hose.

All sorts of oddities hang from the ceiling; macrame pot holders brush gently against dip nets; seine needles nestle against hooded sweatshirts. Behind a hand-carved serving window is a gas grill; an ancient cash register rests on a board next to the pizza oven. An old sink with a calico skirt wrapped around it, and a soft ice cream machine sit to one side. Somehow, they seem in perfect balance with each other.

Just recently, Miss Willie built on to her old store. Now there is a rustic looking dining room, with handmade wooden tables covered with checkered oilcloth. The kids still congregate on Miss Willie's porch; watermen still gather at the tables to play a friendly game of dominoes or checkers, but now Miss Willie also serves meals to tourists in her new dining room that overlooks the Thorofare.

Just up from the rambling old store, there is a graying saltbox with a toilet out back; the privy is still in use. Across the street, there's a modular home with two chrome-fitted bathrooms. In the yard of one, an elderly man stands at an old table, washing dishes in a tin dishpan. Inside the other, a young wife stacks her dishes in an automatic dishwasher. A quilting frame rests on a porch across from the "Big Store," where the proprietor has electric blankets on sale.

Down the Field, a grizzled waterman stops to rest his gear-laden wheelbarrow, while a three-wheeled motor scooter, complete with a cat perched on the handlebars, passes him by. Over the Hill, an old woman in a sunbonnet tends her flowers, and looks the other way as a gaggle of bikini-clad young girls walk down the road.

There is no doubt that time has touched Smith Island. But with all the changes that have come to pass, it is still a world within a world, a world that revolves at a tempo of its own making. Years ago, after a visit to the island, someone wrote a description that, except for the snowy sails, could apply to this day.

> To stand near the chapel on a bright morning, and scan the horizon around, presents a spectacle never to be forgotten. The mingled picture of little green isles; the glistening and rippling streets of water; the scores of snowy sails, like angel's wings dotting the horizon in every direction for miles and converging towards the humble sanctuary; the mingled snatches of cheerful, sacred melodies from many of the approaching crews, floating over the waters from every direction in sweet and witching confusion, stamp an impression on the sensitive canvas of the soul, so weird and picturesque as to forever remain indelible.[25]

Today's Smith Island is still quaint with a picturesque charm that lures the imagination, and some things will never change. Although there are now some houses on the island where no one lives, and other houses that have become the dwelling places of outsiders, the islanders are still very attached to their homes and to each other.

They still draw their living from the combination of land and sea, and the men still gather to swap yarns or discuss the weather. There is a boat a-building in someone's yard, and hand scrapes lean against the shed. And, although the "Temperance Flag" has disappeared and the long blast of the horn is heard only during camp meeting, there is still the feeling that, on Smith Island, man has been permitted to achieve a perfect balance with nature, becoming one with the elements he lives with.

VIII

Tall Tales and Traditions

In them days, your word was your bond. But some
things that is told fer the truth ain't the truth.
—Bain Bradshaw, 1979

FROM early morning until just past noon, the barrel wharf
at Crisfield is a flurry of activity. This long dock at the end
of State Route 413 is where the island freight boats converge
every morning. They bring waxed boxes filled with crabs or
barrels of shucked oysters, and they bring islanders off for a
day of business or pleasure. The packet boats remain at the
wharf all morning, while they load with return freight—the
necessities of life for the islanders.

Island wives call in orders to the supermarkets and catalog
stores in Crisfield; the orders are filled and delivered to the boats.
Watermen send for engine parts, tools, and paint, or other
hardware from the shelves of downtown marine supply shops.
On any given day, the freight is varied: someone needs lumber
for an addition to his house or shanty; there's a new sofa coming
down the road, a new kitchen sink, or a television set.

Before the island boats arrive, cars and trucks are lined up
along the dock, trunks and tailgates gaping to receive barrels and
boxes. Three or four taxis wait with motors idling, to whisk
arriving islanders uptown, or to pick up their own cars. Occasionally, an ambulance stands by to pick up a patient from one
of the islands. Men and boys scurry around, unloading and
reloading, from arrival time to departure.

What seems to the watcher to be completely disorganized
chaos is, in reality, a smooth operation controlled by the boat

135

captain and his crew. As the passengers disembark and the crew and drivers handle freight, the captain gathers up his belongings and sets out to take care of business.

From bank to bank, from pharmacy to hardware store, he delivers messages or orders, and conducts business transactions, making deposits for islanders, paying bills, and cashing checks. Then it's back to the wharf to supervise freight handling and dispense the money to pay for COD purchases. Most of these transactions are kept in the captain's memory rather than in a ledger, and will be settled upon delivery, when the boat makes its return trip.

The barrel wharf is also the center of activity for retired watermen, or for those with nothing particular to do at the moment. They take up space on the green-painted benches, or squat back on their heels to pass the time of day, to watch the comings and goings, to greet their island friends, and as the morning's flurry subsides, to spin yarns. This is Crisfield's famed liar's bench.

While Crisfield has its liar's bench, Smith Island has its general store. When the weather's nasty, and they can't go out to work, or in the evenings when their chores are finished, watermen tend to congregate. In olden days, they gathered 'round on wooden benches at the store, their pews drawn close to the potbellied stove. The weather outside would be forgotten as the men reminisced about the days of yore, told tales of narrow escapes, or just topped each other's yarns.

Nowadays, the potbellied stove has been replaced by a modern oil burner and the store has been expanded. It is no longer a one-room building, but the wooden benches are still there, worn smooth with age and the backsides of generations of watermen who have gathered together to wile away a few hours.

Wherever watermen congregate, it's storytelling time. They are natural storytellers, and they spin yarns in unconscious competition with each other. Outsiders are lucky if they get to hear the tall tales, for islanders have always been suspicious of strangers, or "furriners." Usually, they clam up when one is listening, or at least, they tone down their stories. They are also wary of tape recorders and notebooks, skeptical of those who would write their stories to be retold by "them as don't belong."

In the past, their suspicions have been well founded. More than one islander has befriended a stranger and later been betrayed for his hospitality. Others chafe at the memory of being exploited by a furriner. Some have been bilked by un-scrupulous salesmen who unloaded inferior products on them, or took deposits on orders that were never received.

They have also been interviewed by well-meaning writers, to realize too late, that information given in trusting innocence has been distorted, resulting in unfavorable publicity for them and their way of life. Sometimes they have been pictured as coarse and uncouth, almost barbaric. At other times, the island life-style has been romanticized almost to the point of ridicule.

Most islanders can tell at least one story concerning be-trayal by a game warden disguised as a professor, an artist, a writer, or even a preacher, who came to search out infractions of the rules concerning wildfowl. For a long time, islanders had little use for game laws, or for those who tried to enforce those laws. For centuries, their forefathers had lived off the bounty of the sea and the wildfowl God had given them for food. They didn't always understand the need for conservation.

Back in the thirties, a retired minister came to visit the island. He claimed he was from a midwestern state, and wanted only to rest for a while before starting out on a trip to Florida. The "preacher" stayed for a few weeks, and won the islanders' trust. He claimed that he was a gun collector, so they showed him their favorite weapons and took him to their duck blinds and out-of-season traps. They even disclosed some of the secrets of baiting the birds. For souvenirs of his visit, the preacher took pictures of his island friends and their guns, wrote down their names and addresses, and promised to write.

A week or so later, after the islanders' new friend left for Florida, a government boat pulled up to county wharf, and six game wardens came ashore. They were armed with pictures and names, plus information that could have come from just one source, the retired preacher. Eventually, the islanders came to realize the importance of conservation regulations and recognized the fact that they must abide by the game laws. But the memories of betrayal by foreigners linger. They are still cautious in their dealings with casual strangers.

A few writers have been fortunate enough to record and publish some island folklore. For instance, George Carey told a few island stories in his book, *A Faraway Time and Place*. The superstitions, tall tales, legends, and yarns of the Eastern Shore that he recorded are a treasure, part of the rich heritage of a culture that may soon disappear.

Smith Island, Chesapeake Bay

A part of this culture is superstition. It is a remnant of the time when life was never easy, and often was dangerous, a time when folks needed to take all precautions to ward off evil spirits and bad luck. Even those who were deeply religious felt the need of an extra measure of luck to ensure good health and success.

No one knows the exact origins of island superstitions; some of them go back for centuries. Most are simple beliefs and are accepted as facts of life. For instance, no islander has to be reminded not to hang anything on a doorknob, or not to put his hat on a table. A calamity might befall the household, if he did forget. Also, no sensible housewife sweeps her floor if someone is sitting in the room, nor does she use her broom after the sun sets. She is apt to sweep her visitor's money away or sweep good luck right out the door.

There are tokens of luck, too. Finding a coin with heads up is definitely good luck, while a bird flying at a windowpane is an omen of death. Rocking an empty chair brings bad luck, too, but picking up a pin from the floor brings good luck all day long.

Most household superstitions are familiar ones, like knocking on wood to ward off bad luck or tossing a pinch of spilled salt over the shoulder. But some are less familiar. An island housewife never leaves her wash on the line on New Year's Day. To do so would bring bad sickness to her family or poor times during the new year.

Another superstition concerning the beginning of the year involves an old tradition, New Year's giving. Early in the morning of New Year's Day, children troop from house to house, each one bearing an old sock and crying out at each door, "New Year's Give!" When the first little beggar knocks, the door is opened cautiously, for if it is a girl who has come begging, bad luck is foretold for the coming year. But if it is a boy, the bigger the gift, the better the luck.

Seamen are notorious for being a superstitious lot. They take no chance of inviting bad luck on board their boats. Long ago, sailors learned that their safety and rewards depended upon hard work, skill, knowledge of the weather and the sea—and a good measure of luck. Their knowledge was limited, their equipment often crude; the tools of their trade were few. Fortune was often credited to good luck, while disaster or poor returns were shrugged off as bad luck.

138

Tall Tales and Traditions

Some of the early superstitions have carried over into the twentieth century. Walnuts, for instance, since they grow mainly in cemeteries, are definitely bad luck, and should never be carried on board a boat. A big, burly Smith Island waterman will grow pale and fidgety with the knowledge that a cat has stowed away and sailed with him, but every mariner knows that finding a bone, however small, on his boat brings good fortune.

Black crows can be a symbol of either good luck or bad. An elderly islander says:

> Crows is the smartest birds ever. They'll fly five miles to sally with the wind, just to come across your bow. If you have a good fishing place in mind and one crow crosses your bow, change your direction in a hurry, head away from there fast. But if two fly acrost your bow, keep right on agoin'!

He remembers one time, when he was heading out:

> One old crow was asittin' there on a tump awaitin' for me, to cross my bow, you know. I sneaked out, headed away from him, but here he comes aflappin' by, just a hollerin' to let me know, "You might can't see me, but you sure can hear me." And crows, they're thievin' creatures, too, they'll steal ya blind. Take your pipe or cigar right outten your mouth. Or anything layin' loose on your boat.

That same waterman remembers working for a certain captain who was really superstitious. When one of his crew whistled while on his boat, he suspended work on an oyster rock to return that crew member to shore. He also told of an old belief concerning the new moon:

> If you spy the new moon over your right shoulder, whatever money you have, take it all out and shake it at her. You'll make plenty of money all that month."

He recalls another old salt who had extremely bad luck:

> Well, sir, ever' time he went down to his boat, somethin' went wrong. One time his engine wouldn't start. Or he'd sprung a leak, or the ropes'd break. One thing right after another. First, he'd get one thing fixed. As soon as he got that fixed, somethin' else tore up. He says, "I got the Devil on board of me. He's worryin' me to death.

139

Just got to get that Devil off'n here." So's he got a broom
and started sweepin'. He swept that boat from the bow
back, clear to the starn. Yessir, he swept that Devil right
off the starn. Next mornin' he went right out and caught
a load.

How the color blue became associated with bad luck, no one
remembers. But some watermen refuse to use blue paint, wear
anything blue, or carry anything of that color on board their
boats. The same waterman who paid five dollars to have a blue
wheelbarrow painted another color before taking it home,
blames another blue wheelbarrow for the bad luck he experienced a few years later.

It seems he had gone to Crisfield to pick up supplies for
crabbing, and his daughter went along. She needed a new
wheelbarrow, and without her father's knowledge, bought one
and had it loaded on the boat. The only color available was
blue. In the meantime, her dad rounded up his supplies and
had them delivered to the wharf. Among his supplies were
bundles of crab pot paddles—sixty dollars worth. When they
were ready to leave Crisfield, they discovered that all of the
paddles were missing; they had been stolen from the dock. It
wasn't until they were halfway across the sound, that the
waterman discovered the cause for his misfortune—the blue
wheelbarrow.

Another waterman was also particularly sensitive about
the color blue. His buddies decided to sneak something blue
on board his boat, just to see his reaction. A piece of blue string
was tied to the handle of his water bucket. The string went
unnoticed, and the waterman set out for Crisfield. On the way
over, bad luck set in. The island waterman ran smack into a
Crisfield scraper's boat. He had to tow the man's boat all the
way to Crisfield, but by the time they reached the mainland,
all that could be seen of the scraping boat was the awning
sticks. Considering the cost of repairs to the other man's boat,
and the loss of several days' work, that was a pretty expensive
piece of string. It would be hard to convince that waterman that
there is no such thing as bad luck.

Part of superstition is the belief in tokens, or omens, that
foretell death or disaster. Mysterious happenings, visions, or
unusual sounds are considered by older island people, and
some younger ones, as tokens. Sometimes, hindsight is better
than foresight, as in the case of the islander who heard a

strange tapping at his parlor window in the middle of the night. Before three days had gone by, his daddy was laid out a corpse in that same parlor. Said the islander, "I should a'knowed that tappin' was a token."

Even modern watermen can be superstitious about tokens. For instance, an islander who admittedly liked his good times, and refused to go to church, was haunted all summer by a vision. While working his scrapes on a calm morning, he bent over the low side of his boat to rinse out a bucket. He says that he saw, clearly outlined in the calm water of the crabbing bottom, the face of the Lord. As he knelt watching, the vision floated before his eyes, became brilliantly colored, then gradually floated away. The dreadfully frightened crabber pulled in his scrapes, shook out the bags, and headed for home.

He spent the rest of his summer looking over his shoulder for the catastrophe he knew was coming. The rest of the season was plagued with bad luck: family illness, engine trouble, and poor profits. Toward the end of the season, a badly leaking stuffing box almost caused the loss of his boat, and his own life. If you ask that waterman today, he'll tell you, "When I seen that face in the water that day, I knew it was a token."

Another token story concerns a tiny elderly lady who is remembered on Smith Island as a saintly woman who had dreams of prophecy, or visions, which were taken as forewarnings of disaster. Her warnings were heeded by those who believed; scoffers dismissed them as the wanderings of an old lady. But even scoffers came to believe after one episode:

A few years ago, a group of island men planned to take their tonging boats up the Bay for a week's work. One particular waterman was the proud owner of a beautiful new boat. She was long and sleek, with a brand new cabin, and up-to-date equipment that included a new hydraulic rig. This boat represented an investment of thousands of dollars and many hours of hard work.

The boats were bobbing about down landing, all ready for departure the next day, when the first token occurred. As she rose from her evening prayers, the saintly little lady happened to look out her window. She saw a figure at the bow of the boat with the brand new cabin. The figure was tall and slim, with long, flowing robes moving gently in the breeze. His hand was outstretched, pointing toward the southwest.

That same night, the boat's owner had a dream, a dream in which he saw himself lying in his grave, waiting for his

141

friends to cover him over. The vision and the dream were tokens not to be ignored.

But the fleet sailed off up the Bay. A few days later, after a good week's work, the boats started home. It was Friday, the eve of Halloween. A storm of wind from the southwest blew up, and for some reason, the boatman who had had the dream became separated from the rest of the fleet.

He fought his vessel through the turbulent sea. His bow went down into one wave; the next one filled his boat with water. Later that night, he was found floating on his engine box lid; he was nearly dead from exposure. His boat, oysters and all, still rests on the bottom of the Bay.

A token? A warning? Or just superstition? Regardless, this waterman's life was changed forever.

Not everyone on the island believes in luck and tokens. Some feel, as one of the elders puts it, "Luck is in the Lord, the Devil in the people."

One example of a mixture of superstition and religion is the belief that any work done on the Sabbath does no good. A violator of the Sabbath rule stands a chance of having a lot of trouble during the next week. Even those few who do not declare themselves Christian abide by this rule. As an old friend remembers back to when he was a little boy and not allowed to play on Sunday:

> I was down landin' Sunday mornin' playin' with my boat, makin' engine noises, and lettin' her ride out, and pullin' her back in. My ma caught me and warned me, "You better not do that, pretendin' you're workin' on Sunday. Put that boat up; you'll call 'em down on ye." Well, sir, I played like I was goin' over to Tylerton to church, and let Ma think I was gone. Then I played with my boat. That night, when I went to bed, I heard 'em. Right over my head. They was draggin' chains and makin' boat noises, just like me a' playin'. Yessir, I called ghosts right down on myself. I run and jumped 'tween Ma and Pa, but everytime they'd go to sleep, they'd start in again. I never did play boats on a Sunday after that.

So strong is the conviction about any type of work on Sunday, that there are examples of this belief still talked about.

One crabber from Rhodes Point had his floats full of crabs, but refused to fish up on Sunday. His sons went out to the shanty and saw all the big soft crabs in the floats and fished them out. They packed them and got them ready for shipment the next day.

Monday morning, when the father spotted the boxes, he realized what his boys had done. Immediately, he dumped every box overboard. To the boys, he merely said, "We're going to live, and we're going to die. Them crabs'll neither make us or break us."

It is the same with strong drink and game playing. Out of respect for an unwritten code, those who would take a drink on Saturday night, refuse to do so on Sunday. Island children play quietly on Sunday; there are no games, no rowdiness, no card playing. No cars roar past the church during meeting; none of the stores is open while services are going on, and no business is discussed on the Sabbath. It is a tradition that has been followed for centuries.

Island folklore consists of stories that are so old that no one can remember how some of them started. Perhaps they started with an event that gradually became embroidered into a legend. For instance, a new preacher was called on to perform the first duty of his new charge—an impromptu wedding ceremony on board the packet boat.

Two young visitors were so charmed by the island that they decided it was the ideal place to begin their marriage. They had already obtained their license and had planned to be married at the county seat after their island tour. As word of the wedding got around, islanders chipped in for gifts to make the day a memorable occasion for the couple. Flowers were gathered for a bridal bouquet and to decorate the *Island Belle* when it came in. There was to be music and a real wedding cake.

As the new minister arrived, he was introduced to the couple. While the *Belle* was being decorated, he counseled with the couple, then they all stepped back on board. The new preacher performed the ceremony on the deck of the *Island Belle*.

The *Island Belle* is gone now; it has been replaced by a modern ferryboat. But this wedding made the beginning of a story. It is a story that will grow with each telling, until it becomes a legend, a part of island folklore.

Some of those stories, island folklore, are fantasy, some are truth, and still others have had their origins lost in antiquity.

A few of these stories concern Pittcraft, Colonel Stevens's seventeenth-century plantation. The plantation house was built around 1700, and became the home of Uncle Haney Bradshaw, who called his property "Pitchcroft." On the grounds of Pitchcroft is the grave of an unknown British soldier, whose body was brought to shore from a warship over a century ago.

Some say that the soldier was mortally wounded during the War of 1812, and that he had made a request that he be buried on shore rather than at sea. Years ago, a group of Britons heard about the grave and brought a British flag and presented it to the islanders. Then they went back to England and made a search through military records for the name of the soldier. They found that all of the men on the British ships were accounted for, so the identity of the grave's occupant is still unknown.

The flag eventually became so weatherworn that it had to be taken down. Then someone moved the stone, and now the exact location of the grave is also unknown. Some believe that the grave contains the body of the Englishman; others contend that the body is that of a pirate, and there may be pirate's treasure buried at Pitchcroft. A legend? Perhaps. But few islanders would entertain the thought of disturbing the grave to find out the truth.

Before it burned down, the house called Pitchcroft was large and graceful, with ancient bluish windows that shimmered from years of exposure to salty wind and faded shingles that created an atmosphere of antiquity. Inside, the floors were still the original pine, and the woodwork was just as it was in Uncle Haney's day, pegged together with no visible nailheads marring its surface.

Hand-hewn beams supported the thick walls; large fireplaces graced the parlor and the room that used to be the kitchen. A stately staircase led upstairs to spacious bedrooms, and a narrow set of steps at the back angled up to the garret. It was a gracious old house, where visitors could feel the warmth inside, roam the vast lawn that slopes down to the waterfront, or explore the tiny graveyard out back.

Uncle Haney was a patriarch of the island, an elder of the church who was proud to be given the honor of housing the visiting preachers. The time came when Uncle Haney felt that his Pitchcroft was too small, not nearly grand enough to serve this purpose.

He had his house cut in half from top to bottom. One half was moved a distance of twenty feet from the other half.

144

Between the two parts of the house, Uncle Haney erected a large addition, and joined it all together to make a suitable lodging for his ministerial guests.

Although Uncle Haney was a highly respected individual, his exterior was rough, his appearance uncouth. His manner of speech was unique; he coined words for his own use and punctuated his conversation with phrases of his own making. After returning from church one night with the visiting preacher, Reverend R. W. Todd, he took it upon himself to compliment the preacher on his message:

> I tell you, brother, you had a mighty bunctious tex' tonight. Why, sir, if you'd combusticated at that dyin' rate a little longer, I'd a splodified right out the consanctum! In that way and form, sir, you got things in a solid smother. Why hain't they made you a Bishop long ago?

Another time, he said of a visiting preacher:

> In that manner and form, sir, your preacher's a regular Bonytholimar. Honerated powerful well in the mornin' and then went home with me to dinner and tuck in a cooner load of pervisions. And, I tell you, sir, I didn't think he could preach more of a sermon in the afternoon, and I just rared my head back agin the wall for a good nap. But I tell you, sir, in that way and manner, when he let on the steam and got under full headway, he just funked out the preachin' to excess!

One of Uncle Haney's contemporaries was the legendary Lickin' Billy Bradshaw, who lived at the far tip of Rogue's Point. Billy earned his nickname, not from his ability to lick any man awalkin', although he could, but from his habit of reaching out his tongue to lick his lips and the hairs of his beard. Billy's grandson talks about his granddaddy:

> Lickin' Billy was a big man, way over six and a half feet, a tall, raw-boned man. His wife, Atline, was a little tiny cracklin'. Small, no bigger'n a minute. She come up under his arm. He had a white goatee, chin whiskers, you know. I used to bum 'baccer from him.
>
> He didn't hold nothin' back; what come up, come out. If he didn't like you, he'd tell you to your face, or call you down, right in church. The last Sunday of camp

meetin', the people would all march around the
campground, singin' and praisin'. Billy was the leader,
because he was the biggest, you know.

One year, Cap'n, you know, he went to sleep, and the
people was a marchin'. Atline went there to their tent
and yelled, "William, get up, get up!" She shuck him.

"What fur?" Billy yells.

"They're marchin', William!"

"Let 'em march—they ain't a doin it right!"

'Cause he weren't there, you see, they wasn't doin' it
right. He was the leader, you know.

Old man Lickin' was incredibly strong; they say he wasn't
scared of anything. Legend has it that he had the strength of
six men:

One time, down here on the point, they was tryin' to get
some men together to pull up a boat on shore. It was a
ka'noo, and three or four were tryin' to get it up. Billy
says, "Step aside; I can pull 'er up." And he did.

Another version of this story claims that Billy was offered five
dollars to pull the boat up on shore. Billy hauled her out of the
water singlehandedly, but didn't get paid. So he put the boat
right back where he had found her. When his grandson was
asked to verify this version, he claimed. "I heard that, too. But
I can't swear to that. I wasn't there, you see."

But he was willing to tell one more story:

Lickin' Billy had a big flock of sheep over here on
Bayside. Bayside was a lot wider than it is now. The big
day was sheep shearin' day, in May. Everybody would
come to see the fun. People would come from all over
the island. They built a pen out of trap posts, to put the
sheep in. The youngsters would go down in the marsh,
and chase 'em up and in the pen.

They would take 'em out, tie their feet. Tie their hind
feet and their forefeet, and shear 'em, right out here on
Bayside. Well, sir, Billy had this one big sheep with
horns. He weren't wild none! Now, Billy was in his six-
ties, gettin' old. He'd chase that sheep down, grab him
by the horns, and he'd get loose. Over and over.

Well, Billy was gettin' tired, and people was afraid he'd
have a heart attack. But Billy yelled, "Run him up one
more time, boys!" This time he got a good hold on him
and someone yelled, "What you gonna do with him,
Billy?"

146

He says back, "Well, fellers, if'n his horns stays on,
this gentleman is agoin' over the fence!" They did; and
he did.

Lickin' Billy is at rest now, alongside his Atline in the graveyard
at Rhodes Point, but Lickin' Billy, the legend, lives on in the
hearts of Smith Islanders who cherish his stories.

There are other stories, too, especially the scary ones that
are told around Halloween. Stories like the one about the
woman in white who haunts the road out around where the
coffin house used to be. And the story of the young man who
saw the snake with saucer eyes on the bridge that used to go
to Pitchcroft. The last line of that story goes, "He riz right up,
right in front of him. What was that, but the Devil himself?"

Smith Island had its own witch, too, a real one who lived
all alone in a tiny shack Over the Gut. She was a gnarled old
lady with a long pointed nose, snarly gray hair, and long, dirty
fingernails. Unruly children quieted down when they were
threatened with the prospect of being sent to live with the
"witch." Parents warned their children to behave, or else "she'll
get you in her clutches—then you'll behave!"

How this old crone happened to arrive on Smith Island,
where she came from, who brought her there, or why she
stayed, no one seems to know. Her name was not an island
name; she seems to have had no island relatives. She fit the
general idea of what a witch should be, so witch she was.

According to legend, she was wont to appear suddenly
behind her "victim," and clutch at his clothing with her long,
skinny fingers, to cackle and whine for food or pennies. Once
in a while, a charitable homemaker would hire her for a little
help with the housecleaning. She "proved" herself a witch by
the following incident:

> A certain lady hired her to come to her house one day a
> week. When she was helping with the cleaning, she saw
> this purty cut-glass bowl. My, she wanted that dish; it
> was all sparkly, you know. She asked the cap'n's wife
> for it. "Oh, no," said the lady. "I can't give that away. It
> was one of my wedding presents."
> Whenever she came to clean, the witch'd ask for the
> bowl. Ever' time the lady'd say no. The old witch asked
> one more time, and the lady got mad. "I told you no,
> now finish the dusting!" Instead, the witch marched out
> the door. When she shut the door, that bowl just

jumped off the table it was sittin' on and fell "Wham!" to the floor. That bowl broke into a million pieces!

After that, the witch's reputation was secured; she was given a wide berth by the island people.

Curiously enough, there are graves in the churchyard whose headstones bear the name, Brit, the same first name as the witch. Apparently, some islanders either did not believe in witches, had some affection for the old crone, or else her name was just a lovely name. However, there may be some truth in the witch story. The tiny graves are those of little girls who never lived to grow up.

Islanders may be superstitious, but they can find humor in almost any situation, even one as bad as the terrible fire that took away the church and the tabernacle. Most of the families were just sitting down to Sunday dinner when the fire broke out. All day and all night they fought the fire; their dinners were forgotten.

Eventually, the weary islanders were able to return to their homes. More than one family went home to a mess. An island grandmother remembers that day clearly:

> When we heard them yellin' "Fire!" we was just settin' down to dinner. My, we had us a spread: chicken and dumplin's and all the trimmin's—hot rolls, greens, baked corn, and salad and pie. We jumped up and run, and somebody forgot to shut the door to. Next day, when we got back to the house, you shoulda seen it. Chairs was tumbled over. The tablecloth was all muddy and hangin' on the floor. Food was all over every place. Greens was a danglin' off the table cloth. Dumplin's and potatoes mashed and dried out all over. The pig had got in! The door was wide open—the pig smelled dinner on the table and made hisself to home.

When asked if they had punished the pig, this practical housewife replied, "Punish him? No, we didn't punish him. We ate him."

Then there were the pigs that the candy man brought. Drummers used to come to the island on a regular basis, to sell their wares to the storekeepers, and to take orders for future delivery. One was a candy and tobacco salesman who was called the candy man.

One time when the candy man came, the storekeeper expressed a desire to have some little pigs to raise. Says the candy man, "Why, I know where I can get you some little pigs, and cheap, too." He and the storekeeper made a deal. With the condition that a sturdy pen would be all ready to put them in, the candy man would bring the pigs on his next trip.

The storekeeper labored over the pen, building it big and strong enough to hold six growing pigs. My, but he was proud of that pen. Finally, the big day came. When the candy man made his appearance at the store, the proprietor anxiously asked, "Did you bring my little pigs?"

"Sure did. And that's some pen you built. I dropped 'em in when I come by."

Everyone rushed out of the store and down the lane to the pig pen.

"Why, I don't see no pigs!" yelled the storekeeper.

"Sure you do—right there in the corner."

And, sure enough, right there in the corner of that great big pen were a half-dozen licorice piglets.

Shippies come in for their share of stories, too. On the few dredge boats still working the Bay, the men now work on shares. Usually, it is a good paying job, but it is cold, hard work, with long periods spent away from home. It is hard enough to get a good crew today; in the old days, it was nearly impossible to get enough local men to do the back-breaking work. Captains sometimes had to go to Baltimore to get up crews any way they could.

Most captains hired their men from agencies, but sometimes men were shanghaied, and some were given bad treatment aboard the boats. These men were often referred to as tramps; on Smith Island, they were called shippies.

Many stories have been written of men who were drugged or slugged, forced to work for months, and then were paid off with the boom. Smith Island had its share of cruel captains, but for the most part, the shippies were treated well by the islanders. Some shippies liked island living, and chose to stay. Some even married island girls and settled down on the island.

But according to some of the stories told, others did not fare so well. For instance, it is said that at least one shippie received such harsh treatment from a local dredge boat captain that he chose death by his own hands. To avoid continued beatings, he threw himself overboard and drowned. Three others lost their lives in an attempt to escape in a leaky boat; their bodies are buried behind the campground.

Smith Island, Chesapeake Bay

Another shippie tried to rob his captain; he bashed him in the head with an ax and ended the captain's career on the water. The captain's son, now a retired waterman, carries a scar from the blow that split his own skull. This is his story:

> Me and my daddy left home that day bound up the Potomac to buy oysters. Just a boy I was. I began sailin' with my dad when I was just big enough to reach the wheel standin' on a packin' box. We was on our way up the Potomac; had quite a lot of money with us. Or quite a lot of money for those days, that is. There was just three of us on board, my dad and me and our shippie.
>
> Well, sir, we anchored off in a cove just above Lower Cedar Point to eat, and catch a little shut-eye. We'd just drifted off good in the cabin. The shippie was bunked in, in the hold. Somethin' woke me quicklike, and I saw my dad layin' in a mess of blood, and saw this bloody ax acomin' at me.
>
> They told us later that this man and a little boy was out fishin' and saw our shippie pullin' away from our boat. The boy says, "Paw, did you see all that blood in that boat?"
>
> They hailed us, and not gettin' an answer, they clumb aboard to check us out and found us there. Thought we was goners, for sure. They went to get us help; a navy boat took us to the hospital, and they sent for Ma. Well, sir, my dad never did get much better; never worked no more. Me, I been following the water ever since.

If a captain had a shippie who wasn't particularly needed at a certain time, another captain might take him on. Sometimes, he stayed at the captain's home, to help the women with heavy chores. Others were left to fend for themselves; they slept in sheds and ate wherever they could find a meal.

Often, these men created fear in the hearts of women who were left alone with only young boys and old men for protection. One of the women who lived through those days, remembers one scary night when she was a young girl keeping her grandmother company while her grandfather was gone "up the Bay":

> Granddaddy had a shippie. His name was Derby, I think it was. He'd leave him sometimes, or other men'd take him. He was a great big man and sometimes he'd get real mean. He slept in an old shed, and liked to come to grandma's. She fed him, you see. But grandma got scared of him. He wanted to come to grandma's in the night.

150

The *Mama Estelle*, a round-stern workboat, coming into the dock at Rhodes Point. In the background are crab shanties; in the foreground, overboard floats used for shedding crabs. (Photograph by Marion E. Warren.)

151

There wasn't no electricity in them days, and this night it was raining, pourin' down, and so dark. It was pitch black. Grandma said, "Surely Derby won't come here this night. But just in case, we're goin' to bed early."

Just about that time, I heard him comin'. He had on those big old oilskins; you could hear him rattlin' when he was comin' down the path. I says, "Here he comes, grandma, he's comin'. He's knockin' on the door!" and grabbed a lamp.

Grandma says, "Get upstairs, quick!" I hit the step and dropped that lamp. It was pitch dark. We slipped up the steps in the dark, and when we got to the top, I remembered something. "Grandma," I says, "we got to go back. We forgot the pot!"

Grandma grabbed my arm and said, "Child, I'd do it in the bed before I'd go back to get that pot!"

I looked out the window and Derby was goin' round and round the house. He'd abeen lynched, if he hadn't left. But he left, and no one ever saw him again.

Two more shippies met their fate while aboard a workboat from Rhodes Point. Loaded down with oysters, the bugeye was headed for home. A storm of wind came up, and the seas became rough. The bugeye sank, "out here on the middle ground." Willie B., the captain, got up to the head of the mast, and tied "hisself" there. He was found the next day, drowned, but still hanging from the mast. His two shippies were lost.

Other shippies became members of the community; one was a carpenter who died at the age of ninety-six; he is buried at Rhodes Point. Another became the island handy man. The shippies are now a part of island history, part of an era long past.

In those days of loose law and the oyster wars, it was a struggle just to survive. An old salt from Rhodes Point sums it up pretty well:

Them days was rough days, and they was rough men. Had to be to do what they did. Workin' on the water was dangerous in the old days. Folks did what they had to do. They tell all those tales about how mean the drudge boat captains was. Some of 'em were meaner'n them Egyptian slave drivers. But it was hard times for everybody, captain and crew alike. It was tit for tat. You worked with what you got. If you made a day's work, that's fine. If you lived to tell the tale—that was better.

152

Tall Tales and Traditions

Through long association with each other, and the intimacy that has resulted from this close association, islanders have a relationship that is seldom seen in mainland communities. Because they know each other so well, there is an easy camaraderie. Together, they take pleasure in simple things: steamed clams on a Saturday night, church on Sunday, summer baseball games, a troop through the snow for a community supper, and an evening of rowdy fun and games—or a rousing practical joke.

Practical jokes have long been a source of homemade fun; they are a part of island culture, and there is as much fun in the retelling of jokes played, as there is in the joke itself.

Some of the practical jokes are spur-of-the-moment tricks or gags. Others are complex schemes that require resourcefulness and much hard work. For example, several hours of hard work in the dead of night were required to make a success of one prank that was pulled on an unsuspecting waterman.

To understand the complexity of this particular practical joke, it is necessary to describe its components, a set of patent tongs and a scraping boat. Patent tongs are large, awkward pieces of oystering equipment; they weigh close to three hundred pounds. The tongs are basketlike dredges with iron teeth that are bolted together and fixed to a large hydraulic shaft.

A scraping boat, a boat used by crabbers to tow their crab scrapes through the water, is twenty-five to thirty feet long, with low sides and narrow washboards. Much of the interior of the scraping boat is filled with gear: live box, pumps, barrels, and hand scrapes. There is little room for even one man to maneuver comfortably. Few scrapers have cabins, and if they do, it is a tiny structure just high enough for a man to stand. It, too, is crowded; it houses the steering gear, radio, and extra equipment, and provides a place just big enough for the waterman to get in out of the weather. Because of the lack of space, the cabin's door is extremely narrow. The object of the joke was to somehow fit the patent tongs into the boat's tiny cabin.

To add to the jokers' problems, the boat involved was tied up at the side of a rickety finger of a pier, treacherous enough in broad daylight. First, the heavy tongs had to be taken apart and carried down to the pier. Once there, they were lifted onto the boat, angled through the narrow door piece by piece, then reassembled in the confines of the cabin. So much work, just to

153

see the look of astonishment on the face of the sleepy crabber, as he stepped on board his boat and opened his cabin door.

Hidden behind a nearby shanty, the jokers bent double with laughter as a bellow of rage and frustration erupted from the irate crabber. His friends lost a few hours sleep; the crabber lost a day's work while he disassembled the tongs and removed them from his boat. Together, they provided hours of fun for generations to come in the retelling of one more waterman's practical joke.

This practice of pulling pranks dates back as far as the memory goes, and youngsters beg old-timers to tell their yarns, then sit in quiet awe to listen. One favorite practical joke is the "wedding story."

As the story goes, a very quiet, extremely shy man came to work for an island captain. He was a hard worker, but he was nearly blind without his thick-lensed eyeglasses. The gentleman enjoyed a nip now and then, but he wasn't much of a lady's man. He'd never been married, and his lack of a wife or lady friend let him in for a lot of teasing.

Elaborate planning went into a situation that developed into a serious attraction for the nearsighted handyman and a certain "lady." On an evening when he just happened to be in his cups, a fair-haired, buxom young woman just happened to be visiting the island. She flirted shamelessly, and things progressed until the only answer to the handyman's lovesickness seemed to be an immediate marriage.

The lady was more than willing, and an elegant ceremony was set up. Fortunately, an itinerant "preacher," all dressed up in a parson's black suit, was also visiting the island. He was glad to preside over the solemn rites. The wedding was well attended; a crowd of well-wishers followed the happy couple to the house where the groom had a room.

Amidst catcalls and congratulations, the groom led his blushing bride into his room, only to become stone sober when he realized that his bride was not all that she was cracked up to be. Under the blonde wig, fancy dress, and padding, was a rough Smith Island waterman. No one tells in mixed company the exact words that were used that night, but it was a long time before the groom took another drink—or took another wife.

Jokes have been known to backfire, too, as in the case of the rocking ghost of Wading Place Bridge. The bridge, a wooden structure that crosses the gut that separates the two main islands, is halfway between Rhodes Point and Ewell.

The bridge has a scary past. It has been the site for witch's tales and ghost sightings from way back. There is the story of the headless horses that clatter across the bridge after midnight; an especially farfetched story, since Smith Island has never had a herd of horses, even one complete with heads.

Other tales are told of hearing a baby wailing in the marsh close to the bridge, of hearing his cries choked off, then a silence that is broken by a mother weeping for her lost child. It is stories like these that give Wading Place Bridge a ghostly reputation. It is a stouthearted fellow, indeed, who dares to walk Rhodes Point Road alone after midnight.

Years ago, a young man from North End was courting a girl who lived at Rhodes Point. Night after night, he walked the long road to her house, then back again. There were no street lights or cars, no traffic at all, and no friendly voices, either. Just empty road, with miles of marshland stretching out on either side. One dark, moonless night, the atmosphere seemed ideal for the perfect practical joke.

The pranksters carried a large rocking chair from North End, a distance of almost a mile, and placed it in the middle of the bridge. One of the watermen sat down in the rocker, and to complete the ghostly picture, a white sheet was thrown over him. The rest of the crowd of jokers chose hiding places along the banks of the gut.

Shortly after midnight, along came the romantic hero, marching down the road, whistling to keep up his courage. Warned by the whistle, the ghost set the chair in motion, rocking to the tune of groans and eerie moans. The young waterman approached the bridge and yelled out, "Who's there?" and the ghost rocked harder and groaned louder.

As he neared the apparition in the middle of the bridge, the lad clenched his fists, and took a boxer's stance. Then, dancing around the rocking ghost, he bellowed, "Be ye ghost or be ye human, I'm acomin' through ye or over ye!"

Up jumped the ghost, yelling, "Hell's bells! Don't kill me!" And he ran for his life, his ghostly robes trailing after him. As for the rocker, over the rail it went. The watchers crept away through the night, sneaking off to tell the tale of the ghost of Wading Place Bridge.

This type of prank takes forethought and patience, virtues that have long been traits particular to watermen. The result of these do-it-yourself projects is the enjoyment of good-natured give and take, the humor of people who know and love each other. But, inevitably, this, too, will change. The population of Smith Island is dwindling; there are now less than five hundred people living in the three villages, and outsiders are beginning to move in.

The new people are accepted with traditional Smith Island hospitality. The summer folks and the new residents may pay their share on the well house, and give to the preacher; they may attend church and the community suppers, and join in the fun and games. They may go out with a crabber or stand around in the store listening to the watermen spin yarns. But they are on the outside looking in. They have no need to fear the possibility of being on the receiving end of a practical joke. The islanders are cordial to the newcomers, but the best yarns and pranks are kept in reserve for home folks.

Most of the stories heard on the island are scraps of yarns, pieces of life as it has been lived on Smith Island for centuries. But they are the pieces of life that are a part of an earthy people trying to make for themselves a comfortable living, and to soften their existence by poking fun at each other, while relishing their good times in an attempt to make them last a little longer.

For instance, there are cat stories. There are many, many cats on Smith Island—big cats, little cats, calico cats, black cats, and white cats. There are cats on the doorsteps, cats down landing, in the house, and on the porches. There are always cats underfoot, and when the tide comes up and covers the yards and roads, there are cats overhead as well.

No one has ever taken a full count of the feline population, but it far outnumbers the human population. Although some would have you think differently, the cats are not only tolerated, they are loved. The cats are too well fed for really effective rat control, because nearly everyone feeds them table scraps, and the stores are kept well stocked with cat food.

As this story shows, nearly every household has more than its share of felines:

> An outlander married an island waterman, and came to
> begin her new life on the island. At Christmas time, her
> heart was touched by a very special gift from a small
> child—a tiny gray kitty. It didn't matter much to her
> that the precious little gift just happened to be female.
> At least, not until the first litter came, and the next.

156

Then, those litters started producing, too, until she had a full-fledged nursery set up with large, padded boxes for delivery and separation of litters. By the time that the kitten-count reached twenty-four, she realized that the joke was on her, and printed a sign to tack up on the door of the "delivery" room. The sign said "Shhh! Nursery: Babies sleeping."

The next day, a door-to-door salesman from the mainland stopped in to give his sales pitch. Thinking to please the new mother, and thereby make a sale, he asked about the babies in the nursery. With the straight face of a true Smith Islander, the new "mother" replied, "Oh, we have quite a litter!"

The salesman begged to see the little darlings and was shown into the nursery. At the sight of box after box of mama cats nursing their babies, he beat a hasty retreat, so anxious to flee the "cathouse," that he left behind his sales packet.

This practical joke may very well have boosted this outlander's acceptance as one of the home folks.

The same waterman who will cut short his day's work if he finds a cat on board his boat will offer a big reward if one of his pets is lost. Not long ago, a cat stowed away on a barge that was leaving the island. He was sorely missed by his owner, who instigated a search for the animal, and put up a sum of money for its return. After the cat was finally given up for dead, he was found by his own master. The cat was found roaming the dock at Crisfield; his master swears that his pet was just waiting for a ride home.

Another animal provided the catalyst for an island story that will live forever. Many years ago, several families kept goats as pets. The goats became a nuisance, so they were loaded in skiffs and set loose on a little island across the creek from the mail-boat landing. From those early goats, a large herd has grown. Some are as big as cows; they are all wild and hard to catch.

An island waterman, one well known to get easily upset, had just built a cozy little cabin on his scraping boat. Just before daylight one chilly spring morning, this crabber jumped on board his boat, checked out his engine, and headed for his cabin. As he opened the door, out shot a wild billy goat, who nearly knocked him over in his rush to get out. The goat skittered all over the boat, then went overboard, and swam away.

157

Smith Island, Chesapeake Bay

Inside the cabin, the scraper slipped and fell in the debris left behind by the goat. Total rage built up as he surveyed the damage; wires were chewed up and torn loose, storage boxes and supplies were half-eaten and strewn about, and in the scraper's own words, "It stank to high heaven."

He "seared the ears" of the listeners on the CB radio, those who were waiting to get his reaction. As one of the pranksters put it, "It were a lot of trouble, but it was worth it!"

Of course, as Lickin' Billy's grandson says, "They's some things is told for the truth what ain't the truth." A story begins, based on either fact or fantasy, then grows into a legend. Sometimes, the real details are lost, but the story becomes embroidered while it lives on.

Some island legends are real; some are even documented, but some are told only to be enjoyed. The story of Captain Caleb's granddaddy is based on fact; the legend of Carlos and Hester is a historic romance. Carlos's bravery is lauded when the tale of his daring escape from Pt. Lookout is told, and Hester's beauty and goodness are legendary.

According to family stories, other island ancestors found their way to the island as refugees from the Civil War. In fact, most families have at least one tale to tell about the early days and their own forebears. But the legend of the origin of one family name is romantic, indeed.

According to the story, three brothers of noble lineage were en route to Baltimore on a Spanish merchantman. This was during the Spanish Revolution, and as their ship sailed up the Bay, the three brothers were accused of treason. They were stripped of their finery and thrown into the hold of the ship.

The brothers decided to fight for their lives, and managed to escape their captors by jumping overboard. One of the brothers drowned, another swam to Virginia's Eastern Shore. The third made it to the Tangiers, where the people took him in and cared for him. While recovering from his ordeal, he fell in love with an island girl. They married, and began a family whose descendants still live on the islands.

Like this story, much family history can be told only through legend, and some early family names have disappeared. A stroll through one of the three island graveyards gives mute testimony to this. One gravestone simply says, "Lavinia Poe." Who was Lavinia Poe? Where did she come from? Who did she belong to? What was a Poe doing on Smith Island? No one knows.

Other stones tell their stories. One on the grave of a tiny child asks you to, "Tread lightly, a dream lies sleeping here." At Rhodes Point, a pyramid memorializes a father who never returned from the sea. On other gravestones are symbols of grief: a weeping willow or a willow weeping over a broken monument. In the family plot at Pitchcroft is a rose with a petal for each member of the family, save one. A withered stem is etched in its place.

In one of the graveyards, a large stone covers an entire family, all lost together. Another marks the resting place of a devoted couple who died within hours of each other, one not caring to live when the other left.

The dates on the stones tell stories, too. They mark the time when outlying families gathered into inland communities. They record the dates of death-dealing storms and times of epidemic. They tell the tales of tragedy and grief, of hopes shattered, or of lives lived long and well.

There are the teachers who came to teach in the one-room schools and stayed for the rest of their lives. There are the preachers who led the islanders in worship, the doctors who came to serve, and who died in that service. Here lie Uncle Haney, King Solomon and his consort, the lighthouse keepers, and "drudge" boat captains and their mates.

The three cemeteries are well kept; the graves are trimmed regularly; the dead are treated with respect. Flowering shrubs mark the graves of island ancestors, whose memories are kept alive through legend and tradition.

Just as their ancestors did, the people of Smith Island feel privileged to dwell in this maze of land and water. Their hearts remain attached to the rugged shores that barely rise above the Bay. This tiny bit of land is home.

About the time of the Second World War, it was rough times on the island. The crab season was very poor, and it was hard to make a living. Some of the men were forced to seek jobs elsewhere for the time being. They went to Baltimore, Philadelphia, and other large cities, to work in shipyards and factories. A few came straight back home; some stayed away for the duration of the war.

This was a trying time for the islanders, especially for the wives. Those who went away with their husbands seemed to get lost in the confusion of city life, and they were homesick. The wife of one of those who went away to work remembers how it was:

Smith Island, Chesapeake Bay

When we was moved away, I despised it up there in the
city. I says to Daddy, "Captain, sir, if you don't want to
come home, I am. I'm takin' the children and I'm agoin'.
I was born there, I was riz there, and I've never lived
nowheres else. I'm agoin' home.

He stayed, you know, to make the money to live on,
but soon as he could, he come home, too.

Inevitably, the time will come when the islanders will no longer
be able to call this place home. It will no longer be a shadow
on the horizon; it will no longer be a way station on the great
highway of the Chesapeake. Only a remnant of the original
families will remain, until they, too, are laid to rest beside their
ancestors. But the islanders who leave their watery domain will
take with them a rich heritage, a heritage that will live on
forever.

IX

Bits and Pieces

There is an island
 I'll always call my home.
Only my family lives there,
 I'll never want to roam.
Sometimes when I'm happy,
 Sometimes when I'm sad,
God sends the seagulls
 To tell me to be glad.
Sometimes it is stormy,
 And sometimes there is ice,
But always it's my homeplace,
 And I just think it's nice.
 —Keith, age 12.

M any of those who have written articles about Smith Island
have mentioned the language spoken there. They have
described it as a regional dialect with Elizabethan patterns or
as a mixture of Shakespearian English and the Cockney dialect. It is neither.

The island language may have had its beginnings in old
England, but the dialect is a form of prose that has developed
over the three centuries that the islanders have lived together.
It is a mixture of colloquialisms that are blended together with
love and humor, and spoken with a quaint accent reminiscent
of their motherland.

Through their manner of speaking, the islanders gently
chide each other, use sarcasm to express humor, and use some
phrases backwards, with their meaning exactly the opposite of
what is said. For instance, the phrase, "Well, that ain't ugly

Smith Island, Chesapeake Bay

none!" actually means that the speaker is voicing admiration for something that he thinks is very attractive.

Some of the expressions are easily interpreted. They are nicknames given to islanders during their childhood, or special names given to the different types of boats they use, or terms used to describe certain places. For example, the community of Ewell is divided into two sections. Where the front road joins the back road, there is a slight rise that divides "Down the Field" from "Over the Hill." Down the Field has two roads—Front Road and Back Road.

After rounding Preacher's Corner, the main road winds past Frances Kitching's Inn and the schoolhouse to a lane that is commonly known as Poor Man's Lane. Bayside is the barrier island that lies off the north shore, and "Over the Gut" is an abandoned section of marshland that used to be high ground. Then, there's Marsh Island, Hog Neck, "Shankses," and Round Hammock.

Other expressions are a little harder to understand. A new-comer, if he listens in on the conversation of a group of islanders, almost needs an interpreter. This poem, written with the help of a group of island teenagers, explains some of those expressions:

Talking to Each Other

While listening to our language,
    a stranger gets confused.
Here, in case you visit,
    are some phrases often used.
It's the language of our fathers,
    handed down from year to year,
So if you came to see us,
    this is what you'll hear:
When an islander says he's run ashore,
    he's absolutely filled,
While someone who ain't hurt none,
    is very nearly killed.
If she disappears like Sally,
    she'll ne'er be seen no more,
And a man who states, "There ain't nothin' to do!"
    has *really* got a chore.
Now, "This is where I belong to be,"
    means he's home and island drawn,
While the statement that a man is *weak*,
    denotes that man is strong.
One who claims, "I ain't got no cats!"
    has too many cats to count,

Bits and Pieces

But if he says he ain't caught airy one,
    he's caught a *large* amount.
The phrase, "No, *I* don't think so!"
    asserts he's really sure,
And something that tastes just very fine
    is understated by, "That's poor!"
"I hope to die, that weren't no good,"
    he loved with all his might,
But when he likes the way it looks,
    it's said, "That don't look right!"
Exclaiming, "I didn't tell *him* nothin'!"
    means he really has cut loose,
By shouting, "I didn't harm *him* none!"
    he certainly cooked *his* goose,
And said in no uncertain terms
    what he definitely had to say.
"I'll *do* it—first thing 'fore light!"
    means it'll not get done that day!
But if he says, "Well, now, I'll tell ya',"
    that's what he'll start to do,
And, "I'll swear and kiss the Bible,"
    points out he means it's true.
By announcing, "If that weren't the champ,"
    he insists it was quite a feat,
"That's poor eatin', ain't it?"
    means it sure was hard to beat.
When a man remarks, "I'll swagger, die."
    you know he's indeed amazed,
But, "There ain't nothin' wrong with *him!*"
    actually means he's crazed.
When a kid proclaims, "I *AM!*"
    he'll never get it done,
But if what he says is hilarious,
    they say, "He ain't funny, none!"
About someone who can really sing,
    it's said, "He's overboard!"
And a man can be poor'ern Pern,
    Or richer than a lord.
Or when a body insists, "He ain't ready!"
    you can bet he really is,
But if they say, "He cain't *do* it!"
    it's sure that he's a whiz.
Now, the Graveyard is a tonging place,
    A Bar-cat's a scraping boat,
There's no witch at Witch's Cove,
    and the Barn has neither shoat.
There's certainly no fire at Light'ard Knot,
    no cherries on Cherry Hill,
But you can fish at Fishin' Island,
    or go draggin', if you will.

Smith Island, Chesapeake Bay

Nut Sundae lives just Down the Field,
    with Rooster, China, and Stink,
While Over the Hill live Messer and Spot,
    with Wildman, Boats, and Bink.
You "fish up" to get the softies,
    "melt and run together" in the sun,
Or you're frozen in just "chock-a-block,"
    before the winter's done.
Now please don't be bewildered;
    please don't think we're queer,
Just listen to what we're saying,
    and interpret what you hear.
We know just what we're meaning,
    though you may not understand,
We're just talking to each other—
    in the language of our land.

The people of Smith Island are down-to-earth folks who enjoy the simple pleasures of life. Many of them are talented. Some are artistic; they make amazingly accurate scale models of all types of boats, carve decoys, paint, and draw. Others write plays that are performed at the annual fireman's show; some write and produce religious dramas, or write poetry. Although not well-educated, many are able to express themselves eloquently.

Here are some bits and pieces contributed by islanders. From one who prefers to remain anonymous:

The earth is as high as the heaven,
    The sea as deep as the sky.
Our world as vast as the horizon,
    As we go sailing by.
We're launched on a sea of adventure,
    As we sail upon the tide,
We face our journey boldly,
    And sail on, side by side.
Our future waits before us,
    Together, we are one,
Away from the harbor,
    We set our course,
And sail on—sail on—sail on.

From an island teenager:

A native, both proud and free
    is what I am,
Free to do whatever I can.
    To walk on the shores of my island sand,
To feel the crisp air blowing from the Bay,

The Middleton-Dize General Store, more commonly known on Smith Island as "Chart and Ruke's" or just "Miss Willie's." Although the sign has been changed, Miss Willie's store still looks much like it did more than thirty years ago. The telephone exchange shown on the sign, named for Hurricane Hazel, is still in use. (Photograph by Marion E. Warren.)

Smith Island, Chesapeake Bay

Tells me the island is special, in every way.
To see the watermen sail away,
        out to work the Chesapeake Bay,
And to see and smell the marshland, day by day,
        makes me feel special, in every way.
To ride the waters as far as you can see,
        To watch the sea gulls fly, Oh, so free,
Is a treasured gift from God,
        given to me,
To be able to live on an island,
        so lovely, and so free.

—Valerie Bruce

Island watermen express their humor with straight-faced seriousness. Usually, it is expressed in spur-of-the-moment comments while conversing with other watermen. Jennings Evans, an islander with a delicious sense of humor, has an extensive collection of bits and pieces. Each is typical of "lines that are delivered each day in conversations among watermen."

How Small Were They?

Tonger complaining about culling through heavy small oyster growth: "They were so small you could drop 'em in a jug!"

Waterman complaining about working on a very shelly oyster rock: "I've worked on that rock two times this year—my first and my last!"

Waterman describing another waterman's courage: "He's got more nerve than a jimmy-crab!"

Waterman doubting another waterman's story: "I think he threw me a curve!"

Waterman telling how to avoid a heavy southwesterly wind: "The only place to get rid of a white-belly sou'wester is home in your house!"

Crab-potter describing his outlook for the next day's catch: "Looks bluer than a gizzard out there!"

Waterman commenting on the weather: "Why, it was so windy there was whitecaps in the chamber pot!"

Waterman talking about the large shark he spotted: "Boy, what he could do to a pair of real white legs!"

166

Bits and Pieces

Overheard on the CB: "Let's quit talking about crabs and talk about women."

Waterman (tongue-in-cheek) describing his having overslept two hours: "All I did was lay down my head!"

Waterman describing the horrors of his bald head: "I'd rather pull down my pants than take off my hat!"

Waterman describing a well-dressed seafood packer: "He had on a red tie bigger than a for'sail!"

And a waterman describing early bird rising of another waterman: "He's reached the age where he only needs three nods for a night's sleep!"

Watermen make fun of each other, but they make fun of themselves, too. Both the *Crisfield Times* and the *Waterman's Gazette* recognized Mr. Evans's knack for satire by printing the following essay:

On Scarce Oysters

Oysters are scarce—when you wake up in the morning, dreading to go anywhere, but knowing you must go somewhere, looking for oysters.

Oysters are scarce—when you catch a recently opened sardine can on the spot you're tonging, left by a previous tonger who ate his dinner there, indicating he was there ahead of you.

You're on scarce oysters—when the shells coming up in your tongs look like Kellogg's Special K, and the toad eggs look like raisins.

You're on scarce oysters—when you catch three oysters in one dip, and feel an overwhelming urge to throw a buoy.

You're on scarce oysters—when after throwing the buoy, you wouldn't care if the U. S. Navy came and "bombed" the area.

You're on scarce oysters—when you catch two oysters and a stone in one dip, only to have the stone mash one, and the teeth of the tongs shuck the other.

You're on scarce oysters—when one of the precious bivalves falls from your culling board, and you feel an inward desire to dive overboard after it.

You're on scarce oysters—when you catch an empty whiskey bottle, and wish it were full.

You're on scarce oysters—when you look at the Great Cliffs of Calvert (in flusteration), and holler "Mama!"

Smith Island, Chesapeake Bay

Oysters are really scarce—When the buy captain races wildly to catch your bow line, only to stumble and stick his pencil in his ear.

Oysters are scarce—When after dragging the bottom all day, you feel some consolation in naming the three oysters you did catch—Huey, Lewey, and Dewey.

And finally, you're on scarce oysters when you have enough time between licks to make this crazy mess—as I did one day—while tonging on Hog Island.

See you on the rock!

Islanders stick pretty close to the basics of life: work, food, shelter, nature, their respect for each other, and their love of God. A few of them have written their thoughts on these subjects and don't mind sharing them with others. Jennings shares his collection of thoughts about food:

Sometimes I rise in the morning,
    And pull my firkin out,
And open up the lid
    to pull me out a trout.
Then I put me on a pan,
    just to boil him in,
That's poor eatin', ain't it?
    With grease drippin' off your chin!
Then, sometimes in the winter,
    when we have a little luck,
We have for Sunday dinner,
    a great big corn-fed duck.
Just to smell of one a'cookin',
    nearly drives me crazy,
Do ya think that's any good
    with a sweet tater rolled in gravy?

More thoughts on food:

I tell you now, another dish,
    that we just love to have,
In the summer, ain't they good?
    them stewed up jimmy crabs?
And before you eat your crab,
    just lick from off his claw,
Them steamy little stewed onions,
    Boy—that'll hit your craw!
There's another good dish
    you surely ought to try,
We have it really often,
    it's called good old clam pie.

168

Go fishin' for them dough boys,
    a'swimmin' all around,
Boy, I'll tell you one thing,
    they ain't hard to get down!
I'll tell you another dish that's good,
    after you've tonged all day,
Can't think of nothin' no better,
    you fix it up this way.
Just boil some of that Hake fish,
    in all its natural gasses,
Then top the whole thing off,
    by soppin' up molasses.
And, have you ever come home from crabbin',
    just as hungry as a bear,
And sniff the smell of soft crabs,
    a'fryin' in the air?
I'm tellin' you now,
    you ain't never been fed,
Unless you've tried them little softies,
    'tween two slices of bread.

Traditionally, many island men have had to leave home on Sunday afternoon to go oystering up the Bay. Some work on the Chesapeake's skipjack fleet; others leave their boats in upper Bay harbors and commute to the island ferry. Those who have to leave, do so amid the jeering taunts that are good-naturedly thrown at them from their friends, who get to stay in home port. An oysterman who has to leave sometimes feels this way:

Now, Sunday dinner at home
    is tops if you can stay,
But it's not worth a hoot,
    when you're oysterin' up the bay.
I'd round the preacher's corner,
    at three right on the docket,
With tears a'runnin' down my face,
    and a chicken wing in my pocket.

But, as another waterman says:

Eatin' aboard a boat
    can be a problem, too.
You have to cook what's easy,
    and still be good for you.
We eat lots of beans for dinners,
    they say they're good for your health.

Smith Island, Chesapeake Bay

> But on rainy days with oilskins on,
> It's hard to live with yourself!

A few years ago, a teacher asked her island pupils to put their thoughts into poetry. Nearly all of them mentioned nature, love, or God in their poems.

Bits and pieces from island children:

> Seagulls soaring high in the sky,
> Give me a thought of how gracefully they fly,
> The roaring ocean is great to be near,
> Waves pounding like a heart full of fear.
> Summer . . .
> Warmth of the sun
> Filling the land with glow,
> Lays across the water like jewels,
> Sparkle.
>
> —Anita

> Cold snow is gone
> It melted under the sun
> Summer's here again!
> —Pat

> The Spring day was warm
> Birds chirped and children sang
> For Spring is warming.
> —Lori

> Love is
> Living together
> Sharing
> Caring
> Praying
> And how we show it to each other
> Love is that.
> —Carol

Irma Marshall, a native of Tylerton, gathered a collection of her inspirational verses, and had them made into a small booklet to share with her friends. She dedicated her "Story Poem" to Smith Island ancestors, "who have been the backbone of the island church for decades past. A lot of this is taken from my childhood memories."

Excerpts from "The Old Timers and Their Religion":

> My thoughts often wander back

170

to the times of yesteryears,
When the elder members of our Church
    instilled in our hearts these fears:
That if we followed in the mean old Devil's ways,
    we'd better get on the right road quick,
To the mending of our ways.

They'd tell you in a hurry, too,
    just what they'd seen or heard,
As they didn't care a hoot back then,
    if your feelings they got hurt.
But in those days, you could
    take almost anybody's word.
To tell a lie to most folks,
    was really quite unheard.
The Mamas and Pas would punish their child,
    when they told a fib, or anything untrue.
Not so, like the parents of today,
    I mean, like me and you.
When my thoughts return back to the old time Chris-
        tians,
    Who down through the years have led our Church,
It makes me stop, pause, and wonder,
    even cause my poor heart to lurch.
If some of the old timers could come back,
    and see how things are run today,
I imagine they'd fall down on their knees,
    and just pray their time away.
I know how it was when I was a child,
    and an old timer was called on to speak,
They'd tell you such hair raising yarns,
    you'd be perched on the edge of your seat.
You could fairly picture what they were talking about.
    You could hear the amens,
And, why, some would even shout!

In her little book, Irma mentions some of the old-timers by
name; they were heroic captains who left a vivid impression on
island youngsters:

There was a man called Capt. James
    who could weave a tale so true,
Who could also make you feel ashamed,
    as if your inner thoughts he knew.
There was good old Capt. Charlie
    who could hold you spellbound, too,
By telling some of the good old
    Christian stories that he knew.
Another fine man was Capt. Oscar,
    To him, the Law was the living Gospel.

171

Smith Island, Chesapeake Bay

I've heard him go by preaching
    right aboard of his boat,
Or else lifting up his voice in song
    with such a rejoicing note.
There was my own Grandpa Ira, too,
    who was such a gentle and understanding man.
He always took the time to sing songs to his
    grandchildren,
    And tell them stories about that far off promised
    land.
Marvin was a man who also loved the Dear Master,
    He knew that life without Him could surely bring
    disaster.
Capt. Norman was a quiet sort of man,
    he knew that God was always near at hand.
Now, Asbury was a man of few words,
    but this one thing I know,
He had God's help from up above,
    towards making his gardens grow.

Irma closes her booklet with these thoughts, profound poetry from an islander who has lived simply and still follows the example of those who have gone before:

I just wanted to share with you
    some of my fondest memories,
But if you've lived longer than I have,
    You have greater ones than these.
I guess sometimes we wonder
    what this life is all about!
Or reasons things happen and why!
    We must all have had some doubts,
why we were born in the first place,
    When to everyone there has been
A time appointed to die.
    So the choice is really up to you
which place you choose to dwell,
    So just remember this, my friends,
It's how you live your life,
    Will determine how it ends!

This narrative poem, also by Irma Marshall, sums up the way an islander feels about his life:

A Waterman Talks With God

Lord, it's been quite a while since I've talked things over
    with you in a regular prayerful way,

172

Smith Island crabber, Harold Smith, in his low-sided scraping boat.
(Photograph by Marion E. Warren.)

Smith Island, Chesapeake Bay

But I'm thankful, Lord, and I'd hoped you'd know,
    We depend on your love each day.
Times we've stopped, my trusty old boat and me,
    On a high and wind-swept sea,
And I saw your glory in the sun rise,
    as you spoke through the skies to me!
"What have you been doing?" you asked me out plain,
    "Since I've made you to be a Waterman?"
I'm just fishing my pots, to make a living for my family,
    Lord, and trying to do the best that I can.
Some men like to crab-scrape or have crab traps,
    while some older men like to net.
There's not many crabs can wander astray,
    As long as these types of crabbing is done,
    day after day.
Now in early spring, when it's starting up time again,
    we put out a few crab pots at a time,
Our catch isn't too much until
    the temperature starts to climb.
There could be a storm, Lord,
    or gale warnings headed our way,
To scatter our pots
    all over the Sound and the Bay.
Lord, you know this job gets more expensive,
    each year without a doubt,
And to lose a lot of pots,
    could completely wipe us out.
But since I've asked you to be my partner, Lord,
    and to always be my guide,
You've never failed me yet, my Lord,
    I'll make it—with you by my side.
Now the winter time is colder, the going's getting rough,
    the temperature keeps falling fast,
I'm praying out loud, as onward I go, to find an oyster
    bed,
    and hope for a good catch.
The market price rises when there's a bite in the air,
    and a freeze-up looks sure to come true,
It seems to come after Christmas each year, Lord,
    so you know we'll be depending on you.
After January passes, things start to look up,
    there's no need for us to complain,
We get right back in the swing of oystering,
    the season will last until Spring.
The market prices go up and down, but somehow
    we all manage to survive,
We are our own boss, and have the freedom of choice,
    of not punching a time clock from nine until five.
Now teach us, dear Lord, to be fair to our fellow man,
    in our measure and in our count,

Bits and Pieces

Shaken down and running over,
    not so stringent with our amount.
For remember, God supplies our every need,
    But this doesn't account for our own personal
      greed.
We know on Him we have to rely,
    As he is our source, and our means of supply.
Well, it's been nice having this talk with you, Lord,
    I guess you're tired of hearing my complaints,
But it's nice to know you're always there,
    to listen to sinners or Saints.
And this is my prayer for us watermen, Lord,
    Watch over us all, I pray,
And head us at last to that home port in the sky,
    And see that not one goes astray.
But give us courage and strength, dear Lord,
    to be something like you have planned,
To walk in a plain, humble way, Lord,
    and to be your kind of Waterman!

This narrative sums up the waterman's work, his hopes and dreams, his appreciation and respect for nature, his fears, and his dependence upon God.

But, even the best of watermen grow old and eventually have to retire from active work on the water. Most retired watermen rest at home, surrounded by their families, while they wait for the time to come when they should "cross the bar" to that "home port in the sky." They gaze out their windows at the magnificent waters of the highway of the Chesapeake, and reminisce about their years on the Bay.

Occasionally, it is necessary for an islander to spend his waiting time in a mainland nursing home, where medical help is readily available. An island octogenarian told a visitor, "I may not be home, but my heart is." With a voice still strong and full of emotion, he recited a poem that he had written long ago and still remembered. He said:

I live on an island,
    My home is on the bay,
My heart is island drawn,
    Whenever I'm away.
I live with the wind and the water,
    and the mighty waves that roll,
For here is communion with nature,
    and here is the home of the soul.

175

X

Charting the Course

The north end of Hog Neck has washed at least one
hundred yards in my day, and is now cut through by
two small creeks.
—Charles Marsh, 1872

We are also concerned about the fact that if the island is
eroding at 7.5 feet a year, in not too many years that
bay is going to be breaking through right on Rhodes
Point.
—Jim Kohler, Chesapeake Bay Foundation, 1980

SEVERAL years ago, a flotilla of the Coast Guard Auxiliary
received an unusual request. They were asked to teach a
piloting course to a group of Smith Island watermen. The
watermen, whose knowledge of the water is well known, needed
help. In order for them to pass the tests required to
obtain their captain's papers, it was necessary for each of them
to be able to understand and answer the questions correctly.
These men knew the water intimately; they were as familiar
with the highway of the Chesapeake as city dwellers are with
expressways. But they lacked the education needed to
pass the tests. Those who had tried had found the questions
and answers on the written tests too technical and con-
fusing.

The flotilla was glad to oblige. They supplied teachers and
equipment for the classes, and the brawny, work-hardened,
thick-fingered watermen struggled, night after night, with
textbooks and slide rules. They worked with charts and com-
putations, watched safety films, and committed the rules of the

176

road to memory. Then they bombarded each other with questions and sample tests until they were able to decipher the samples and mark the appropriate answers.

Finally, the entire group journeyed to Baltimore, and returned bearing captain's papers and sporting gold-leaf insignia on their caps. Their certification enables them to operate vessels for hire, take out fishing parties, work on tugboats, or pilot tour boats. For the first time, these island men had felt a need they barely recognized, the need to begin preparation for an uncertain future.

This uncertainty has been brought about partly because of the changes the islanders have seen in recent years. They have managed to adapt to some of the changes by combining the old with the new. For instance, they adapt innovative devices for their own use, while discarding ideas and tools that seem too "new fangled." The same boat that sports a fish finder, radar, or a depth-sounder in its cabin still drags for oysters with rope and chain. A scraper with a brand new winding rig still hauls his peeler crabs along behind his boat in a rough wooden float. They suit themselves, finding their own level, waging their own war against too much progress too soon.

But the changes that have been made and the accompanying growing pains they've experienced are not the main problems for the islanders. They are facing their biggest battle, the real reason for their uncertainty, the relentless battle that is being waged against them by the Chesapeake Bay.

In no uncertain terms, they have been told that Smith Island's days are numbered. Erosion has taken its toll on all of the Bay islands; only two remain as living examples of island fishing village culture. One, of course, is Tangier in Virginia; the other is Smith. Both are facing imminent destruction. The inhabitants of the islands know that, within their children's lifetimes, both islands may be uninhabitable. They are facing a precarious future.

Smith Island is constantly exposed to the damaging forces of nature: high tides, wave action, tropical storms, and ice. The southwestern edge of the island is losing land at the rate of over seven feet per year.[1] In less than one hundred years, the entire island has lost twelve hundred acres. Also, the barrier island that protects the narrow spit of land that holds the homes of Rhodes Pointers has washed through in two places, and continues to erode by several feet annually. In turn, this erosion causes silting of the navigation channels and creates sandbars across the existing natural channels. This shoaling causes potentially dangerous navigational difficulties.

Rhodes Point is particularly susceptible. Most of the houses there are barely above sea level, and are close to the unprotected shoreline; several are frequently flooded. They are bombarded by devastating storms like the August storm of thirty-three, and Hurricane Hazel that caused water levels from two to eight feet above their first floors. At times, tidal waters make roads impassable and suck away at the road-beds.

According to a recent U. S. Army Corps of Engineers report, the Bay shoreline will continue to erode, and in less than twenty years, this loss of shoreline will allow waves to pass over or through the barrier islands more frequently.[2] As a result, the Rhodes Point shoreline will begin to recede rapidly, causing the ruin of homes, road, and sewer lines. Rhodes Point has a bleak future; it may be faced with complete destruction within fifty years.

The same report claims: "With the exception of Smith Island's sister island to the south, Tangier, there is no other area within the great expanse of the Chesapeake Bay where man and the environment interact so closely. The inhabitants of Smith Island literally fight the Bay for their existence. Annually, the Bay claims acres of their island as wetland and prized upland areas wash away."[3]

The village of Tylerton is eroding, too, a little more slowly than Rhodes Point, but just as surely. Tylerton is partially bulkheaded, but without additional bulkheading, it may take just a little longer, a matter of a few more years, for the people of Tylerton to see destruction of their property. Justifiably proud of their homes and their heritage, the people of Tylerton suffer much anxiety about the future.

North End, or Ewell, is the largest of the three island communities. It is the commercial center of the island and the terminal for the freight boats. It is the most prosperous of the villages; the medical center and parsonage are located here, as are the busiest stores, the fire hall, and the largest recreation center.

The Bay entrance channel to the basin at North End is plagued with continuous shoaling that causes a real problem for navigation. The silting increases steadily until it becomes difficult for a fully loaded boat or barge to make deliveries. In spite of periodic dredging by federal navigation projects, the shoaling is rapid.

The village of Ewell is not directly exposed to the Bay; it is on the Tangier Sound side of the island. Therefore, the rate of erosion is slower. Few homes are on the immediate shoreline; that space is taken up by the oil dock, crab houses, and packing plants. The houses here are in neat rows, two or three deep, along lanes that branch off from the main road. Most are far enough away from the water to prevent damage in the near future.

The road leading to Pitchcroft is a different story. Water often laps at the edge of the road; windows of the houses that line it are showered by wind-driven spray. It has been estimated that at least a three-hundred-foot section of this road will begin to wash away by 1990.[4]

Sections of the Ewell shoreline are bulkheaded, and north of this area is the island that is the location of the Martin Wildlife Refuge. Just outside are a few smaller barrier islands which were once a solid landmass. These small bits of land help provide protection for North End.

But these barriers are washing away at a rate similar to that of those outside Rhodes Point. The optimistic view is that Ewell will survive Rhodes Point and Tylerton by at least half a century, or maybe a little longer.

The length of survival time depends largely on the whims of nature. Since Hurricane Hazel, several smaller storms have bombarded the coast, but Smith Island has been fortunate to escape the devastation of a severe hurricane. The U. S. Army Corps of Engineers reports that:

> Erosion in the vicinity of Ewell is not occurring at a rate rapid enough to cause any damage to the community's structures. This fact greatly increases the margin of security afforded the residents in terms of physical, psychological, and economic well-being weighed against Tylerton and particularly Rhodes Point. Indeed, the one foot per year erosion rate, if continuous to the year 2030, would not result in any significant damages to structures. Given these overall but carefully docu-mented erosion factors, the socio-economic profile of Ewell will most likely remain in its present condition save the occurrence of a catastrophic storm that would affect the whole island.[5]

But the report also says that erosion along the shoreline of Ewell and adjacent landmasses is threatening the community and two anchorage basins with exposure to the forces of the Chesapeake Bay.[6]

Since the average elevation of land is two feet above mean sea level, the island is extremely vulnerable in the event of the direct force of a hurricane. Should the island be swept by a massive storm, the dwindling barrier islands would afford little protection against tidal surge and wind. To the islanders, it would be a disaster of major proportions.

In September of 1979, the village of Rhodes Point received only the edge of Hurricane David. When they knew the storm was coming, the people of Rhodes Point battened down to wait it out. From their windows that faced the Bay, they could see nothing but water as terrific winds racked their homes.[7] After the storm subsided, they used razor blades to scrape the salt from their windows, and recalled the violent storm of forty-four, when waves crashed over tiny Watts Island, a few miles to the south and east. That storm finished the destruction of the lighthouse on the island. Watts was almost completely under water, and today, no one lives on Watts Island.

Rhodes Pointers wonder about their own fate. The Railway, the harbor for boat repairs, is on the very tip of the point. How many years does it have? The village church is a remarkable little building. Its woodwork has a timeworn sheen; light filters through the stained glass windows and casts a soft glow over the pews and the rich molding that was handcrafted in a time long past. Will the church go the way of the Watts Island lighthouse?

The Senior Citizens' Center is housed in the old community hall that used to be the church. How much more buffeting can this historic building take? Miss Livy's old red store, a source of memories for all islanders, is slipping into the water. Attic sections of the oldest houses are beginning to tilt away from the wind, and sometimes the water crosses the road and laps at the doorsteps.

As early as 1973, members of the Christian Women's Society began writing to state and federal officials. They expressed concern about the erosion and asked for help to stop the flooding. Various congressmen, Corps of Engineers personnel, and the District Engineer visited the island to survey its problems and determine its needs, and a meeting was held with the Somerset County Commissioners. Then, at the initial public meeting with the Corps of Engineers, the islanders were given an opportunity to express their concerns and their desire for aid to protect their homes.[8]

Previously, the corps' involvement had been limited to navigational assistance, and maintenance of the twin jetties off Bayside, where the channel enters the deep water of the Bay. But in 1973, Congress had authorized the Corps of Engineers to conduct a study to determine the economic feasibility of providing necessary improvements, such as flood control, shoreline erosion control, and navigation improvements.[9] In 1977, the engineers began an intensive study that included a broad range of preventive or corrective measures. They considered the possibilities of constructing breakwaters, stone revetments, and bulkheads, along with groin fields and artificial beach nourishment, wetland habitat development, and, as a last resort, the relocation of the entire island population.

The economic, social, and environmental effects of each proposal were determined by taking into consideration the expense of each, the environmental impact, the protection of existing wetlands, and—to ensure the availability of resources for future use—the preservation of the natural environment.

The cost of each plan that met all requirements was then weighed against the economic benefits accrued by the project, including the prevention of loss of structures and businesses, the county road, and the sewer line. Since the beneficial effects of any plan must meet the requirements of economic benefit over cost before implementation of any Corps of Engineers project, most of the plans were pronounced to be "not economically justified."[10]

Plan after plan was assessed, evaluated, and rejected. When compared with the tremendous cost of preventing its loss, the historic significance of the preservation of this water-related culture was little in monetary terms.

Finally, two workable plans were presented and approved.[11] One, Plan C, was a navigation project only, the entire cost of which would be borne by the federal government. The other, Plan D, combined navigation improvements with an erosion control project for Rhodes Point only. Under this plan, a breakwater would be constructed, and an upland habitat created at the barrier island that lies west of the community.

181

The federal government would share the cost of Plan D with nonfederal interests.

However, no real help was available. This was confirmed by correspondence from the Somerset County Commissioners.[12] In a letter to Colonel Peck of the Corps of Engineers, the commissioners said, "The required financial contribution. . . is too costly. Therefore, Somerset County is unable to provide the required assurances for Plan D." The county supported Plan C, navigational improvements only.

The Corps of Engineers had no alternative other than to conclude that Plan C would better serve the public interest than "the remaining alternative, which is no action."[13]

Negotiations concerning the protection and preservation of Smith Island have come to an end. All reports are in; the decision has been made. Further argument is futile; no more can be done without financial support by nonfederal interests. Other than the continued maintenance of the existing navigation channels, no action will be taken.

Where does this leave the people of Smith Island? Elwood Marshall, a resident of Tylerton, collected littoral environment observation data for the authorities: measurements of wind, waves, and amount of transported sediment. At one of the meetings, Captain Elwood asked, "What figures do you use to measure the contribution of people to human life? The value of a place is what the people contribute."[14] The president of the local waterman's association, Jennings Evans, expressed his opinion that taking measures to save the island would be a valuable investment for the whole nation.

Jennings also posed the question, "Are we worth a million dollars?" Then he answered his own question by stating that federal investment would be more than justified by the island's contribution to the seafood industry, as well as by the preservation of an original life-style.

Preservation of their life-style is important to the watermen and their families. For over three centuries, the island has been the only home generations of islanders have known. Every inch of this bit of land is dear to the present islanders. Their parents' homes are now their homes; these are the same homes that belonged to their parents' parents.

The islanders know that they will be allowed to live in these homes a little while longer, and that they will be able to work out of home port for a few more years. It is possible that their

The *Miss Whitelock*, one of the first Smith Island packet boats that provided passenger service, mail delivery, and the freighting of necessities to the island. (Photograph by Marion E. Warren.)

sons will be able to take their boats out through the channel to oyster bed or crabbing ground.

But as the team of engineers predicted, "As erosion continues, an increase in the number of youths who turn to the mainland for economic opportunity can be expected . . . "[15] And, as it did in the last century, when the islanders moved their houses, "Distribution of the residents will follow the patterns of land changes caused by wind and water."

Within a few short years, the islanders must make a choice: to leave their homes, or to stand by and watch helplessly, as their homeland deteriorates before their eyes.

A retired sea captain once lived at Rhodes Point in a tall, weather-beaten house. His wife is buried close by in the churchyard. As he sat on his back stoop, with his cats rubbing against his legs, Captain Winfred put his feelings into words: "We don't want to move to the mainland. My father lived here and followed the water. So did his father, and his father, and his. Nope, if we'd awanted to go, we'd abeen there long ago."

The engineers made it clearly understood that if Smith Island is to be saved for future generations, a way must be found to make the project economically feasible for federal or nonfederal interests. So, the islanders speculate on the prospects for the future.

Some fear that the government has plans for the island. There have been rumors concerning the establishment of an island naval base or refueling station. Other rumors concern the possible construction of a nuclear power plant. Although there seems to be no basis for these rumors, there is a real anxiety among island people over the eventuality of a complete government takeover of their homes.

There are nearly sixty thousand acres of wetlands in Somerset County.[16] Nearly half of that acreage belongs to the state or federal government, including a large section of Smith Island, the Glenn L. Martin National Wildlife Refuge. Over four thousand acres of marshland and estuary are maintained by the government at the refuge. Part of this land, which was formerly used as a hunting club, was donated by Martin; the rest was acquired by the Migratory Bird Conservation Commission.

At one of the public meetings, it was pointed out that "the island is the only possibility for a national wilderness area in Maryland."[17] A delegate who supported the islanders' fight against federal regulation, opposed this idea, and a retired waterman voiced the opinion of many of his neighbors. He said, "We have been on Smith Island for three hundred years, and now the federal government comes in and wraps its arms around everything and takes it away from us."[18]

In his simple way, the old waterman was putting the islanders' fears into words. It is natural for them to feel that, since the government controls the refuge, sets up regulations that they must observe, and even owns property on other parts of the island, they must dread the encroaching government, as well as the erosion. As the marsh spreads to cover low-lying areas, trespassing on yards and gardens, there is conjecture concerning the possibility of the entire island becoming a part of the refuge.

However, this is a possibility that could hold some hope for the future. For instance, if the refuge were to be expanded to include more of the outlying areas of marshland, leaving only the three villages on the higher ridges, perhaps the worth of Smith Island would be increased, and the engineers' proposals would be more economically feasible. Measures could then be taken to prevent further erosion, preserve the wetlands, and in the process, give the islanders the hope of clinging to their heritage.

This would be one possible answer to the existing problem, a problem that is easily explained. Property values on the island are low; the amount of taxes paid is comparatively small; there is no industry other than the seafood industry. There is nothing here to merit the expenditure of the amount of money necessary to save the island.

The solution to the problem is complex. If island resources could be developed enough to benefit the public, if its historic significance were to be recognized, if an industry could be established that would boost island economy, then it would be worth saving. Several suggestions come to mind; each is a possible answer to the problem.

One such possibility is that of making the island a state recreation area. State authorities must feel that there is some kind of future in this direction, for in 1981, a proposal was made in the interests of yachtsmen for a marina for pleasure boats in the vicinity of Pitchcroft.[19] A wetlands hearing was held, and since no wetlands opposition was presented, the state gave the go-ahead and agreed to pay all costs for a large basin and two long piers with finger piers running up both sides.

185

Smith Island, Chesapeake Bay

A pier in this location would relieve the congestion at the workboat basin during the summer months, when visiting yachts need a place to tie up, but the practicality of the project is questionable. Although it is somewhat protected by the barrier islands, the selected site is subject to silting. As the barriers continue to erode, the basin would be threatened even more. In the meantime, constant care would be required to maintain sufficient depth for safe docking.

At a public meeting, island watermen claimed that unless further measures to control erosion were taken, funding for this project would eventually be wasted. And if, as the Corps of Engineers' report says, sections of the road leading to the basin are washed away, or even badly damaged within a few years, the purpose of the project would be defeated.

Some citizens protested the pier proposal by circulating a petition. They voiced their anxiety over the possible influx of strangers, their dread of exposing their lives to the public, and the fear of increased crime and the possible need for policing. The project was shelved.

Three other possibilities exist for the future of Smith Island. Each would require financial investment by the islanders or by outside interests. Each would provide the means of increasing economic value, thereby opening the way to a new feasibility study.

Among these possibilities are the establishment of an island-based marine biological laboratory and research center, designation of the entire area as a historic district, and the development of tourism as an island industry.

The first possibility is an interesting one. The island is a natural arena for observation and study; it is composed primarily of salt marsh, with tidal creeks and shallow water areas, a highly productive habitat for a wide variety of fish and wildlife. Diamondback terrapin lay eggs along the shoreline; muskrat, mink, otter, and red foxes inhabit the area. By harboring submerged beds of aquatic vegetation, the surrounding waters serve as spawning, nursery, and feeding ground for marine life.

A number of independent groups, as well as state and federal agencies, are already involved in data collection—water quality analysis, commercial catch studies, and educational programs. Smith Island offers an invaluable location for such research; this locale could well provide the proper setting for the study of shellfish and commercial fin fish.

186

Charting the Course

In his book, *Understanding the Chesapeake*, Arthur W. Sherwood quotes the director of the Natural Resources Institute of the University of Maryland: "The Chesapeake Bay is the crown jewel of the 850 estuaries and bays along the several coasts of the United States. It is the largest bay in the country, more valuable for human uses than any other estuary, and vulnerable to destruction from human use and abuse."[20] What better location could be found for a center engaged in the study of the estuarine system, than an island surrounded by this valuable mixture of salt and fresh water?

In 1978, the Chesapeake Bay Foundation established a center at Tylerton. This foundation is a nonprofit organization working to involve citizens in the management of the natural resources of the Bay. By emphasizing education through estuarine fieldwork and publications, the foundation performs a very real service to the public. It contributes greatly to those interested in conservation and pollution control. It is one example of the type of program that could be conducted from Smith Island.

As the U. S. Army Corps of Engineers Plan of Study stated, "The cyclic patterns of tide and weather will certainly continue making it uncertain as to whether or not Smith Island can survive as a land mass and consequently as a habitat for terrestrial creatures."[21] With the establishment of an island research center, it is possible that the survival of this habitat could be ensured. If so, the islanders could remain in their communities while performing valuable services in connection with a new source of employment.

Another possibility yet to be fully explored is the designation of Smith Island as a national historic district. According to the Maryland Historical Trust, a historic district is described as a geographically definable area possessing a significant concentration, linkage, or continuity of sites, buildings, structures, or objects united by past events, or aesthetically by plan or physical development. A district may also comprise individual elements separated geographically but linked by association or history.[22]

Smith Island certainly meets the criteria. It is a classic example of a historic area worth preserving. It is a geographically definable area that possesses the continuity of a life-style that has existed for over three centuries. There is certainly a significant concentration of people whose life-style and culture

187

reach back into the history of early America. They are linked with national history through their involvement in the early wars, the beginning of the seafood industry, and the struggle over state boundary lines.

There is also a continuity of buildings, sites, and individuals united by past events, and some island structures have historical significance. Although the house at Pitchcroft, which was the oldest structure on the island, no longer exists, other homes are more than a century old. Many have been remodeled, but their basic structures have not been altered. One home at Rhodes Point still has visible signs of its "colonett," the structure that was built to connect the kitchen to the main house.

Other homes are from the Victorian period, and one of the old camp meeting houses is still standing. None of the structures are on the register of historic sites, but the island has never been surveyed by representatives of the Maryland Historic Trust.[23]

There is also historic significance attached to the archaeological sites found on the island. In response to the Corps of Engineers' request for information, the Maryland Geological Survey wrote that, since only one systematic survey had been made, archaeological investigations at Smith Island were limited, but that there is still a potential for undiscovered archeological remains.[24] Artifacts found on the island date from early archaic to the woodland period, indicating a prehistoric occupational sequence of at least 8,000 years. Both the Geological Survey and the Historic Trust recommended that surveys be made to inventory cultural and archeological resources.[25]

Other factors have historic significance. Rhodes Point was once the pirate village, Rogue's Point; Kedges Straits was the site of the Battle of the Barges. Joshua Thomas was an important figure in the history of Methodism; he lived for a time on the island and married an island girl. All of these factors add up to a considerable concentration of history in one small geographical area.

One of the most important elements that should be considered in a project of this kind is that Smith Island is different. It is "a unique island habitat supporting the water-oriented lifestyles of its 600 plus inhabitants."[26] It is different from rural communities on the mainland, vastly different from urban areas, and certainly different from other fishing communities on the Eastern Shore. As Williamsburg is an example of colonial history, Smith Island is an example of early American fishing village culture.

The advantages of designation as a historical area would be numerous. Island people already have a special pride in their heritage. With the knowledge of their importance to national history, there would be a renewed interest in the preservation of existing structures and the restoration of those falling to ruin. Through association with people interested in this preservation, the islanders would be able to retain their life-style while achieving a balance with the outside world. Those who come to see and enjoy this watery dominion would be able to view, firsthand, a working example of an early culture.

There would also be a strong likelihood of private, social, or business organizations becoming interested enough in preservation to invest in erosion control measures. Even minimal efforts such as the installation of floodwalls, stone bulkheads, or pilings placed in strategic locations, would retard the rate of erosion and save Smith Island for a little while longer.

The third alternative, and perhaps the most advantageous proposition, is the promotion of tourism as an island industry. Because people are enchanted by the unusual, the charm of the neat little island villages, the isolation, and the rugged scenery seem to hold a fascination for visitors. The windswept marsh, the vast expanse of water, the intriguing tangle of guts and thoroughfares, all provide a sense of adventure to travelers who desire to see something different from their own surroundings.

In their study plan, the Corps of Engineers report that there is a recreational potential for tourist facilities. They said that given the nature of an island fishing community, it can be expected that tourists will continue to visit Smith Island to sample the island's natural and social environment.

So far, there has been no concerted effort to fully utilize this potential, but the natural surroundings could be enhanced by comprehensive planning. Native ability could be put to use for the enrichment of island life. For instance, island women are well known as expert cooks; they also do beautiful handwork. Island men have mastered the arts of decoy carving, handcrafting models of boats, and sketching and painting nautical scenes. Utilizing these talents would attract tourists and add another source of income to the island economy.

There are many ways of promoting tourism while increasing island economy. Overnight accommodations in the form of

189

country-style inns or vacation cottages operated by local people would provide income. Development of local enterprises, such as supply centers, grocery stores, souvenir shops, and other conveniences to attract and serve vacationers would give islanders an opportunity to increase family income and a sense of participation in a project of community interest.

If the islanders could come to understand that such a project would benefit them, an island council could be formed to help control development and growth. Tourism, if kept within the bounds of simplicity, would increase the island's value, and as its worth increased, erosion control would become more economically feasible, and Smith Island could be saved.

One of the alternatives presented by the Corps of Engineers was permanent evacuation of the island people as a means of preventing flood damage and eliminating potential loss of life. This tentative plan was, of course, rejected by the islanders. In the evaluation of measures considered, relocation or evacuation and flood warning was charted as being highly beneficial in respect to local economy, population distribution, life-style, and protection of life. However, this plan was dropped from consideration.

Perhaps life would be easier for the watermen and their families if they sold their property and moved away, as some have already done. They would be absorbed into the life of the mainland, as those who have already left have been absorbed. After all, they could follow the water from any bayside community. But no other place would be a part of their heritage; they do not want to leave the home of their ancestors. Most of those remaining will stay and fight disaster until they are forced to leave by the Bay itself.

> Any island and its inhabitants are at the mercy of water and its controlling elements such as climate, weather, tides, and topography. Being surrounded by water makes it necessary for an island people to compensate for changes in the local land structure caused by the ever changing conditions of the wind and water. Island life is often precarious and threatening to life and property; other times, life can be tranquil with the water barrier serving as a buffer from noise, pollution, and other costs of high density urban life. The island must compensate for the demands that storms, tides, and the unceasing process of erosion make on the land. All too

often, the physical, psychological, and social well-being of inhabitants (human, animal, and plant) suffer losses. Land is flooded and eroded, wildlife habitat is lost, structures destroyed or demolished, and boats sunk . . . Often life is lost and effects are long lasting . . . Without some form of assistance to counteract the forces of nature, the future for the existence of Smith Island is questionable. The cyclic patterns of tides and weather will certainly continue making it uncertain as to whether or not Smith Island can survive as a land mass and consequently as a habitat for terrestrial creatures.[27]

This statement by the U. S. Army Corps of Engineers puts into print the facts that islanders have known and feared for a long time. They feel helpless against the eventual loss of their homes, and are beginning to make provisions for the changes that are sure to take place. They are concerned for the future generations of island children, and fear that there may be nothing left to pass on to them.

Today there is no economically feasible plan for erosion control on Smith Island, but periodically, there are mud-diggers working in the channels that lead to island harbors. The heavy auger bit tears up the bottom, and throws it aside to deepen the channels. Meanwhile, the tide sucks away at the roadbeds, and the marsh creeps farther inland.

The islanders continue to make their living on the water, and come home from work to enjoy their homes and families, to tell tall tales on the store benches, and remember how it used to be. They go on with their lives as they always have.

Smith Island was created by the natural action of the Chesapeake. Perhaps it is fitting that the Bay island species of man disappear along with his natural habitat, to succumb to the voracious appetite of the Mother of Waters. But it is also fitting that these people, who are island born and island bred, believe that through their faith, a way will come to save their homes.

But if a way does not come, they will accept it as the will of God, as they have accepted calamities throughout the centuries. As Bay captains, as mainland-based watermen, or as shipyard workers—wherever they may go—they will carry their heritage with them, and a part of Smith Island will live forever.

191

Notes

I. An Introduction to an Island

1. William H. Rodgers, "A Wet and Windy Kingdom," *Maryland Magazine* 11 (Spring 1979): 3–7.
2. Woodrow T. Wilson, *Crisfield, Maryland, 1676–1976* (Baltimore: Gateway Press, Inc., 1977), 25–28.
3. Johanna Wilson, "The Death of Holland's Island," in Woodrow T. Wilson, *Crisfield, Maryland, 1676–1976*, 7–9.
4. J. Thomas Scharf, *History of Maryland, 1600–1765*, vol. II (Baltimore Press of John B. Piet; New Edition, Hatboro, Pa.: Tradition Press, 1967), 2.
5. Alice Venable Middleton, interview with author, Ewell, Md.
6. Alice Venable Middleton, interview with author, Ewell, Md.
7. Winfred Evans, interview with author, Rhodes Point, Md.
8. Rodgers, 3.
9. Lynette Hoffman, interview with author, Rhodes Point, Md.
10. Alice Venable Middleton, interview with author, Ewell, Md.; Olivia Tyler, interview with author, Rhodes Point, Md.; Caleb Jones, interview with author, Ewell, Md.
11. Betty Tyler, interview with author, Ewell, Md.

Note: A complete list of Smith Island residents who were interviewed in preparation for this book may be found at the end of the Bibliography.

II. From the Beginning

1. Lyon Gardiner Tyler, ed., *Narratives of Early Virginia, 1606–1625* (New York: Barnes and Noble, Inc., 1946; reprint, 1959), 82.
2. Geological information is taken from a study of "Environmental Dynamics" in *Prehistoric Peoples of Maryland's Coastal Plain*, Maryland Department of Natural Resources, Tidewater Administration, Coastal Resources Division, 1979.
3. Information about the Indians who occupied this area is taken from a study of "Cultural Dynamics" in *Prehistoric Peoples*, and Wm. A. Gardner, Robert D. Wall, and others, *A Cultural Resources Reconnaissance of a Portion of Smith Island, Somerset County, Maryland* (Front Royal, Va: Thunderbird Research Corp., April 1978; rev. May 1979).

Notes

4. *Prehistoric Peoples,* 3.

5. Gardner, 17.

6. Hulburt Footner, *Rivers of the Eastern Shore* (New York: Farrar and Rinehart, 1944; reissued by Tidewater Publishers), 13, 14.

7. Tyler, 143.

8. *Report and Journal of Proceedings of the Joint Commission to Adjust the Boundary of the States of Maryland and Virginia, 1872* (hereinafter referred to as *Report and Journal*). (A partially decomposed and rat-eaten copy of this booklet was found by Howard and Louise Atkins of Salisbury, Maryland. They allowed me to make a copy for my files. The inside title page of the booklet was missing; no publication data are available.) Transcript and translation of grant to Lord Baltimore is on pages 220, 221.

Mr. and Mrs. Atkins are the authors of *To Speak of Many Things,* a series of regional booklets filled with genealogical data.

9. *Report and Journal,* 68, 69. See also Footner, 24–39.

10. *Report and Journal,* 70–72, 78, 79.

11. *Report and Journal,* 71, 72, 325; John L. Bozman, *The History of Maryland: Its First Settlement in 1633 to the Restoration in 1669,* 2 vols., a reproduction of an 1837 set (Spartanburg, S.C.: Reprint Company, 1968), 2:586; "Opinion and Award on the Maryland and Virginia Boundary Line, Washington, 1877" (hereinafter referred to as Black and Jenkins Award), Md XF 177.821364, Enoch Pratt Free Library, Baltimore, 19.

12. *Archives of Maryland* (hereinafter referred to as *Md. Arch.*) 1:332, 2:327, 3:435, 436; *Report and Journal,* 76–78.

13. Hennings Statutes at Large (An Act Against Quakers), Ninth Act of the General Assembly of Virginia, 1662, 1:532, 533; *Report and Journal,* 260-62. *See also:* Charles B. Clark, *The Eastern Shore of Maryland and Virginia,* 2 vols. (New York: Lewis Historical Publishing Co., Inc., 1950), 2:683–97, 1000, 1001.

14. *Report and Journal,* 83 (Formation of commission for granting lands). Note: Conflict over location of Watkins Point and the Calvert-Scarborough Line are discussed in chapter 6.

15. Woodrow T. Wilson, 25.

16. *Report and Journal,* 218–20 (Memoranda of colonial and commonwealth grants).

17. *Md. Arch.,* Patent Liber 7, f 262 (1664); Patent Liber 8, ff 435, 436. Note: On old records there are several spellings of Cager—Cadger, Cager, Kedger, Cajer; on patent, the spelling is Cadger.

18. *Md. Arch.* 1:293, Test. Proc. 2:189, 190 (Will of Robert Cager [father]); *Md. Arch.* 2:530, 531, Liber W H L, 109, 110 (Robert Cager [son]).

19. *Report and Journal,* 315, 316 (Discussion of Russell Isles grants, including the patent for 3,804 acres).

20. *Md. Arch.* 5:43–45; *Report and Journal,* 96–99, 261, 269–73.

21. Somerset County Land Records, Princess Anne, Md., Liber L, #1, 113, 114, 115.

22. *Md. Arch.* 67:173, 174, Feb. 22, 1677/8.

23. Somerset County Land Records, Princess Anne, Md., Liber L, #1, 113, 114, 115.

24. Hennings Statutes at Large, Eastville, Va., 13:242; 15:439; 17:194; 19:338; 23:193.

25. The following island lore is taken from personal interviews with island residents: Alice Venable Middleton, Olivia Tyler, Lucy and Bain Bradshaw, Lula Bradshaw, Lynette Hoffman, Caleb Jones, and Laban Evans.

26. Ullie Marshall, interview with author, Tylerton, Md.

27. "Last Maryland Frontier," *Evening Sun*, Hanover, Pa., April 25, 1967, Author unknown. Note: For further reading about the religious freedom offered to settlers on the Eastern Shore, *see*: Doris F. White, "Religious Freedom is a Proud Local Heritage," in *Lower Eastern Shore Patriot*, Bicentennial Edition; Anna Brotemarkle and others, eds., Consultant, John E. Jacob, Jr., (Salisbury, Md.: Peninsula Press, The Bicentennial Committee of Somerset, Wicomico, and Worcester, 1976). *See also*: Frank Gouldsmith, *Indians of the Eastern Shore of Maryland* (Sykesville, Md.: Springfield State Hospital Press, 1922).

III. The Islanders Meet the Enemy

1. Old Accomack Co. Records, Eastville, Va., 19:202.

2. Arthur Pierce Middleton, *Tobacco Coast, A Maritime History of Chesapeake Bay in the Colonial Era* (The Mariners Museum, Newport News, Va.; reprint, Baltimore: Johns Hopkins University Press, 1984), 327. *See also*: Elmer Green, *The Making of Maryland* (Baltimore: E. and M. Green, 1934) and Donald G. Shomette, *Pirates on the Chesapeake* (Centreville, Md.: Tidewater Publishing, 1985).

3. For affidavits, accounts, and further information, *see*: Md. Arch., 17:32, 50, 51, 116, 189, 332, 333, 349–51, 372, 374; and An Act for the Punishment of Privateers and Pyrates, 17:568.

4. Winfred Evans, interview with author, Rhodes Point, Md.

5. For an interesting discussion of Delmarva's role in the events leading to the Revolution, *see*: Charles J. Truitt, *Breadbasket of the Revolution* (Salisbury, Md.: Historical Books, Inc., 1975), 14–18.

6. *Md. Arch.* 16:422, 440, 442.

7. *See:* Truitt, 30–33.

8. *Md. Arch.* 12:144, 166; 16:27, 123, 124; 21:333; 45:440, 446

9. For numerous references to depredations committed by the British, requisitions of supplies by Patriot forces, and accounts of picaroon activity, *see: Md. Arch.*, 11:46; 16:27, 31, 41, 105, 110, 122–25, 128, 129, 132, 440, 539; 25:19; 45:440; 47:140. *See also:* Clark, vol. I, and Truitt, chapters 6 and 22.

10. *Md. Arch.* 16:157, 159, 386; Truitt, 63, 64.

11. *Md. Arch.* 16:157.

12. *Md. Arch.* 12:154, 156.

13. *Md. Arch.* 12:152–156 (Deposition of Mariman & Yell).

14. *Md. Arch.* 12:160, 270.

15. *Md. Arch.* 12:408.

16. *Md. Arch.* 12:156. Note: Other Whayland references found in 12:152; 21:333; 45:201; 48:288–89, 334, 419.

17. *Md. Arch.* 16:141, 390; 2:194, 195; 45:390.

Notes

18. *Md. Arch.* 16:422, 440; 45:439–41.

19. *Md. Arch.* 2:194, 195, 196; 16:132, 141, 422; 45:390, 413; 48:227, 228.

20. *Md. Arch.* 47:163 (Joseph Dashiell to Governor Lee, March 4, 1781).

21. *Md. Arch.* 45:413; 47:164; 48:129–32.

22. *Md. Arch.* 45:603; 48:131

23. *Md. Arch.* 45:413, 439, 440, 441, 483; 48:97, 100, 148, 344.

24. Part of Commissioner Grayson's story is told in Adam Wallace, *The Parson of the Islands* (Philadelphia: Methodist Home Journal, 1861; reprint, Cambridge, Md.: Tidewater Publishers, 1961), 179.

25. *Md. Arch.* 47:148; Truitt, 179.

26. *Md. Arch.* 47:140.

27. *Md. Arch.* 45:500; 16:124; 47:263, 388, 392 (Continued picaroon activity).

28. *Md. Arch.* 17:608; 47:140; 48:218; John H. Jeffries, *Maryland Naval Barges in the Revolutionary War*, A monograph researched by John L. Bond (Princess Anne, Md., 1978), 15

29. *Md. Arch.* 47:140; 48:608; Jeffries, 11, 17.

30. *Md. Arch.* 45:476; 48:218, 225–30, 265, 266.

31. *Md. Arch.* 48:267–69.

32. These accounts include: Log account of Captain Frazier, November 27, 1782–December 3, 1782; Account of Captain Speddin, not dated; Colonel George Dashiell to Governor Paca, December 5, 1782; Captain Robert Dashiell to Governor Paca, December 5, 1782; Colonel Henry Dennis to Governor Paca, December 5, 1782; Lieutenant Cropper to Governor Paca, December 6, 1782; Captain Levin Handy to Governor Paca, December 13, 1782; John Cropper to William Davis and Major J. Poulson, December 6, 1782; Colonel Robert Done to Governor Paca, December 7, 1782. (Copies of these communications are in the possession of the author). *See also: Md. Arch.,* 48:313, Liber #78, 394; 48:148, 325, 336, 356; Virginia Calendar of State Papers, Eastville, Va., 39; and Barton Heyall Wise, *Memoirs of John Cropper* (Richmond, Va.: Historical Society, 1951).

33. This quote and following account are taken from: Levin Handy to Governor Paca, and Colonel R. Done to Governor Paca.

34. Account of George Dashiell.

35. Colonel George Dashiell to Governor Paca; Captain Robert Dashiell to Governor Paca.

36. Smith Island legend; Wallace, 179-84. Note: This legend is told by Smith Islanders (interview of Alice Venable Middleton) and by Adam Wallace, as told him by Solomon Evans in 1850. According to Wallace, Mr. Evans combines his story of the battle with his story concerning "Grissom" (Grayson), who was killed in another skirmish. Grayson had orders to proceed to the mouth of the Potomac (*Md. Arch.* 47:344) and was killed in the ensuing battle (*Md. Arch.* 47:148). Truitt (p. 179) says that Grayson was killed while approaching Tangier Island, which is south of Smith Island. The Battle of the Barges took place in Kedges Straits, north of the island. Mr. Evans, who

Smith Island, Chesapeake Bay

was nearly 100 years old when he talked to Wallace, said that "the engagement began just opposite my door." He and his brother, Richard, buried twenty-two men. This number coincides with the number of men killed in the battle, other than the officers, who were taken to Virginia.

37. Colonel Henry Dennis to Governor Paca; John Cropper to Governor Paca; Robert Done to Governor Paca; Levin Handy to Governor Paca.

38. *Md. Arch.* 48:323, 328, 329 (Liber C. B. #24, 370).

39. *Md. Arch.* 48:327–29, 332, 392.

40. *Md. Arch.* 48:322, 328, 336, 364-67, 388, 401, 419.

41. Henry Dennis to Governor Paca, December 5, 1782.

42. *Md. Arch.* 48:322, 328, 332, 333, 366, 391, 397.

43. *Md. Arch.* 48:364, 376, 384, 387, 401, 402, 418.

44. *Md. Arch.* 48:361; Red Book #28, Letter 64.

45. *Md. Arch.* 48:160, 161.

46. Mortality Schedule, Accomack County, Va. (Courtesy of Jean Mihalyka, Cherry-Core, Cheritan, Va.) *See also:* John E. Jacob, Jr., "Battle of the Barges," in *Lower Eastern Shore Patriot*, Anna Brotemarkle et al., eds.

47. Alice Venable Middleton, *Maryland's Right, Tight Isle, Smith* (Ewell, Md.: Private printing, A.V.M., 1967), 4.

IV. The Enemy Tests a New Faith

1. W. P. Taylor, *A Brief History of Smith's Island, Maryland* (Wilmington, Del., Hubert A. R.————, Printer, 1910), 1.

2. Alice Venable Middleton, interview with author, Ewell, Md.

3. E. Frank Dize, *Something Fishy From Tangier: An Island History* (Private printing, E.F.D., 1974; 6th edition, 1975), 12, 13.

4. Wallace, 47–57.

5. Wallace, 61.

6. Wallace, 63.

7. Wallace, 67–71; Clark, 691.

8. Wallace, 330, 331; Footner, 105

9. Wallace, 175–83; Taylor, 5, 7.

10. Wallace, 99, 100; Taylor, 2.

11. David S. Muzzy and Arthur S. Link, *Our Country's History* (Boston: Ginn and Co., 1968), 178; John Dos Passos, *The Shackles of Power* (Garden City, N. Y.: Doubleday, 1966), 119, 120.

12. Muzzy, 186.

13. Carl Bode, *Maryland, A Bicentennial History* (New York and London: W. W. Norton, 1978), 53; Walter Lord, *The Dawn's Early Light* (New York: W. W. Norton, 1972), 19, 20.

14. For examples of looting, plundering, boat burning, and general harassment, *see: Niles Weekly Register* 1812–1814 (hereinafter referred to as *NWR*), 5:179, 187, 206; 6:150; Bode, 55; Lord, 46, 51, 52, 53.

15. Lord, 43, 44.

16. *NWR* 5:79, 187.

Notes

17. *NWR* 5:206; 6:150.
18. Wallace, 128.
19. Wallace, 131; *NWR* 4:344; Lord, 346. Description of fort also in Clark, 602.
20. Lord, 52
21. *NWR* 4:244, 344.
22. *NWR* 6:150.
23. *NWR* 4:245, 356, 374, 375; William M. Marine, *British Invasion of Maryland, 1812–1815,* edited by Louis H. Dielman, reprint of 1913 edition (Baltimore: Genealogical Publishing Co., 1977), 59ff.
24. Alice Venable Middleton, interview with author, Ewell, Md.
25. For account of Washington campaign, *see* Lord, chapters 3 and 8.
26. *NWR* 5:77, 79, 187, 206; 6:150.
27. Wallace, 144–48; Clark, 605.
28. Wallace, 151; Clark, 603.

V. On the Border of Rebellion

1. John R. Wennersten, "The Almighty Oyster; A Saga of Old Somerset and the Eastern Shore, 1850–1920," *Maryland Historical Magazine* 74 (March 1979): 80–93.
2. This tradition verified by the Joint Comission of 1872; Depositions of Witnesses: Testimony of John Marshall, 158, 159; John Evans, 194; personal interview with Addie Florence Dize, direct descendant of John Evans. *See also:* Brian Schuel, *The National Trust Guide to Traditional Customs of Great Britain* (Exeter, England: Webb and Bower, 1985).
3. *Report and Journal:* Multiple references to registration and voting practices are given by Smith Island witnesses on pp. 164–94.
4. *Report and Journal,* Depositions of Witnesses: Testimony of John Marshall, 161; Testimony of Henry Dies, 198.
5. *Report and Journal,* Depositions of Witnesses: Testimony of Severn Bradshaw, 173; Testimony of John Cullen, 150, 151; Black and Jenkins Award, 13, 14.
6. Lincoln Proclamation, April 15 and 19, 1861.
7. For more information concerning steamboat service on Chesapeake Bay, *see:* Alexander Crosby Brown, *Steam Packets on the Chesapeake* (Cambridge, Md: Tidewater Publishers, 1961); Robert H. Burgess and H. Graham Wood, *Steamboats Out of Baltimore* (Cambridge, Md.: Tidewater Publishers, 1968); Clark, 583–89; and Woodrow T. Wilson, 42–45.
8. *Official Records of the Union and Confederate Navies in the War of the Rebellion* (hereinafter referred to as *Official Records,* available at Civil War Room, Salisbury State Teachers College, Salisbury, Md.), Series I, 5:619; Virgil Carrington Jones, *The Civil War at Sea,* 3 vols. (New York: Holt, Rinehart, & Winston, Inc., 1962) 1:105.
9. *Official Records,* Series I, 5:619; Jones, 1:105.
10. In the *Official Records,* Series I, there are multiple references to smuggling activity in the vicinity of the Tangiers; *see* 5: 27, 47, 101,

197

204, 208, 226, 477, 618, 738, 743; *see also*: Clark, 2:605.

11. *Official Records*, Series I, 5:743.

12. *Official Records*, Series I, 5:743; *NWR* 5–47 (Flag Officer G. S. Pendergrast to Lieutenant Braine, June 23, 1861).

13. *Official Records*, Series I, 5:738, 739.

14. *Official Records*, Series I, 5:743.

15. *Official Records*, Series I, 5:767.

16. Edwin W. Beitzel, *Life on the Potomac* (Private printing, Abel, Md.: E. W. Beitzel), 188.

17. *Official Records*, Series I, 5:769; *see also:* 5:27, 58, 101, 151, 204, 226, 399.

18. *Official Records*, Series I, 6:73, 74.

19. *Official Records*, Series I, 6:73 (Lieutenant Crosby's report).

20. *Official Records*, Series I, 5:58, 101.

21. *Official Records*, Series I, 5:204, 226, 399, 401.

22. *Official Records*, Series I, 4:208.

23. *Official Records*, Series I, 5:400, 401; 9:529; Jones, 3:139, 140.

24. Jones, 3:106; 1:44.

25. *Official Records*, Series I, 5:510 (Thomas Nelson to Lieutenant Commander Edward Hooker, Feb. 25, 1865).

26. *Official Records*, Series I, 9:310, 311.

27. *Official Records*, Series I, 5:220, 226.

28. Jones, 1:135–42.

29. Jones, 3:89–95.

30. *Official Records*, Series I, 9:203: Jones, 3:89–95.

31. *Official Records*, Series I, 9:318.

32. *Official Records*, Series I, 9:304, 305, 311, 318.

33. Jones, 3:368, 369.

34. Note: For an interesting and accurate account of conditions at Camp Hoffman, *see*: Edwin Beitzell, *Escape from Point Lookout* (Private printing, Abel, Md.: E. W Beitzell).

35. *Official Records*, Series I, 5:63, 313–17, 331, 346.

36. *Official Records*, Series I, 5:359; 10:281.

37. Caleb Jones, interview with author, Ewell, Md., 1978.

38. *Official Records*, Series I, 10:281, 288, 289, 346.

39. *Official Records*, Series I, 10:721.

40. *Official Records*, Series I, 10:721, 722.

41. Caleb Jones, interview with author, Ewell, Md.

42. National Archives, 1864: Special order #12 and General order #49, Provost Marshall's Office, U. S. Forces on the Eastern Shore.

43. *Official Records*, Series I, 5:476, 477.

44. *Official Records*, Series I, 5:477.

45. *Official Records*, Series I, 5:489.

46. *Official Records*, Series I, 5:510.

47. *Official Records*, Series I, 5:510.

48. *Official Records*, Series I, 5:514, 519, 520.

49. *Official Records*, Series I, 5:516.

50. *Official Records*, Series I, 5:519.

51. *Official Records*, Series I, 5:555.

52. *Official Records*, Series I, 12:123; *see also* 11:109.

53. *Official Records*, Series I, 12:124.
54. *Official Records*, Series I, 5:556.

VI. The Dividing Line

1. *Journal of the House of Delegates*, 1874-75 (Richmond, Va.: Superintendant of Public Printing, 1875), 10–12.
2. April Fehr, "An Exploration of Settlement Patterns and Agriculture, Smith Island, Maryland: 1860–1900," Diss., Catholic University of America, 1979, 6.
3. Wennersten, 80–93. Note: Joseph Conlin, in "Consider the Oyster," *American Heritage* (February/March 1980), says that at least fifty were known to be killed and fifty more injured.
4. *Report and Journal*, Final report of Virginia Commissioners, 28; Statement of Va. Case, 275, 308.
5. *Report and Journal*, Va. Correspondence, Commission to Governor Kemper, 28.
6. *Report and Journal*, Va. Correspondence, Henry Wise to William J. Aydelotte, December 26, 1870, 40.
7. *Report and Journal*, Va. Correspondence, Henry Wise to Governor Gilbert Walker, December 31, 1870, 45.
8. *Report and Journal*, Va. Correspondence, Watts to Wise, March 3, 1871, 49.
9. *Report and Journal*, Va. Correspondence, DeJarnette to Wise, 62-66.
10. *Report and Journal*, 237, 238.
11. *Report and Journal*, 245, 246, 254.
12. For the story of William Claiborne and the Isle of Kent, *see* Footner, 24–39.
13. *Report and Journal*, 77.
14. *Report and Journal*, 267–69.
15. *Md. Arch.* 3:473; *Report and Journal*, 84–86; Hon. Levin Claude Bailey, "Maryland's Boundary Controversies," Address to the Maryland State Bar Association, Atlantic City, New Jersey, June 22, 1951 (Reprint from *The Daily Record*, June 23, 1951), p. 4.
16. *Report and Journal*, 86; Clayton Torrence, *Old Somerset on the Eastern Shore of Maryland*, reprint of a 1935 edition (Baltimore: Regional Publishers, 1979), 36.
17. Accomack County, Va. Circuit Court Records, 1:43, Scarborough's Report; copy is also appended to *Report and Journal*, Va. Case.
18. Henning's Statutes at Large, 2:183, 184; Torrence, 37, 38; copy is appended to *Report and Journal*, Va. Case.
19. *Report and Journal*, 87–89; Torrence, 48, 49.
20. Black and Jenkins Award, 19, 20. Note: Even Black and Jenkins deplored Colonel Scarborough's actions. They said, "His conduct throughout violated the Act of Virginia Assembly as grossly as it violated the Maryland charter."
21. *Report and Journal*, 89; Torrence, 48, 49.
22. *Report and Journal*, 86–89; Black and Jenkins, 19.

23. *Md. Arch.* 5:43–45; *Report and Journal,* 96-99, 269–73; Black and Jenkins Award, 21; Bailey, 6.

24. *Report and Journal,* 264.

25. *Report and Journal,* 114, 121, 247, 248, 254, 259; Bailey, 11.

26. Lines approved by Virginia Assembly, 1748; Bailey, 12.

27. Maryland grants: *Report and Journal,* 134–37; List of Colonial and Commonwealth grants, *Report and Journal,* 212–20; Patents issued during the Regal Govt. of Va., Accomack Co., *Report and Journal,* 313–25; Commonwealth grants, *Report and Journal,* 316–22; Black and Jenkins Award, 19, 24. Note: In the possession of the Maryland State Historical Society, there is a map of Virginia, Maryland, Pennsylvania, and East and West New Jersey. It is signed by John Thornton, 1700. On this map, the divisional line begins at Smith's Point on the south bank of the Potomac and crosses the Bay on a due east course, leaving Smith Island entirely in Maryland.

28. *Report and Journal,* 305, 306.

29. *Report and Journal,* 121, 309.

30. Bailey, 12.

31. *Report and Journal,* 138–40 (Copy of Compact of 1785); Black and Jenkins Award, 11, 12; Bailey, 16.

32. *Report and Journal,* 41, 122, 124–27; Bailey, 13.

33. *Report and Journal,* Va. Correspondence, Commissioner Wise to Governor Walker, December 28, 1873, 144; Commissioner Wise to Governor Kemper, 28.

34. *Report and Journal,* Depositions of Witnesses, Testimony of John Cullen, 149, 150; Copy of commission is appended to Cullen's testimony, 153, 154; Liber G H #8, Election District, Folio 35 & 36.

35. *Report and Journal,* Va. Correspondence, Commissioner Wise to Commissioner Jones, November 27, 1871; Wise to Jones, November 30, 1871, 97.

36. *Report and Journal,* Depositions of Witnesses, Testimony of Stephen T. Dize, 194; Testimony of Henry Dize, 199.

37. *Report and Journal,* Va. Correspondence, 97–100.

38. *Report and Journal,* 107–13, 138.

39. *Report and Journal,* 139.

40. *Report and Journal,* Final Report of Virginia Commissioners, 23–27; List of Proposals, 152–59.

41. *Report and Journal,* Final Report of Virginia Commissioners, 21. Note: The arrest of the *Edington* and the *Amelia Ann,* the seizure of the vessel, *Fashion,* and the ensuing legal action are covered in chapter 5.

42. Mr. Wynne's involvement with the missing volumes is discussed in the following correspondence: Va. Commissioners to Governor Walker, 110–13; Commissioner Wise to Governor Walker, 130, 131; Thomas Wynne to H. Wise, 133.

43. Black and Jenkins Award, 24; Bailey, 14.

44. Black and Jenkins Award, 28.

45. *Report and Journal,* Md. Case, Lieutenant Michler quote, 132.

46. Fehr, 7, 8.

47. Rodney W. Dize, interview with author, Ewell, Md., 1979; Ullie

Notes

Marshall, interview with author, Tylerton, Md., 1979; Tom Horton, "Maryland Watermen Sue Over Boundary", *The Sun* (Baltimore), March 8, 1981; Wennersten, 90.

48. Rodney W. Dize, interview with author, Ewell, Md.
49. Ewell Scrapbook, 1888–1893 (Maryland Historical Society, Ms. 351) p. 5, excerpt from *The Sun* (Baltimore), November 28, 1889.
50. Rodney W. Dize, interview with author.
51. Ewell Scrapbook, 6.
52. Case #1054 (Wharton-Wise); *see also* Wennersten, 90, 91.
53. Horton, March 8, 1981; Rodney W. Dize and Ullie Marshall, interviews with author.
54. Rodney W. Dize and Ullie Marshall, interviews with author; Bailey, 17.
55. Jennings Evans, Past President, Tangier Sound Watermen's Association, interviews with author, 1980 (Ewell, Md.) and 1988 (by telephone).
56. Rodney W. Dize, interview with author, Ewell, Md.; Winfred Evans, interview with author, Rhodes Point, Md., 1978; also quoted by R. P. Harris, *The Evening Sun* (Baltimore), April 27, 1938.

Note: Although I have not used specific references from his files in this chapter, Woodrow T. Wilson, author of *Crisfield, Maryland,* and other very informative books, allowed me to use his files. These files contain copies of articles from *The Crisfield Times* from 1908 to present. For more information *see:* Woodrow T. Wilson, "Corbin Library Accepts Crisfield Times Microfilms," *The Crisfield Times,* May 3, 1989, pp. 1 and 3.

VII. Smith Island: Then and Now

1. Blanche H. Phillips, "Somerset—Our Nook in the Nation," in Clark, 994.
2. Taylor, 1.
3. Fehr, 3.
4. Taylor, 5.
5. Taylor, 5.
6. Wallace, 333, 334.
7. Alice Venable Middleton, interview with author, Ewell, Md. This settlement shift verified: Fehr, 1; Gardner, Wall, et al., 16.
8. Personal experience; *See also:* interview with Lieutenant Colonel Thomas F. Donovan, *The Sun* (Baltimore), February, 17, 1977.
9. Bain Bradshaw, interview with author, Rhodes Point, Md.
10. Tom White, "They Never Made it to Icy Tangier," *Baltimore News American,* January 18, 1981, and "The Hunter Freeze," *The Crisfield Times,* February 4, 1987.
11. Alice Venable Middleton and Addie F. Dize, interviews with author, Ewell, Md.
12. Harry Reed Evans, interview with author, Ewell, Md.
13. Alice Venable Middleton, interview with author, Ewell, Md.; Taylor, 5.
14. Taylor, 1.

15. Harry R. Evans, interview with author, Ewell, Md.
16. Addie F. Dize and Essie Mae Dize, interviews with author, Ewell, Md.
17. Lucy Bradshaw, interview with author, Rhodes Point, Md.
18. Stanley Taylor, "Tangier and Smith Islands Now Talking to Mainland," *The Transmitter*, 1941.
19. Printed information received from Henry Guy, C & P Telephone Company.
20. Mrs. Mabel Evans, interview with author, Ewell, Md.; John C. Ahlers, "Telephones Now Link Smith Island with Mainland," *The Sun*, (Baltimore), November 24, 1952.
21. Rodney W. Dize, interview with author, Ewell, Md.
22. Bain Bradshaw, interview with author, Rhodes Point, Md.
23. Harvey Bradshaw, interview with author, Crisfield, Md.
24. Joe Kyte, interview with author, Ewell, Md.
25. R. W. Todd, "Patriarchs of the Chesapeake," *Methodism on the Peninsula*, publishing data unknown.

VIII. Tall Tales and Traditions

Some of the contributors to this chapter are no longer living. This chapter is dedicated to all those who shared their memories with me. The stories, legends, and traditions were drawn from personal interviews with:

Bain Bradshaw, Rhodes Point, Md.
Lula Bradshaw, Rhodes Point, Md.
Lucy Bradshaw, Rhodes Point, Md.
Addie F. Dize, Ewell, Md.
Essie Mae Dize, Ewell, Md.
Rodney L. Dize, Ewell, Md.
Rodney W. Dize, Ewell, Md.
Willis Dize, Ewell, Md.

Alva Evans, Ewell, Md.
Harry R. Evans, Ewell, Md.
Mabel Evans, Ewell, Md.
Raymond Evans, Ewell, Md.
Caleb Jones, Ewell, Md.
Garrett (Joe) Kyte, Ewell, Md.
Seymour Kitching, Ewell, Md.
Earl Marshall, Baltimore, Md.
Alice Venable Middleton, Ewell, Md.
Woodrow T. Wilson, Crisfield, Md.

X. Charting the Course

1. U. S. Army Corps of Engineers, Baltimore District, Public Meeting Record, December 15, 1980, 3; U. S. Army Corps of Engineers, *Plan of Study Concerning Shore Erosion Control, Flood Control, and Navigation for Smith Island, Maryland and Virginia* (hereinafter referred to as *Plan of Study*), December 1973, 6–1, 6–4.
2. U. S. Army Corps of Engineers, *Main Report and Environmental Impact Statement* (hereinafter referred to as *Main Report*), June 1981, 20, 27.
3. *Main Report*, 27.

Notes

4. *Main Report,* 30.
5. *Main Report,* 30.
6. *Main Report,* 30–31.
7. Maxine Landon, Sara Marsh, and Lula Bradshaw, interviews with author, Rhodes Point, Md.
8. *Plan of Study,* 4–3.
9. *Main Report,* 1.
10. Public Meeting Record, December 15, 1980, 4–18; Major General E. R. Heiberg III, *Record of Decision,* U. S. Army Corps of Engineers, January 21, 1982.
11. *Main Report,* Description of proposed plans, 56–69.
12. *Main Report,* A-16, A-17; Letter to Colonel Peck, U.S.C.E. from Somerset County Commissioners, April 14, 1981.
13. *Main Report,* 68.
14. *See:* Mary Corddry, "Smith Islanders Seek U.S. Help on Erosion," *The Sun,* (Baltimore) November 18, 1979.
15. *Plan of Study,* 5–2.
16. *See:* U. S. National Wildlife Refuge System, *Martin Wilderness Study,* September 1971.
17. Mary Corddry, "Smith Islanders Opposed to U. S. Takeover of Refuge," *The Sun,* (Baltimore) September 17, 1971.
18. Corddry, September 17, 1971.
19. Paul Bedard, "Island Pier Will Be Built Despite Protest," *Salisbury Daily Times,* July 31, 1981.
20. Arthur W. Sherwood, *Understanding the Chesapeake* (Cambridge, Md.: Tidewater Publishers, 1973), 39.
21. *Plan of Study,* 5–1.
22. Maryland Historical Trust, "Guidelines for Completing National Registration Applications," RA/2/1980.
23. Correspondence: Clark Gibson, Maryland Historical Trust, to the Baltimore District U. S. Army Corps of Engineers, March 18, 1977.
24. Correspondence: Tyler Bastion, State Archeologist, to Baltimore District U. S. Army Corps of Engineers, July 18, 1977.
25. Correspondence: Maryland Historical Trust to U. S. Army Corps of Engineers, March 18, 1977.
26. *Plan of Study,* 7–1.
27. *Plan of Study,* 5–1.

Bibliography

Accomack-Northhampton County Circuit Court Record Books, Accomack County, Virginia; Old Accomack County Records, Eastville, Va.

Ahlers, John C. "Telephones Now Link Smith Island With Mainland," *The Sun* (Baltimore), November 24, 1952.

Archives of Maryland: Correspondence of the Governors, Journal of Maryland Convention, Proceedings of Provincial Court, Proceedings of Council, and Proceedings and Acts of General Assembly.

Bailey, The Hon. Levin Claude. "Maryland's Boundary Controversies." Address to the Maryland Bar Association, Atlantic City, New Jersey, June 22, 1951. (Rpt. *The Daily Record*, June 23, 1951).

Bedard, Paul. "Island Pier Will Be Built Despite Protests." *Salisbury Daily Times*, July 31, 1981.

Beitzell, Edwin W. *Life on the Potomac.* Private printing, E. W. Beitzell, 1968.

———. *Escape from Point Lookout.* Private printing, Abel, Md.: E. W. Beitzell.

Black, J. S. and Charles J. Jenkins. "Opinion and Award of the Arbitrators on the Maryland and Virginia Boundary Lines, Washington, 1877." Md. XF 177.82164, Enoch Pratt Free Library, Baltimore, Md.

Bode, Carl. *Maryland: A Bicentennial History.* New York and London: W. W. Norton, 1978.

Bozman, John L. *The History of Maryland: Its First Settlement in 1633 to the Restoration in 1660.* 2 vols. A reproduction of an 1837 set. Spartanburg, S. C.: Reprint Company, 1968.

Brotemarkle, Anna, and others, eds.; John E. Jacob, Jr., consultant. *Lower Eastern Shore Patriot,* Bicentennial Edition. Salisbury, Md.: Peninsula Press (The Bicentennial Committee of Somerset, Wicomico, and Worcester), 1976.

Brown, Alexander Crosby. *Steam Packets on the Chesapeake.* Cambridge, Md.: Tidewater Publishers, 1961.

Burgess, Robert H. and H. Graham Wood. *Steamboats Out of Baltimore.* Cambridge, Md.: Tidewater Publishers, 1968.

Clark, Charles B. *The Eastern Shore of Maryland and Virginia.* 2 vols. New York.: Lewis Historical Publication Co., 1950.

204

Bibliography

Conlin, Joseph. "Consider the Oyster." *American Heritage.* February/March 1980.

Corddry, Mary. "Smith Islanders Opposed to U. S. Takeover of Refuge." *The Sun* (Baltimore), September 17, 1971.

Dize, E. Frank. *Something Fishy From Tangier: An Island History.* Private printing, E. F. Dize, 1974, 6th edition, 1975.

Dos Passos. *The Shackles of Power.* Garden City, N. Y.: Doubleday, 1966.

Everstine, Carl N. Research Report #26. Research Division, Maryland Legislative Council; reprint by Chesapeake-Potomac Study Commission, Baltimore, 1946.

Ewell Scrapbook, 1888–1893. Maryland Historical Society, Baltimore, Md. Ms. #351.

Fehr, April. "An Exploration of Settlement Patterns and Agriculture, Smith Island, Maryland: 1860–1900." Diss., Catholic University of America, 1979.

Footner, Hulbert. *Rivers of the Eastern Shore.* New York: Farrar and Rinehart, 1944; reissued by Tidewater Publishers.

Gardner, Wm. A., Robert D. Wall, and others. *A Cultural Resources Reconnaissance of a Portion of Smith Island, Somerset County, Maryland.* Front Royal, Va.: Thunderbird Research Corp., April 1978; rev., May 1979.

Gouldsmith, Frank. *Indians of the Eastern Shore of Maryland.* Sykesville, Md.: Springfield State Hospital Press, 1922.

Green, Elmer. *The Making of Maryland.* Private printing, Baltimore: E. & M. Green, 1934.

Harris, R. P. Untitled article. *The Evening Sun* (Baltimore), April 27, 1938.

Horton, Tom. "Maryland Watermen Sue Over Boundary." *The Sun* (Baltimore), March 8, 1981.

"The Hunter Freeze." *The Crisfield Times,* February 4, 1987.

Jeffries, John H. *Maryland Naval Barges in the Revolutionary War.* (A monograph researched by John L. Bond). Private printing, Princess Anne, Md.: J. H. Jeffries, 1978.

Jones, Virgil Carrington. *The Civil War at Sea,* 3 vols. New York: Holt, Rinehart & Winston Inc., 1962.

Journal of the House of Delegates of Virginia, 1874–75. Richmond, Va.: Superintendent of Public Printing, 1875.

Lord, Walter. *The Dawn's Early Light.* New York: W. W. Norton, 1972.

Marine, William M. *British Invasion of Maryland, 1812-1815.* Edited by Louis H. Dielman. Reprint of 1913 edition. Baltimore: Genealogical Publishing Co., 1977.

Maryland Department of Natural Resources. *Prehistoric Peoples of Maryland's Coastal Plain.* Tidewater Administration, Coastal Resources Division, 1979.

Maryland General Assembly Senate Document E. (sixty-two-page report) W. T. Iglehart and Co., January 14, 1874.

Smith Island, Chesapeake Bay

Maryland Historical Trust. "Guidelines for Completing National Registration Applications." RA/2/1980.

Middleton, Alice Venable. *Maryland's Right, Tight Isle, Smith.* Private printing, Ewell, Md.: A. V. Middleton.

Middleton, Arthur Pierce. *Tobacco Coast. A Maritime History of Chesapeake Bay in the Colonial Era.* The Mariners Museum, Newport News, Va.; reprint, Baltimore: Johns Hopkins University Press, 1984.

Moore, Frank. *The Rebellion Record, 1861–1864* (A Diary of American Events). Reprint Salem, N. H.: Ayer Publ., 1976.

Muzzy, David S. and Arthur S. Link. *Our Country's History.* Boston: Ginn and Co., 1968.

Niles Weekly Register. 1812–1814 and 1861–1865.

Official Records of the Union and Confederate Navies in the War of the Rebellion, Series I. Civil War Room, Salisbury State Teachers College, Salisbury, Md.

Report and Journal of Proceedings of the Joint Commission to Adjust the Boundary of the States of Maryland and Virginia, 1872. Publishing data unknown. Courtesy of Howard and Louise Adkins, Salisbury, Md.

Rodgers, William H. "A Wet and Windy Kingdom." *Maryland Magazine,* 11 (Spring 1979): 3–7.

Scharf, J. Thomas. *History of Maryland, 1600–1765.* 2 vols. Baltimore: John B. Piet, 1879; reprint Hatboro, Pa: Tradition Press, 1967.

Sherwood, Arthur W. *Understanding the Chesapeake.* Cambridge, Md.: Tidewater Publishers, 1973.

Shuel, Brian. *The National Trust Guide to Traditional Customs of Great Britain.* Exeter, England: Webb and Bower, 1985.

Shomette, Donald G. *Pirates on the Chesapeake.* Centreville, Md.: Tidewater Publishers, 1985.

Somerset County Records, Princess Anne, Md.

Taylor, Stanley. "Tangier and Smith Islands Now Talking to Mainland." *The Transmitter,* 1941.

Taylor, W. P. *A Brief History of Smith's Island, Maryland.* Wilmington, Del.: Hubert A. R. ———, Printer, 1910.

Todd, R. W. "Patriarchs of the Chesapeake." *Methodism on the Peninsula.* Publishing data unknown. Courtesy of Alice Venable Middleton.

Torrence, Clayton. *Old Somerset on the Eastern Shore of Maryland.* Reprint of 1935 edition, Baltimore: Regional Publishers, 1979.

Truitt, Charles J. *Breadbasket of the Revolution.* Salisbury, Md.: Historical Books, Inc., 1975.

Tyler, Lyon Gardiner, ed. *Narratives of Early Virginia, 1606–1625.* New York: Barnes and Noble, Inc., 1946, reprint, 1959.

U. S. Army Corps of Engineers, Baltimore District. *Plan of Study Concerning Shore Erosion Control, Flood Control, and Navigation*

Bibliography

for Smith Island, Maryland and Virginia, December 1973.
———. *Main Report and Environmental Impact Statement,* June 1981.
———. *Public Meeting Record, Smith Island, Maryland and Virginia,* December 15, 1980.
U. S. National Wildlife Refuge System. *Martin Wilderness Study.* September 1971.
Virginia Calendar of State Papers, Eastville, Va.
Wallace, Adam. *The Parson of the Islands.* Philadelphia: Methodist Home Journal, 1861; reprint, Cambridge, Md.: Tidewater Publishers, 1961.
War Department Records, National Archives, Provost Marshall, Eastern Shore of Virginia, Eastville, Va.
Wennersten, John R. "The Almighty Oyster: A Saga of Old Somerset and the Eastern Shore, 1850–1920." *Maryland Historical Magazine* 74 (March 1979): 80.
White, Tom. "They Never Made it to Icy Tangier." *Baltimore News American,* January 18, 1981.
Wilson, Woodrow T. *Crisfield, Maryland, 1676–1976.* Baltimore: Gateway Press, Inc., 1977.
Wise, Barton Heyall. *Memoirs of John Cropper.* Richmond, Va.: Historical Society, 1951.

Personal Interviews:

Bain Bradshaw, Rhodes Point, Md.
Harvey Bradshaw, Crisfield, Md.
Lucy Bradshaw, Rhodes Point Md.
Lula Bradshaw, Rhodes Point, Md.
Addie F. Dize, Ewell, Md.
Essie Mae Dize, Ewell, Md.
Rodney L. Dize, Ewell, Md.
Rodney W. Dize, Ewell, Md.
Willis Dize, Ewell, Md.
Alva Evans, Ewell, Md.
Elizabeth Evans, Rhodes Point, Md.
Harry R. Evans, Ewell, Md.
Jennings Evans, Ewell, Md.
Laban Evans, Salisbury, Md.
Mabel Evans, Ewell, Md.
Raymond Evans, Ewell, Md.
Winfred Evans, Rhodes Point, Md.

Lynette Hoffman, Rhodes Point, Md.
Ann Elizabeth Jones, Ewell, Md.
Caleb Jones, Ewell, Md.
Seymour Kitching, Ewell, Md.
Garrett (Joe) Kyte, Ewell, Md.
Maxine Landon, Rhodes Point, Md.
Herman Marsh, Rhodes Point, Md.
Sara Marsh, Rhodes Point, Md.
Earl Marshall, Baltimore, Md.
Irma K. Marshall, Tylerton, Md.
Paul Marshall, Tylerton, Md.
Ullie Marshall, Tylerton, Md.
Alice Venable Middleton, Ewell, Md.
Wilson Sneade, Ewell, Md.
Alma Somers, Ewell, Md.
Betty R. Tyler, Ewell, Md.
Estelle Tyler, Rhodes Point, Md.
Olivia Tyler, Rhodes Point, Md.
Woodrow T. Wilson, Crisfield, Md.

Index

(Ships are indexed alphabetically under "vessels.")

Index

Calvert, Phillip, 26, 94
Calvert-Scarborough Agreement
    and Line, 26, 92, 94, 96,
    100, 103, 104
Calvert Cliffs, 168
Cambridge, Md., 58
Campbell, James, 40
Camp Hoffman, 81
Carey, George, 137
Carlos and Hester, 82, 158
Cedar Pt., Md., 150
Cedar Straits, Md., 100
Charles I, 23
Charles II, 94
Charles, Lord Baltimore, 95
Charley Pole, 125
Charlie, Captain, 171
Chart and Ruke's, 164
Cherry Hill, 163
Cherrystone, Va., 77
Chesapeake Bay Foundation,
    10, 176, 180, 186, 187
Chester, Md., 37
Chestertown, Md., 58
China, 163
Chincoteague, Va., 76, 126
Chincoteague Inlet, 86
Choptank River, Md., 6, 49, 58,
    59
Christian Women's Society,
    180
Cinquack, 24, 91, 95, 97, 101
Civil War, 67–87, 88, 89, 109,
    158
Claiborne, William, 23, 24, 92
Clarkson, Basil, 41
Coan River, Va., 84
Cochrane, Sir Alexander, 60
Cockburn, Sir George, 59, 60,
    61, 63
Coffin House, 127
Cohongaroota River, Md., 95
Compact of 1785, 91, 96, 97,
    100, 101
Confederate Volunteer Coast
    Guard, 80
Cook, Captain, 38
Cosby, Lt. Pierce, 76
Cow Ridge, 72
Creek, The, 98

Crisfield, Md., 5, 8, 89, 90, 96,
    97, 98, 104, 106, 107, 113,
    114, 116, 117, 121, 125,
    127, 128, 135, 136
Crisfield, John, 73
Crisfield Senior High School, 116
Crisfield Times, 121, 161
Crocket, _____, 47
Crockett, John, 53, 54
Crockett, Thomas, 54
Cromwell, Oliver, 92
Cropper, Col. John, 47, 48, 49
Cross the Creek, 72
Cullen, John, 72, 73, 97, 102

D

Dashiell, Joseph, 44
Dashiell, Robert, 45, 47, 48,
    49, 50
Davis, Edward, 38
Davis, Jefferson, 82
Deal Island, Md., 65, 66
DeJarnette, D. D., 91, 102
Delaware, 24
Delmarva Peninsula, 20
Derby, 150, 152
Dize, E. Frank, 53, 54
Down the Field, 122, 133, 162,
    163
Dungan, Captain, 85
Dunmore, Lord, 41
Drum Point, 53, 120

E

Early, Gen. Jubal, 82
Eastville, Va., 37, 46
Eldridge, J. H., 86
Elzey, John, 93
Europe, 37, 38, 58
Evans (surname), 53
Evans, Captain, 15
Evans, Jennings, 166, 167,
    168, 183
Evans, John, 27, 41
Evans, John T., 104
Evans, Johnson, 98
Evans, Rachel, 56
Evans, Richard, 41, 57, 111
Evans, Solomon, 49, 57, 77,
    111, 159

Evans, Winfred, 37, 184
Ewell School, 123

F

Fairfax, Lord Thomas, 95, 96
Fallin, Major, 42
First Regiment of Eastern
  Shore, Md. Volunteers, 80
Fishin' Island, 163
Fog's (Fogg's) Point, Md., 111,
  112, 116, 123
Florida, 18, 74, 137
Fort Jackson, 64
Fort McHenry, 64, 80
Fort Monroe, 76, 80
Fox's Island, 4, 25, 47
France, 38, 58, 96
Frazier, Capt. Solomon, 45, 46,
  47, 49, 50
Frederick, Lord Baltimore, 96
French and Indian War, 96
French Marine at York, 46

G

Gabriell's Island, Va., 25
Garden Island, Md., 41
George III, 96
Gilbert, Bartholomew, 23
Glenn L. Martin National
  Wildlife Refuge, 9, 51, 178,
  184
Grant, Gen. U. S., 86
Grayson, Commodore, 44, 45
Gwynn's Island, Va., 46

H

Hammond General Hospital, 80
Hampton Roads, Va., 59, 74,
  75, 83, 86
Handy, Joseph, 48, 49
Handy, Levin, 45, 47, 48, 49, 50
Handy, Samuel, 47, 49, 50
Harvey, Sir John, 24
Hayes, Senator, 106
Henry, Lord Jermine, 95
Hog Island, 104, 105
Hog Neck, 22, 71, 99, 108, 176
Holland's Island, 4
Hooker, Lieutenant Com-
  mander, 84, 85

Hooper Straits, 49
Hopton Grant, 94, 95
Horse Hammock, 27, 72, 98,
  99, 103
Howith (picaroon), 41
Hudson River, 6
Hungar River, 6
Hunter, Sgt. Wilbert, 114, 115

I

Ira, Captain, 173

J

Jackson, General, 64, 79
Jackson, Governor, 104, 105
James I, 91
James, Captain, 171
James River, 6, 91
Jamestown, Va., 23
Jefferson, Governor, 42
Jenkins, Charles, 102
Johnston, General, 86
Joint Commission of 1872, 72,
  101, 102
Jones, Caleb, 158
Jones, Isaac, 100, 102
Jones Island, 4

K

Kedges Straits, 25, 41, 47, 49,
  50, 51, 60, 64, 76, 112, 188
Kemper, Gov. James, 88
Kent Island, 23, 24, 92
Kidd, Captain, 38
Kidd, Commodore John, 48, 49,
  51
King Richard, 57, 111
King Solomon, 57, 111, 159
King's Commissioners of Planta-
  tions, 24
Kitching, Frances, 162
Kizzie's, 111
Kohler, Jim, 176

L

Lane, Sir Ralph, 22
Lazarus, 41
Lee, Adm. S. P., 81
Lee, Governor, 44
Lee, Robert E., 86

Index